Up for
Renewal

ALSO BY CATHY ALTER

Virgin Territory: Stories from the Road to Womanhood

Up for Renewal

What Magazines Taught Me about

Love, Sex, and Starting Over

Cathy Alter

ATRIA BOOKS

New York London Toronto Sydney

ATRIA BOOKS

A Division of Simon & Schuster, Inc.
1230 Avenue of the Americas
New York, NY 10020

First Atria Books hardcover edition July 2008

ATRIA BOOKS and colophon are trademarks of Simon & Schuster, Inc.

For information about special discounts for bulk purchases,
please contact Simon & Schuster Special Sales at 1-800-456-6798
or business@simonandschuster.com.

Designed by Jaime Putorti

Manufactured in the United States of America

10   9   8   7   6   5   4   3   2   1

Library of Congress Cataloging-in-Publication Data
Alter, Cathy.
  Up for renewal : what magazines taught me about love, sex, and
starting over / by Cathy Alter.—1st Atria Books hardcover ed.
      p. cm.
1. Conduct of life—Humor. 2. Women's periodicals—Humor. I. Title.

  PN6231.C6142A48 2008
  818'.602—dc22

                                                            2007042817

ISBN-13: 978-0-7432-8840-8
ISBN-10:   0-7432-8840-8

AUTHOR'S NOTE

Names and identifying characteristics of some people portrayed in this book have been changed to protect the innocent—as well as the guilty, who already know who they are.

For my parents,
who hopefully won't disown me

Up for
Renewal

Subscribe Now!

the noise was overwhelming. The clashing mastheads, the unbridled exclamation points, the multiple Heidi Klums, all boobs and eyes, all at full volume.

And the sex. The sex was everywhere. *Easy Sexy Hair. 803 Sexy Looks. Your Best Sex at 20, 30, 40. Flab to Fab: A Plan to Reveal Your Sexy Muscles.*

Three rows of beautiful faces, arranged on risers, looked down on me, like a choir of genetic perfection. To either side of me, the ponytailed and manicured congregation reached for their Klums, opening them like hymnals.

I don't know how long I remained parked in front of that wall of women's magazines, motionless and mesmerized in an overly lit bookstore, listening to the rhythmic flip-flap of pages being turned. The sensation was similar to being in a Las Vegas casino, where there are no windows or clocks and you could be playing blackjack for either ten minutes or ten years.

What was I doing here? More important, how had I gotten here in the first place?

For starters, I was a recently divorced thirty-seven-year-old who by day wrote painfully dry sales and marketing materials for a legal publishing company in our nation's capital. It was the kind of ephemera—Dear Subscriber letters and densely worded product brochures—that most people, especially our recipients, would label as junk mail.

By day, I was also screwing a colleague, in my cubicle, with the constant prattling of our two other quadmates providing ambience, mere inches away from the other side of the shared high walls. The literal nine-to-five grind. How we kept it a secret was a mystery to me (frankly, whether I had a cone of silence around my cubicle or just hard-of-hearing coworkers was of no concern to me); how we kept it quiet was Bruno's hand over my mouth. Bruno was a supremely arrogant art director who did asinine things like nibble his toast into the shape of Argentina, his homeland, and then try and impress the waitress—and everyone else in the vicinity—with his artistry. Being bigheaded, he fought any efforts to correct his work—as in, this should be a period and not a comma; or, the company logo is blue and not red—by completely ignoring anyone's attempts to manage him.

Dave, my gay work boyfriend, applauded my steamy open-office romance and thought that Bruno was good for my skin. A fellow writer and voyeur, he agreed that the best stories were often in the telling, and nothing pleased him more than listening to me deliver the latest cubicle installment, with pornographic gusto. In a sense, I was getting off two men, one right after the other.

Bruno would go to creative extremes to get me to touch his penis, and Dave especially loved these narratives because I'd adopt a fantastically exaggerated Latin accent in the recounting.

"Cat, Cat, check it out."

It was always the same prelude. Bruno would enter my cubicle and deftly extract his dick from his fly.

"Can you feel a lump here?" he'd query. "Do you think it could be dangerous?"

Dave and I would howl over Bruno's latest medical inventions, and marvel at how he always managed to up the ante.

"Congratulations, Bruno"—I'd eye-roll—"this is your most pathetic attempt to date." And then I'd hike up my skirt and reward him anyway.

So really, who was more pathetic?

I'd like to say that I was punishing myself for the guilt I felt in leaving my husband, taking up with a guy who was clearly using me as an instrument of his own depersonalized, self-serving pleasure (his music, not mine), but I didn't think the excuses were that interesting. The truth was, I just missed having sex.

I used to joke that I had sex more with Bruno in the first week of our affair than I did in my five years of marriage. But it wasn't a joke. That my husband had gained more than one hundred pounds since our engagement wasn't the only reason I stopped sleeping with him, but it was the most convenient one. A better reason was anchored in desolate anger—at my husband for who he was and at myself for never accepting it. My sadness was so profound and so deep that it circumnavigated itself and looped back around, pulling me under with its weight until I was numb.

My desire to desire was absolute, and Bruno, a Botticelli with excellent table manners, the lean and graceful body of a dancer, and the proximity of being on the other side of the cubicle wall, was the perfect receptacle for my id. He was a no-brainer rebound. But after the glow of frequent, open-office sex had been stubbed out, I realized that Bruno was not only a bad idea, he was career suicide. Plus, I didn't even like him that much.

I knew this. I *knew* this.

And yet I was unable to stop the feeding frenzy of poor decisions.

When I wasn't bent over in my cubicle, I was yearning desperately for Glen, who lived in the apartment building next door (as if fishing off the company pier wasn't enough of a risk), a sweet-faced guy who thought he created a trend the day he pushed his floppy blond hair back with a terry-cloth sweatband. Glen had parlayed an obsession with cowhide into a successful retail business by turning the soft fur of fetal calves into chic clutches and tote bags. If I were lucky, a rare occurrence, he'd let me blow him and sleep over. But mostly I just hung around him, like the girl at last call, hoping that tonight was the night he'd condescend to go home with me, since no one prettier was around and his buddies had taken off and what the hell, he was horny and it didn't really mean anything as long as we technically didn't fuck.

Besides my stellar dating choices, I was running with a pretty fast crowd. I had taken up with two of Glen's clients, the fabulously gay duo of Richard and Ronald, whose "Sunday Fundays" began with cocktails at 11:00 AM and didn't stop until nightcaps at midnight. In the first winter of our friendship, I was on antibiotics four times.

Drinking required smoking, and I easily picked back up where I had left off in my NYC twenties, reuniting with my Marlboro Lights with great big drags of zeal. I was selecting my lunch based on the contents of the office vending machine and had developed an unhealthy addiction to pepperoni Combos and Cherry Coke. And I was spending like crazy—$800 custom-made cowboy boots, spur-of-the-moment weekends in South Beach, a hand-forged silver necklace by an Israeli sculptress I had never heard of before. Sometimes the balance in my checking account was so measly in between paychecks that I was reduced to paying for my morning coffee with fistfuls of pennies.

And I was crying. All the time. Silently, in my cubicle; publicly, walking through Georgetown on my way to meet a friend; inconsolably, at a crowded truck-stop diner while my mother passed me handfuls of paper napkins and men with dirty necks and meaty hands stared at me in bug-eyed astonishment.

But the worst casualty of this excessive living was my writing. As a freelance journalist, it was up to me to hunt up story ideas and pitch them to editors. If they liked an idea, they'd assign me the story. In just two years of freelancing, my byline had appeared in the *Washington Post,* on the cover of the *Washington City Paper,* in the pages of *Spin* and *Self,* and in a continuing, Dave Eggers–commissioned series for *McSweeney's.* I saw everyone I met as a potential profile and always seemed to have something in the works.

But not anymore. My priorities were clearly out of whack, and I was wasting way too much time running after dead-end relationships instead of maintaining and cultivating healthy ones with current and potential editors. For six months, the only thing I had managed to write was a piece for the *Post's* Home Section about Glen and his cowhide business. But that was really more of a love note.

When I was going through my divorce, I reestablished contact with an old boyfriend who was simultaneously ending his marriage.

"What age do you think we are right now?" he had asked, even though he knew we were both thirty-five. "Do you think when people divorce, they regress to the age they were right before they got married?"

"I've gone further back," I admitted. "I'm behaving like I'm still in college."

"Me, too." He laughed.

The last time we spoke, he was dating someone in an

open marriage who had become unreasonable when he told her he wanted to see other women.

My life was taking on a similar car-wreck mentality. But after experiencing the initial jolts of bad behavior, I found that my self-destructiveness had become painfully boring. I knew the gig was up when my best friend Jeanne phoned me early one Sunday and said, "Cathy, we are at a low point in our friendship."

Jeanne and I met as students in the Johns Hopkins part-time graduate program, where we were both earning masters in nonfiction writing. She remembered me, with horror, as the woman who pulled a Pop-Tart out of her pocketbook on the first night of class. I remembered her as the woman who organized weekly brown bag lunches at her office to vilify me as the author of "Bitch Hunt," a recently published cover story in the *Washington City Paper*, which detailed (rather tongue-in-cheek, I thought) why women in Washington were such alacritous ballbusters.

"You live in my neighborhood," she informed me, a few weeks after the Pop-Tart incident.

"How do you know?"

"Because I saw you looking in our kitchen window the other night," she said matter-of-factly.

This was true. I was a flagrant peeping Tom. And in Georgetown, with the sidewalks practically scraping up against the open-draped windows of its grand homes, certainly more lavish than those in my apartment building, the urge to see how the other half decorated was highly irresistible. And now that she mentioned it, I vaguely remembered peering into a set of open shutters and discovering, along with a Sub-Zero and a rack of impressive cookware, another pair of eyes staring back.

We began to walk. First, tentatively, home from class, where we soon began to gleefully demolish our weaker classmates with our mental red markers. We advanced to longer walks along the C&O Canal, a paved trail alive with cardinals and raspberries. We started with businesslike back-and-forths on Saturday mornings, soon tacked on a stop for coffee at Dean & Deluca, and eventually agreed to walk on Sundays as well, occasionally accompanied by Jeanne's husband Paul, a brilliantly funny guy who loved to comb the sidewalks for spare change. Our friendship progressed along with the seasons, and our walks became longer and full of ritual as we paused to watch a blue heron, *our* heron, fish for breakfast, or to collect tight bunches of the wild parsley we discovered growing along the banks of the canal.

Jeanne was my most trusted friend who truly wanted to see me happy and centered. Fifteen years older than I, Jeanne was too young to be my mother and too agenda-less to be a big sister. With this phone call, I knew I had let her down profoundly.

"I don't think I can be around you any longer," she said quietly.

"I can't be around me," I agreed, and then set the phone down on the pillow and cried like the idiot I knew I had become.

This was not the life I wanted. So I sat down and asked myself what I did want. It proved to be a surprisingly diffi-cult question, a Riddle of the Sphinx for the newly divorced. For so much of my marriage and the messy aftermath, I had never found a quiet moment to even ask—never mind answer—that elegantly elemental question.

Eventually, I scraped together a wish list.

1. I want to be loved and to love someone that I also want to have sex with every day for the rest of my life.
2. I want to be successful in whatever I do—whether it's writing a book or paying bills on time or paint-ing my bedroom.
3. I want to stay young forever, and I don't want any more wrinkles or gray hairs than I already have.
4. I want to save money for the future so I can travel at whim or buy a nineteenth-century oil painting.
5. I want to not hurt emotionally so much, and when I do hurt, I don't want to feel it as deeply.
6. I want to not feel guilty for saying no, as in *No, I don't want to have dinner, call you back, or be your friend.*
7. I want to see failures as small victories.

Like the guy who accidentally invented the Post-it note, I had suddenly stumbled on something useful. When I took a closer look at my wants, I noticed something in each one's wording that seemed annoyingly familiar to me: my list could easily be transformed into the cover lines that screamed out from every women's magazine on the planet. All I needed to do was rejigger a bit, switch into second person, and add an exclamation point at the end. As in:

Stay Young and Wrinkle-Free Forever!
Be More Successful in Whatever You Do!
Save More Money and Buy That Monet!
Say No Without the Guilt!

I know what you're thinking. You're thinking the same thing I was thinking. Who would be dumb enough to believe that a bunch of magazines, women's magazines, would have the power to transform her life?

It's not like I didn't grow up with a mother who wore her hair like Gloria Steinem and patiently explained why she would have burned her bra if she actually didn't need to wear one. And it's not like I didn't discover *The Beauty Myth* at the same time I took a job in a NYC advertising agency and walked around saying stuff like, "The media is manipulating women into feeling insecure and unhappy about themselves by creating and marketing a standard of femininity that is impossible for them to attain." Yes, I saw *The Vagina Monologues* and participated in the postshow discussions.

But why can't an undying devotion to *Cosmo, Glamour,* and the slew of other glossies work wonders for my life? Why can't a cerebral, unconventional, authority-questioning woman still believe in the power of the perfect mascara?

Can't I still retain my headstrong nature under a supercute beret?

And I ask you . . . is it so wrong to want to be bossed around by Helen Gurley Brown?

Magazines have rescued me in the past. A major *Seventeen* devotee in junior high, I madly tore through each issue like it was the Holy Grail. Surely, this would be the month that explained it all: my horrible skin, lackluster hair, dismal luck with boys. What's more, not only would I get the explanation, full of upbeat, we're-in-this-together copy, I'd finally get the solution, in a bulleted, step-by-step format.

I talked to my first boy by memorizing the script helpfully provided in "How to Get His Attention." (The phrase "Are you enjoying yourself?" uttered, as *Seventeen* instructed, sotto voce, worked wonders for me. Unfortunately, I uttered it at a party where I had no business being, and the boy I said it to was twenty-eight and stoned off his ass.)

So I made a decision.

For the ensuing twelve months, I resolved to turn my life over to a stack of today's women's magazines and follow their advice without question. The method would be pretty simple: to focus on one specific beauty, fashion, fitness, diet, spirit, relationship, or job-related task and then adhere to, for that entire month, the articles that best addressed my goal. Every month, a new challenge, another damage zone to assess and improve upon.

By the end of my subscriptions, I would have gotten rid of upper-arm jiggle, crawled out of debt, hosted the perfect dinner party, run a mile without puking, engaged in better bathtub booty, asked for a raise, rehauled my apartment, mastered the blowout, and faked a perfect complexion.

And then there was the relationship part. I had recently begun to contemplate one with Karl, a peripheral friend who, one night at a party, quietly reached for my hand and told me I deserved better. So far Karl, or at least Potential Karl, was a lot better, and I really didn't want to send him shrieking for the hills—a talent I innately possessed. I knew my cubicle days with Bruno and random nights with Glen were numbered, and basically amounted to unhappy topics for daytime television. With Potential Karl, who was handsome and forthright and had a refreshingly goofy obsession with building his own robot, the risk of losing something legitimate became very real, and I didn't want to mess things up. After all, I had messed up every single relationship I had ever been in, from my marriage to my ability to enjoy cheap sex—what made me think I wouldn't do it again? In the past, when my inner annihilator asked me that same question, I'd shrug and look away. But now, finally, at last, I was tired of having this conversation. And I knew that in order to successfully change my love life, I was going to have to seek some outside counsel.

So I had come to the fancy bookstore in Georgetown, to select the governing body of magazines that would define, shape, and rule the next year of my life. In a real sense, I was standing in front of that wall because I had hit a metaphoric one.

I voted out some magazines immediately. *Essence* and

Working Mother didn't exactly speak to me and my status as a single honky. And as I flipped through *Redbook*, I imagined their reader dressed in Eddie Bauer no-press chinos and being outstandingly skilled at scrapbooking. Then there were the ones that didn't offer enough how-to ethos. This translated to having the word *you* on the cover, as in "Exotic and Erotic Sex Tricks for You," a cover line from June's *Marie Claire*. So even though I idolized Jane Pratt for *Sassy* (and I'm talking about the early, unadulterated years), her *Jane* had always struck me as identityless (yet somehow self-congratulatory about it), and was conspicuously devoid of the kind of dictates I was after. *Vogue* was also devoid of bulleted lists, makeup lessons, and perf-out advice. If ever an editor anthropomorphized into a magazine, it would be Anna Wintour. She was better than me, and I knew it.

Eventually, I started playing a game of "What famous magazine would I invite to a dinner party?" This set the table pretty quickly. *Ladies' Home Journal*, you're a bit of a fuddy-duddy. Come sit next to me, *Cosmo*!

In the end I went with a core sisterhood of nine women's magazines: *Elle* for its European high fashion and *Marie Claire* for how to get that same je ne sais quoi for less money; *O, The Oprah Magazine*, for her pretty on the inside and *Allure* for its paint job on the out; *Self* to tighten my ass and *Cosmopolitan* to help me use it. For sheer chutzpah, I picked *Glamour*, for doling out their wisdom with manicured nails and an iron fist. Because I sincerely wanted to know where all of Hollywood bought their jeans, I allowed myself the guilty pleasure of *InStyle*. And for shelter, I chose *Real Simple* (as someone who has never turned on her oven and used only one burner at a time, I was not about to tangle with Martha Stewart).

These magazines, I thought as I fanned them out on the checkout counter, were my Rosetta stone. The ads for watches and face creams, the splay-legged models, the exclusive new surveys—if I deciphered their codes, I'd understand all that had been previously unknowable. My wishes, losses, hopes, and shame.

The cashier was clearly not thinking any of this. "Are you opening a nail salon?" she inquired, bagging what she perceived to be reading material for women waiting for their polish to dry.

Anything can change a life that's ready to be changed.

I can't remember if I heard this on *Dr. Phil*, if I read it on a coffee mug, or if I happened to make it up myself. Whatever the source, it was an aphorism that I thought important enough to print out and tape to my computer monitor. It had been staring me in the face for over a year now.

I believed in getting a better life. I was totally convinced that in following the advice found in these magazines, I would be able to show that life—my life—was a work in progress. It was okay that I wasn't there yet. The journey was all in the souvenirs picked up along the way. Maybe tighter triceps, an entrance-making dress, and the map to his secret pleasure zones were the meretricious emblems of true happiness.

What follows is a social experiment on myself, a real-life application of women's magazines—in all its triumph, asskicking, and unfortunate choices in lipstick.

Do or Diet

taking baby steps into a new life seemed like the most humane way to slap myself in the face. I was not mentally prepared to take on a month of money matters or transform anything with paint. My inaugural challenge should be familiar and manageable. Because personal experience showed that I had more control over what (and not who) I put in my mouth, my first foray into self-improvement was to be food-related.

At five-eleven and a size 6, *diet* is a noun for me, not a verb. I didn't need to lose weight. I just needed to stop eating the insides of the vending machine for lunch. Plus, an official lunch would provide balance and structure to my routine, elements of a normal life that had been AWOL from mine.

If I didn't have a digestive system more fragile than most tropical fish, I would eat anything put in front of me. Here's a partial list of foods most deadly to me: shrimp, lobster, ice cream, tuna fish, yogurt, cheese, pumpkin seeds, black beans, white wine, Brazil nuts, soybeans, calcium-enriched orange juice, tiramisu, lamb, and anything from Fuddruckers. I also stopped eating red meat when I was poor and living on my own in New York City. Now that I'm more gainfully employed, I'd like to begin incorporating a bit of beef into my diet, but I'm convinced that first hamburger will send my body into seismic shock.

Because I suffered from so many food allergies, I defaulted to bread. And more bread. I kicked off my days with a jumbo cinnamon raisin bagel and often repeated the same breakfast for lunch when I couldn't think of anything else to eat. And if I wasn't eating popcorn for dinner, I was slapping together a peanut butter (protein!) and jelly sandwich or eating a Dunkin' Donuts corn muffin directly out of the bag.

I thought hard about bread and how much I was going to miss a nice crust. I didn't need to open up a single June issue to know that the only acceptable baguettes I'd find would come from Fendi, not France. What I didn't know was what directives were going to come down from the mountain of magazines that were currently piled on my coffee table—and whether their instructions would result in anything suitable for eating. I imagined a month of shelling snow peas and discovering 10 Tricks for Tastier Tofu. I pictured myself the way I envisioned other healthy eaters—clear-eyed and vibrating with sunshine—and realized I was smiling.

Food has always been a vehicle of change for me, and June was always when the drive began. The moment school let out for summer, I was preparing for fall, when I'd reenter school a different person. Tanner, prettier, shorter (I was heads taller than most of the boys in my class), more confident, magically popular, and finally, FINALLY, kissed. Naturally, I thought the last three would happen only if the first three did.

My first attempt at self-improvement took place the summer between seventh and eighth grade, when my mother and I went on the Scarsdale diet. The food, or lack thereof, was practically prison fare: a scoop of cottage cheese, a piece of skinless chicken, cantaloupes ad nauseam. Breakfast, which consisted of a single slice of dry protein toast the size and consistency of a cocktail napkin washed down with a hellish glass of grapefruit juice, was a key hardship.

Sensing the historic significance of a first diet, I documented my regimen with tedious precision; my quilted Holly Hobbie diary soon took on the qualities of an actuarial spreadsheet. When I wasn't suffering through a dressing-free salad or immortalizing it with Dickensonian aplomb, I was breaststroking like crazy in our swimming pool.

I lasted a week, at which point Gail, my best friend since fifth grade, took me to the snack bar at her country club. I became a spectacle of nutritional noncompliance. I happily purchased a bag of Doritos and a cup of hot fudge (for dipping purposes), and we watched a gang of deeply tanned women play mah-jongg with the same gaping interest we normally reserved for the Matt Dillon classic *Over the Edge*. I had never seen mah-jongg before and assumed that the women, with their coral lips, python-print caftans, and numinous ivory tiles, were gypsies, despite the fact that we were deep in the suburbs of Farmington, Connecticut, at a private club that admitted only Jews.

Not that I should have been on a diet in the first place. I wasn't fat, in spite of my father pinching my "love handles" and nicknaming me Butterball. "Are your thighs still hungry?" he'd ask, whenever I reached for seconds or asked if I could order dessert.

Photos of me at this time show an immature face with full, smooth cheeks, my hipless torso and ribbon legs predicting the shape I would eventually own in adulthood. Yet, at twelve, I had neither the therapy nor the vocabulary to tell my father that he may have been projecting—or getting even with me for every time I poked him in the stomach and asked him to laugh like the Pillsbury Doughboy.

My mother, a six-foot-tall glamazon with a closet pulled from her own clothing boutique, sent the most powerful message to me by way of her dinner plate. I took a nightly inventory of what she ate. "Why don't you want a baked potato?" I'd wonder. "Don't you like the Colonel's special biscuits?"

"I'm on a diet," she'd respond, without fail. To ensure she stuck to it, she'd only stock our cookie jar with Mallomars and our freezer with rainbow sherbet—textures and flavors she found repellent and unworthy.

I grew up accepting the inevitability that once you

became a woman, you were always on a diet. Being a woman equaled loss.

As I reached for a bright orange *Cosmopolitan* with an equally orange (-haired, -skinned, -dressed) Jessica Simpson on the cover, I wondered what was I about to give up—and what I would eventually gain. Flashy and obvious, with page after page of bite-size true confessions about sex in predominantly public places, *Cosmo* was like diving into a big bag of penny candy. Before I knew it, I was in some sugar-induced euphoria, taking the *Cosmo* Quiz "Do You Make Men M-E-L-T?"

1. You're checking into a resort with friends when you notice a group of hot guys. You:
   a. Pray your pals don't embarrass you
   b. Say, "Hey boys, we're in room 508!"
   c. Smile. If they start a convo, you'll say "Maybe we'll see you by the pool."

Can you believe that I really took the time to consider these lettered possibilities? Neither could I. But I chose C, the milquetoast of the trio, and moved on.

2. The guy you're casually dating excitedly asks if you've ever kissed a girl. You say:
   a. "Wouldn't you like to know."
   b. "Gross, never!"
   c. "Sure! Wanna see me do it now?"

HILARIOUS! Had this quiz been written in irony? This was funny by design, right? I liked that I was in on the joke and circled A, because seriously, guys love when you toy with your sexuality.

3. You're chilling at the park next to a stud. What do you
   do to get his attention?
   a. Some provocative yoga poses
   b. Sunbathe in your bra
   c. Pull out your romance novel

I knew a coked-out hairdresser in my neighborhood who would have selected A without a moment's hesitation. I once saw her pull her leg around her head at a dinner party, her crotch aimed directly toward the one straight man in the room.

It didn't take me long to determine the obvious. *Cosmo* had divided the female quiz-taking population into three groups: Sluts, prudes, and everyone else. Did this prevent me from immensely enjoying the discovery of the apparent? Did this stop me from inserting myself into the rest of the seven scenarios? No, it did not. After I decided the television character I most related to was Elliot from *Scrubs* and that I'd most likely wear cropped pants and a T-shirt to an outdoor party, I tallied my score and learned that I was a simmering seductress. I "project come-hither vibes that don't scream desperate."

Rather than being dismayed that I had turned to *Cosmo* to tell me who I really was, I felt oddly validated (as well as highly entertained) and congratulated myself for coming up with this genius idea. In the past, I had to speed-read my way through the latest installments of *Glamour* or *InStyle* in the poorly lit waiting room of my dentist's office. Now, I had an actual excuse, a job, a *responsibility* to read all these magazines every single month for the next year. I could hardly wait for my subscriptions to kick in.

Even though I was supposed to be limiting myself to healthy-eating articles, it was hard not to devour every magazine cover to cover, which took me approximately five hours (not counting the hour I spent online trying to locate the necklace Katie Holmes wore throughout her "Single in the City" photo spread in *InStyle* magazine).

Spending an afternoon with the ladies, I realized how much voyeuristic, diversionary amusement was available to me, like the article in *Marie Claire* about a woman who recruits a wingman to help her land a date. It was a different kind of pleasure, this sort of reading, compared to tackling a ten thousand-word profile on Gertrude Stein in the *New Yorker*, for example. I forgot how much dumb fun regular reading could be. I was both thrilled and horrified by the thought of filling my head with the latest developments in teeth whiteners and wondered what kind of parlor tricks I'd be performing for friends: Look, everyone! Watch how Lucy's jawline softens when I give her a deep side part!

Even if an article was wildly out of sync with my June mission, I tore out whatever I saw as having value for future months. *O, The Oprah Magazine*, for instance, had devoted the month to "religion," with her *Ah, Men!* special issue. Inside, there were all sorts of articles with captions like "How to Get Through to a Man," "Bald Is to Male as Fat Is to Female," and the highly educational, "Getting Him to Open Up, or How to Interview a Brick Wall," by Seth Kugel, a *New York Times* reporter who wrote that getting a man to talk is comparable to cracking a tough subject, like asking Dick Cheney "where the undisclosed location is." And even though David L. Katz's The Way to Eat column was male-oriented, I ripped it out. I figured I could still put it to use the next time I was entertaining my own lab rat, since Katz offered guidance on the healthiest alcohol to serve to a guy who still wanted to pound a few cocktails.

While I built the ultimate reference library, I continued to look for anything food-related. It was pretty slim pickings. Perhaps all the healthy-eating articles appeared in April, with umpteen variations on the "Get Bikini-Ready by Memorial Day" theme plastered across covers. I mostly found articles that offered advice and encouragement for sticking to a diet, not for beginning one. *Allure* had an ongoing monthly feature called Total Makeover, where a weight-loss specialist had been downsizing three pear-shaped women since January. Next to a full-body shot of each participant (who all got the memo from Marcel Marceau to wear black mime tights on their lower halves) was a chart comparing their current weight, waist, hip, and body fat measurements to their January stats. One of the women, a pretty pale blonde with muscular calves, revealed that she sticks to her diet by rewarding herself with a manicure. Below her profile was a photograph of a cassette tape with words of encouragement recorded by the specialist, who had labeled the tape, "Nothing tastes as great as thin." A little cannibalistic, but the sentiment was well placed. I tore out the page and decided to apply the reward strategy to my own battle with junk food. A manicure would look much better without a fringe of orange Cheetos powder under my fingernails.

Cosmo had a twist on caloric slip-ups, with an "Informer" piece on celebrity binges. I was surprised to learn that Eva Mendes sought solace in tuna sandwiches with "extra onions and Doritos smashed inside." There was even a photo of Eva sitting in a café, shoving something that resembled a Gorton's breaded fish fillet in her mouth. No wonder she was wearing dark sunglasses.

I put off reading *Real Simple* until the end—mostly because I was tempted by the sheer razzle-dazzle of the other magazines. But it was here, among ample white space, unfussy graphics, and a calm, reassuring tone, that I found my centerpiece for June: four beautifully art-directed pages devoted to covering things in plastic wrap. (This was not to be confused with *Cosmo*'s more faithful interpretation of package wrap. Number 8 in their "Sex Trick Hall of Fame" called for covering a man's testicles with a square of plastic wrap, pressing your lips against the parcel, and humming gently. I made a mental note to file this one away for sex month.)

Besides giving step-by-step pictorials for swathing half an

onion and a hearty slice of what looked like frosted lemon cake in plastic, *Real Simple* had grandly spotlighted a tutorial in sandwich wrapping.

The potential for my personal success was multifold. For one, I would be brown-bagging my lunch, a phenomenon that hadn't occurred since junior high school. Not only was I taking preventive measures against a meal of pretzels and animal crackers, I would be giving my quarters a higher purpose—the washing machine in my building.

I have a thing about cling wrap, aka the kitchen equivalent of a wire hanger. Both menaces share the exact same characteristic—the ability to completely fuck with you. Cling Wrap, wily, born of static, and with a gravitational pull toward its home planet, simply demanded too much work. Maybe I have poor motor control, but I just can't deal with this runaway-train aspect. Aluminum foil is malleable, predictable, and to my aesthetics, so much prettier.

But this project was all about self-improvement. Perhaps learning how to encase a sandwich in plastic would also serve as a meditation on tolerance and acceptance.

■

Because my kitchen is the approximate size of a welcome mat, with a toaster, microwave, and coffeemaker vying for space on the only counter, I rarely made anything that required a surface area larger than a dinner plate. A sandwich, however, fell within the zoning limit, so I was not feeling any performance anxiety as I set out to prepare my lunch. At 8:30 AM, a good twenty minutes before I left for the ten-

minute walk to work, I made a peanut butter and jelly sandwich and set about wrapping it.

Real Simple testers selected Glad's Press'n Seal as the best
all-around stick-to-iter (can you imagine what circle of hell
the job of analyzing plastic wrap occupies?), but my local supermarket is too low-rent to carry such an advanced piece of
technology. I had to slum it with an earlier generation, the
classic Cling Wrap.

When I studied the three photos demonstrating the
proper wrapping procedure, the first thing that came to mind
was jazz hands. Because the only things moving from photo
to photo were the hands, which were expressive and dramatic looking. The sandwich maintained the same canted
position from one photo to the next. I recalled that scene in
The Bird Cage where Robin Williams analogously choreo-
graphs his backup dancers. "Now Fosse, Bob Fosse. Martha
Graham, Martha Graham!"

I've always been a more verbal interpreter, so maybe the
visual cues weren't that important here. I ripped out the
sandwich triptych and hung it on the cabinet above my
workstation.

STEP 1

Tear off a piece of wrap about 14 inches long and put
the sandwich in the middle of it.

I took notice of the time as I began: 8:42 AM. Acing this first
step was critical, and getting the exact size of the plastic
would definitely ensure my success. So I took it slow—

especially with the tearing of the wrap, my usual point of departure for disasterville.

Remarkably, being vigilant paid off. It was the first time I hadn't either sliced my finger on the box's serrated edge or encased my arm in wrap that had run amok.

> Fold the end closest to you up and over the sandwich, pulling it down over the far edge to secure everything firmly.

This assumed that I had positioned everything for a vertical wrap. I had not. My narrow strip of counter runs horizontally. So I had to rearrange the entire operation, which pissed me off in an admittedly disproportionate way. Which further pissed me off.

STEP 2

> Holding the sandwich by its sides, flip it away from you once, bringing the bottom face-up (make sure you have enough wrap to cover the sandwich entirely after you flip it).

The photo showed a sandwich standing up on its end, with jazz hands on either side, fingers aimed downward, like some bizarre cookery gangsta sign. After reading the instructions another time, I realized that all I had to do was turn the sandwich over, which sealed the open edge. It was the same muscle memory as paying rent, folding a piece of paper around a check to conceal the true contents of the envelope.

STEP 3

Press the excess plastic on the right side together and
fold it tightly over the top of the sandwich, pulling the
flap snug and pressing down gently so it sticks. Do the
same on the left side. Flip it over once more; gravity
will help the seal stay tight.

Believe me, this was not as complicated as the above instructions may have indicated. The fact that this sort of verbal hi-
jinks appeared in a publication called *Real Simple* should not
be overlooked.

By the time I patted down the left and right sides, despite
the exhaustive play-by-play above, the sun had not set, the
hens had not come home to roost, and the clock read just
8:44 AM. I vowed to get my wrap time down to less than a
minute by the end of the week. And of course, the true test
would be the sticking factor. When lunchtime rolled around,
would the package still be this masterpiece of hermetic engi-
neering?

Whereas I arrived at my cubicle around nine, Bruno usually
started his day at eleven, took a two-hour lunch, and multi-
tasked by chitchatting on the telephone, listening to Spanish
talk radio, and surfing the Internet. Normally, I would applaud this ability to buck the system and earn a solid pay-
check—if I didn't have to work with him. As an art director,
he was responsible for taking my words and doing something
visually interesting with them—like creating, for instance, a

four-color advertisement in a trade journal or a humongous sign to suspend above a conference booth.

While I hung up the picture of Eva Mendes and her Dorito sandwich on the edge of my computer monitor (a visual reminder not to eat anything out of the vending machine), I listened to Bruno on the phone. He was obviously conducting another seduction, emitting scratchy-throated *heh-heh-heh*s and validating his enamored listener with "Yes, yes, exactly!" After two years of occasionally being on the other end of the phone line, I could tell when he was talking to someone he was fucking.

I used to feel a deep pain in my heart when he'd have phone conversations like this while we were still screwing. It showed a lack of respect on his part that was unfathomable to me. And yet, even though I knew he was courting countless women, I still welcomed him to my cubicle—oftentimes right after he'd hung up the phone with one of his mistresses. I needed to be reassured, and his visits meant (I told myself) that he still desired me, that I still mattered to him in some small way.

For a while, I'd torture myself by listening to Bruno on the phone, hoping I'd finally discover, in my anger, the self-worth I had misplaced since beginning the affair. But the attempts at aversion therapy didn't work. It never got easier for me to hear him sonically caress someone else, but it didn't make a difference to my cravings: I wasn't ready to put the kibosh on our quickies anytime soon.

So I put my head in the sand. I didn't want to hear what I already knew. The split second Bruno's phone rang, I'd reach for my headphones and drown out his greasy seductions by blasting the White Stripes into my brain. Or, I'd play a constant loop of my theme song, L7's "Stuck Here Again." ("Yeah, yeah, I'm stuck here again. I've learned to make bad situations my friend. It starts all over just where it should end. Yeah, yeah, I'm stuck here again.")

As I pulled out that first semi-wrapped sandwich (one side had flopped open like a limp handshake), I toyed with the possibility that Bruno had ruined me. Not in the broken-shell-of-a-woman sort of way, but more subtly, more gradually. Like pushing his thumb in the dirt, Bruno had planted another small dot of disappointment in me, and the delicate new roots, gnarling with older, thicker, and deeper ones, reinvigorated them and spread them everywhere.

What if this was my lot in life, to be internally and eternally infected? Bruno wasn't responsible for all of the damage, but seeing him, hearing him, interacting with him every Monday through Friday was definitely picking at my scabs. And learning how to wrap a sandwich suddenly seemed a futile exercise, like fiddling while Rome burned. Where was an article like "How to Survive an Office Romance" when you really needed one?

I responded to this latest bout of Brunitis by weighing my options. Again. Even while Bruno and I were still, and I use this term loosely, involved, I always had the good sense to go out with other men. A few months earlier I had met a guy on JDate whose profile read like a Jonathan Franzen novella.

An economics professor at Georgetown University, Zelly appealed to me immediately, both for his erudite wordplay and his resemblance to my secret fantasy lover, Beck. However, after our first date, it was pretty evident (to me, at least) that we'd just be friends. I stood nearly six inches taller than Zelly, and I just couldn't shake the feeling of giganticness all evening. Zelly, on the other hand, freely admitted to having a tall blond shiksa fantasy, so the fact that I towered over him (and was Jewish to boot) didn't crush his hopes at all. In Zelly I saw the chance to expand my social dance card, and I figured that if I liked Zelly, I'd probably like his friends, so I allowed him to extend the fantasy. And when I learned that Zelly rode a motorcycle, I extended one of my own: the dream of becoming someone's bitch.

I had tried to fulfill this desire through Glen, the guy who loved cowhide and not me. As a marketing tool, he was riding around town on a BMW with a seat reupholstered in brown-and-white-spotted hide. With the hopes of becoming his bitch, I had purchased my own white motorcycle helmet, which began gathering dust in the corner of my apartment as soon as Glen found out about it.

At the end of our first date, Zelly gladly rode me home on the back of his motorcycle. And even though, holding on to his tiny shoulders, I felt like I was riding behind a squirrel, I knew my helmet would finally be seeing some action. When Zelly mentioned he was unhappy with the fit of his riding gloves, I offered to introduce him to Karl, whom I had met when the *Washington Post Magazine* hired me to cover an event at the ritzy boutique selling Italian high fashion where he worked. That day, while a Hugh Grant look-alike from Milan tried like hell to sell $6,000 made-to-measure suits to the loyal Brooks Brothers population of D.C., Karl and I had talked about his new Harley, which was parked, at a gravity-defying tilt, in the front window of the store.

Karl's boutique was having a huge sale the weekend Zelly and I met, and after hearing a dissertation the previous evening on Hugo Boss, I knew that Zelly was a fanatical shopper (and his small stature made him the perfect candidate for slim-fitting Italian clothing). So I asked Zelly if he'd like to swing by on his motorcycle and accompany me to the sale. Not only would I have another chance to ride on Zelly's motorcycle, I'd be putting two similarly interested guys together and maybe brokering a new friendship—a selfless gesture that canceled out my prime motive for wanting to take Zelly shopping.

It turned out that my matchmaking skills were top-notch, and Zelly and Karl quickly bonded over an equally distributed love of Italian clothing and Japanese motorbikes. Zelly quickly incorporated Karl into his inner circle, and as long as I played the unattainable Jewish WASP, I had a lifetime membership to Zelly's clubhouse. As I tried hard to extricate myself from the fickle grips of Bruno and Glen, I began to rely on Zelly more and more for my social livelihood. Coincidentally, so did Karl, who had up until recently been dating one of Zelly's friends.

After a while, Zelly found a taller, leggier blonde to chase, and he and I slipped comfortably into an easy, uncharged friendship. Karl and I continued to run into each other, mostly late at night, usually on someone else's couch, always with me regaling Karl with yet another story of love, my love, gone wrong. It was on one of those couches, at about 2:00 AM, that Karl reached for my hand, told me I deserved more than I was getting, and gave me that sly glimmer of possibility.

■

"If you're not busy after work, stop by my place for a drink."

Had I been emailing a friend, the above would have taken me around seven seconds to type. However, I was not emailing a friend. The recipient of the invitation was Karl, and I spent over an hour trying to achieve the casual tone and perfect balance of "It's cool, no biggie if you can't, but I am awesome, so why wouldn't you want to hang out?"

I counted to three and pushed send. Then, in a rare display of optimism (not to mention the uncharacteristic pairing of it with a man), I walked to a liquor store near my office and bought a nice bottle of Australian Shiraz and a six-pack of Miller Lite. Oprah had said that the healthiest alcoholic beverage for a man is red wine because, unlike most booze, it has a high concentration of antioxidants called bioflavonoids, which help decrease the risk of heart disease and cancer (although, Karl's smoking might cancel that last benefit right out). Beer supposedly helps protect bone mineral density, and the hops contain some B vitamins.

Back at the office, I bit the bullet and checked my email.

sure hows 7:30

There were no capital letters or any attempts at punctuation, but so what? With those sort-of words, I had turned into a breathless girl about to walk into her first boy/girl party. On those banner occasions when I met Glen for happy hour at our neighborhood bar, I had always felt anxious and unsure, like I was his Plan B. And with Bruno, there was always a catch. Like the time he invited me to his place for dinner, reheated some leftovers, and then asked for help with his tax return.

Once home, I walked though my front door and experienced my apartment for the first time, through Karl's eyes. I saw the haphazardly hung art, the butt-laden ashtray, the hideous venetian blinds, and, in the middle of the living room floor, the empty brown grocery bag I had left for my cat Raymond to play in. Welcome, Karl. I am a wacky cat lady with the refinement of a garage sale. Care for a cocktail?

Again, I considered the futility of sandwich month and wished I had started off with something more observable, like sexy hair month. But Karl already knew that I had wavy, dirty blond hair, usually with an errant bobby pin or two. While I waited for him, I killed time with an article in *Cosmo* that dissected what a man's food cravings (salty, sweet, or spicy) revealed about his personality—both in and out of bed. I had never seen Karl eat anything other than peanut M&Ms, which sort of qualified him for two categories, salty ("He hungers for the company of others so much that he can't stand to sleep alone") and sweet ("A true hedonist, this pleasure pursuer isn't afraid to indulge his deepest desires").

I was tempted to set out a bag of potato chips, a plate of cookies, and a bowl of five-alarm chili to see what he reached for first, but the chance of finding anything like that in my kitchen was, big surprise, zero.

At 7:25, I considered what sort of music Karl might enjoy. Once, when I asked Bruno what kind of music he liked, he mulled it over for a while and then answered, "I like very much what Jay Leno's band plays before the commercials." Not wanting Karl to think I had similarly questionable taste, I thoughtfully scanned my library and selected the Shins' first album, which was neither too fey (Belle and Sebastian), too estro-fest (Sleater-Kinney), or too ironic (Echo & the Bunnymen). Karl showed up just as "New Slang," my favorite song, began to play. As someone who has always believed in the portentousness of music, this was a very good sign.

"Nice hide," Karl said, walking over to the cow-shaped rug in the middle of my living room. "Did you get it from that guy who makes things out of cows?"

"Oh, do you know Glen?" I asked, trying to sound breezy.

"Everybody knows fucking Glen."

Karl's boutique carried some of Glen's handbags, and Karl and I sat down and immediately started ragging on Glen's P. T. Barnum–esque style of self-promotion.

"I've never met anyone so impressed with himself," Karl said, laughing.

"And one so completely unaware of his own bullshit," I continued. There was no way I was coming clean that I once desperately prayed for the attention of this blowhard.

We sat around drinking beer, talking about ourselves in the way you do when you have a completely new audience, and after a while, Karl shook his head slightly and said, "It feels like we're catching up. Like we've known each other our whole lives, but just haven't seen each other in a while."

"I've really missed you," I said.

I still can't believe what happened next (this coming from the same woman who regularly hiked her skirt up during office hours). But this time was different. This time there was no sex in cubicles, no sex on the roof of the Standard Hotel, no sex on South Beach while people practically stepped over us while strolling the shoreline, and no sex on the hood of a rental car in the Detroit airport (oh, Bruno and I got around!); there was no sex at all, actually. It was just that Karl kissed me like he had read my diary, holding my face in his hands, with an intimacy and tenderness that belied our brief history.

"I can't remember the last time anyone kissed me like that," I told him. Of course I realized that I sounded like a Drew Barrymore movie. But the fact was, I really couldn't remember what real kissing felt like.

And because I couldn't think of anything else to say, and because I always looked for trouble when things were going fine, I said, "How old are you?"

I knew Karl's mother was Chinese, and his father was American and Jewish. I knew Karl was born in New York and moved to Virginia as his parents were divorcing. I knew that the part of the Torah he read for his bar mitzvah was about a woman's menstrual cycle. I also knew he was younger than me. I just didn't know how much younger.

"Twenty-nine."

If he had asked me my age, I would have told him. But he just continued to kiss me.

After a few weeks of sandwich wrapping, I didn't even have to look at my cheat sheet anymore. Besides packing the PB&J standby, I dabbled in sliced turkey, smoked chicken, and even egg salad. I bought mustard again. And lettuce. I don't think I'd ever bought lettuce. When it wasn't too humid outside, I walked through Georgetown and down to the canal, the same canal I walked along on weekends with Jeanne, and ate my sandwich al fresco. It was relaxing, and I sort of felt like a schoolgirl, carrying my lunch in a Neiman Marcus bag. Sometimes I stopped by Karl's store on the way back to work and said hello or stood outside with him while he smoked a Camel. When I returned from those walks, especially the ones when I visited with Karl, I began to realize the only time I put on my headphones was when my other cubicle mate slurped her coffee. (And when she did, I thought, *How can anyone who's been to Italy so many times slurp her coffee?*) And, miracle of miracles, perhaps through some divine intervention of sandwich fixing, I no longer felt stung by Bruno's heartlessness. Lunch had gotten me out of more than just the office.

I also realized that in a small way, I'd overcome my resistance to doing something, even something as insignificant as grappling with Saran Wrap. In the aggregate these trivial accomplishments—baby steps really—did add up to quite significant somethings. Maybe that's why these magazines are so popular among women. What's contained inside shows the reader a perfectly imagined future where they won't eat junk food for dinner or become mired under the weight of a cruel and uncaring lover. And that is surely worth the cover price.

As I wrapped up June, I started to get hit with my July issues. It was incredibly hard not to peek, to flip through the upcoming month and get a *Christmas Carol*–like tour of my future exploits. But that would be cheating. I needed to do the month I was in.

Do the month you're in. It was a good strategy in general—even if it did sound like it was pulled out of a fortune cookie. Or off the cover of a magazine.

Roughing It

the subscription fulfillment process was in full swing. July and August issues monopolized my mouse hole of a mailbox, leaving little space for actual mail and causing me, in my gimme-gimme impatience, to scrape the skin off the knuckles of my retrieving hand.

As I hauled the latest cache back to my apartment, I felt pretty confident. After all, I had subjugated plastic wrap, thrown Bruno out with the Doritos, and Karl and I were nearing the one-month anniversary of whatever it was that we were doing (I wasn't *that* confident to label us as dating). I had even decided not to refill my prescription for Prozac, which I had been scarfing down like Pepperidge Farm Goldfish ever since my divorce.

But it didn't take long for my confidence to nosedive, belly flopping right into Oprah's pool of soul-affirming good-ness. It was there that I met Martha Beck, O magazine's pixie-haired life coach and my new sunny-faced nemesis. I may have kicked Saran Wrap's ass in June, but Beck was about to serve mine up on July's platter.

"Do you need a push to be more outgoing?" asked Beck in the title deck of her column. This month, Beck had developed an Index of Dread, an exercise aimed at achieving "superior social fitness" by logging daily activities in a journal and then rating how inclined or averse you are to actually doing each task. The story art showed a color-drenched photo of four peas nestled in a pod. A fifth pea had already jumped ship and was about to roll off the page.

I have never been a renegade pea. Safe and cautious, afraid to try new things, I never even bothered to learn how to parallel park. My worries reach far back and are troubling and unusual. In nursery school, I developed a profound fear of eye patches and beards. (But strangely enough, not pirates.) I wouldn't eat in restaurants that displayed dead animals on their walls—deer heads, stuffed pheasants in flight, stunned-looking raccoons balancing on tree stumps. This fear was very hard to manage, by the way, in Vermont, where my aunt had a ski house and I routinely ruined any stabs my family ever made at dining out.

"You came out of the womb worrying," my mother told me.

More recently, I dreaded the horrible things Karl was going to do to me. The likelihood of romance had stirred up a big pot of neuroses and I, shifting into anxiety overdrive, had begun to fantasize about all the ways Karl was going to fail me. The last time we had been together, I told him the suspense was unbearable. "Can you just do it already?" I begged.

"Do what?" he answered.

"Drop the other shoe."

My vulnerability triggered an overflowing fear of abandonment that would gush, if history predicted current behavior, into a twisted maze of inner voices and self-doubt, releasing a wooden mallet to Karl's knee, sending another tasseled loafer into the stratosphere and down onto my head. Ta-dah! I was the Rube Goldberg of neediness.

It was time to build a new contraption. One that puffed out confetti every time I tried something new or scary. One that held up a pair of prescription glasses so I could begin to see change as a gorgeous cinematic adventure. One that kicked me, with a tender foot, to just get out there and stop worrying about what, specifically, was out there.

At least this is what I was thinking about as I was swimming around in Oprah's pool with Martha Beck. "Keep fear from running your life," she enthused from the shallow end. And what I first saw as a pair of lead boots was, in fact, Martha holding out a life preserver.

So I grabbed it. This month, I would jump into unfamiliar waters. "If you consistently avoid a particular type of social interaction—perhaps professional situations in which you fear being criticized, friendships that invite disclosure of personal secrets, or any discussion that might lead to an argument," explained Beck, "it might help to do a little resistance training of your own." Martha was right. There was something really transformational in taking an active role in my life. To do this, I had to get out of my comfort zone, away from my laptop, away from my merlot and must-see television.

I had to go camping.

It was an idea that I had been batting around since Karl invited me to join him and a few of his friends in Monterey, California, to watch the American leg of the MotoGP, an around-the-world race on motorcycles. To defray the cost of the trip, the group was going to camp on the sanctioned grounds of the racetrack, which they had reserved for the low, low price of forty dollars.

With a complete lack of experience with the great out-doors, I wasn't just getting out of my comfort zone—I was excommunicating it entirely. But the giddy realization that Karl wanted to spend three solid days with me overrode any fears I had about bathing in a lake or cooking beans over an open flame—that's what you did when you camped, right?

Only after I accepted the invitation did the compound subject of *tent* and *me* really sink in.

"Does he realize he's camping with the princess and the pea?" was my mother's response upon hearing my plans. She urged me to inform Karl that most Jews prefer hot and cold running water and toilets that flush. "Tell him you want to stay in a five-star hotel."

Obviously, I don't come from an outdoorsy family. In all the years my brother David and I enjoyed the pool in our backyard, I never saw my father go in above the waist. He usually avoided touching the water altogether and preferred instead to lie on a floating king-size mattress, a red velvety extravaganza whose presence was the signal for my brother and me to STOP MONKEYING AROUND!

And my mother, who puts on full makeup just to take out the trash and refuses to visit me in Washington between April and September because she thinks it's too hot, my mother thought I had joined a cult when, as a Brownie, I told her how much I liked singing campfire songs.

My experiences with sleeping bags were all indoors and on carpet, at various preteen slumber parties. (Where I always unfurled my bed in the room's most isolated spot and still never slept more than a few hours.)

I phoned my brother David, the only person related to me with authentic open-air experience, which he gained when his best friend Ken gave him a fishing pole for his bar mitzvah.

When I informed him that I was about to go camping on the side of a motorcycle speedway and asked if he had any pointers, he laughed his head off for about ten minutes and finally said, "Get ready for a lot of drinking and farting."

Even though I knew this camping weekend would be good for me, I had a panic attack as soon as I'd purchased the roundtrip ticket to California. On the phone with the airline, I even had absentmindedly doodled some important instructions to myself. I had written, over and over in pressed-hard ballpoint pen, *Do not freak out!* I left in just eight days.

I needed Martha Beck to talk me down from the ledge. Her Index of Dread exercise was created precisely for precipice-teetering moments like this, and drafting my own Index of Dread was the first step toward solid ground. To begin, instructed Beck, "Take a few minutes every evening to jot down a list of things you plan to do the following day, and with whom."

Below, printed on the first page of a green spiral notebook, I imagined my to-do list for the upcoming camping trip.

ACTIVITY	ACTIVITY MATE(S)
Sleep in a tent	Karl
Not bathe/wash hair	My inner critic
Use Porta-John	The great unwashed
Watch motorcycles whiz by	More of the above
Pretend to like others	Larry/Amy/Tim/Ellen

Next, I assigned each item a score, which represented the actual Index of Dread (IOD) or "level of resistance to that activity." A score of zero meant I was not anxious at all. A score of ten, however, meant I'd rather lick the floor of a Greyhound bus terminal.

"Picture one event at a time," Beck continued, "as vividly as possible." In my head, I did a Hollywood movie montage of me interacting with each listed element and then awarded my points.

ACTIVITY	IOD
Sleep in a tent	8
Not bathe/wash hair	9
Use Porta-John	10
Watch motorcycles whiz by	4
Pretend to like others	11

And here I thought the facilities were at the root of my anxiety. But after completing this portion of Beck's exercise, I saw that my true fear rested in the company I would be keeping. The truth was, Karl's friends scared the shit out of me. They were like a Brett Easton Ellis novel come to life. I was afraid that I wouldn't be able to keep up—with their drinking, late hours, and general need for speed (motorcycle- and drug-related). Mostly though, I feared these people were well aware of my weaknesses and were just waiting for the right moment to expose and seize upon them for sport. ("I predict a lot of crying around the campfire," was how my friend Daragh, who knew this crowd, sized up the situation.)

Before I could wrap up Beck's lesson in social unrest, I had to carry out all the activities on my IOD list. Once I completed each task, I had to stroll down memory lane and reconsider how much I actually enjoyed doing it. Beck called this last step the Enjoyment Evaluation, or EE. I saw it as perception versus reality. Because I wasn't at this part in the experiment yet, I set the article aside, so I wouldn't spoil the ending. But without reading too much ahead, I predicted that by the time I got to the EE, I would have derived more pleasure from each experience than my majestic pessimism originally allowed.

This made a lot of sense. Isn't the anticipation of an unpleasantness, a flu shot, say, usually much worse than the actual experience? It was one of the reasons I stayed married for far longer than I should have. The prospective feeling of abandonment was unbearable—until he was actually gone.

After I finished with Oprah, I wanted the rest of the magazines to give me a pep talk. On a conscious level, I was looking to them for any advice they might have about preparing
for a camping trip. But what I was really asking for was vali-
dation, in story or picture form. I needed them to give me a
sign that I would be okay.

That I was looking for safety in a magazine with Lindsay
Lohan on the cover did not sneak by me. (Bedecked in a
marigold silk Dior tunic and a diamond Bulgari necklace,
Lohan didn't strike me as the sort of girl who would wear
Merrell hiking boots and convertible nylon pants.) I had
gotten into the habit of reading the magazines back to front
(to me, the meatiest stuff seemed to fall after all the front-
of-the-magazine product kowtowing). Which meant, in *Elle*,
the first thing I hit was the Numerology page. After doing
some surprisingly complex calculations to determine my
special number, here was what I read about the number 4.

> With or without your permission, July picks you up and
> sends you out of town. You'll be refreshed and revived
> by the experience, and you may even learn something
> new. Leave your safe ways behind (they will still be
> there when you return) and expand your horizons.

Elle was giving me a clear sign from the integer gods, an
arithmetical thumbs-up! In an instant, I stopped feeling like I
was heading off on a death march. It was exactly the brand

of encouragement I had craved from my shrink, a pink-faced
Swede named Dr. Oskar, who sat in direct opposition to this
trip. ("I don't like this for you," he said in an accent even
more fun to impersonate than Bruno's. "Yah, yah. You need
to stay in the hotel and look at the pretty mountains over
brunch.")

The planets continued their alignment in British *Harper's
Bazaar*, a souvenir from Jeanne's recent trip to England for a
writing seminar in Chichester. (Now that she was seeing
some forward action on my part, Jeanne had dropped her
suit against me and made a contribution to my cause with
this magazine, and I, seeing this as an emblem of forgiveness,
had decided to bend the rules to allow for it.) In a piece on
trends called "Dirty Pretty Things," Kate Spicer reported,
"Getting down to nature in the great outdoors is the hottest
new pastime for modern glamour girls." According to Spicer,
bluebloods have embraced "getting grubby" as "a statement
of style, not a dirty, windcheater-wearing secret."

Look what a little reframing could do to a once horrifying
idea. Camping was hot! With the right spin, a North Face
backpack had the potential to unseat the Balenciaga Le Dix
as the new "it" bag.

And Patagonia, I told myself as I walked into their chalet of a
store, was just like Barneys—but with more Polartec. I had
brought along the article from British *Harper's* as my style
guide. One of the women pictured wore a mod white anorak
and Jackie O sunglasses, so I was aiming for a Courrèges-

goes-high-performance look. Unfortunately, most of the clothing at Patagonia looked like it was made out of the Snuggles bear. The fact that I was going to resemble a mascot concerned me. This was an appearance I drastically wanted to avoid, so I sounded the alarm, announcing to anyone who looked my way, "I'm going camping!"

"No WAY!" high-fived a guy who could have been Keanu Reeves, if Keanu ever decided to move through life with a bandanna tied around his neck.

Patagonia Keanu had actually camped in Monterey before, which really shouldn't have come as such a surprise.

"Do they have real bathrooms there?"

"That depends where you're camping," he said, pulling various things made out of nylon and zippers from the racks.

"At the Laguna Seca Racetrack."

Keanu's expression turned to one of Big Sky country. In other words, his mouth was wide and open. "Um, that's kind of not real camping," he finally said, putting back some of the items he had originally pulled for me.

I walked out with a curry-colored pullover and a performance base layer (Patagonia-speak for long johns), items that would be functioning as my pajamas. I also left secure in the knowledge that there probably won't be any "facilities" where I'm going.

"Pet, you need to get out of this," begged Richard, of the formerly fabulously gay duo. Richard had gone solo ever since he sobered up and cut his ties from Ronald, who had sunk even deeper into drink, drugs, and debt (to Richard, mostly).

Richard and I trolled the aisles of Filene's Basement, consulting a page torn from *Real Simple* headlined "If You're Packing for a Weekend." Specifically, we were hunting for two items: a pair of sneakers that would pancake flat in order to save valuable suitcase space, and an appropriate bag into which to pack them. The visual of me wheeling my monogrammed Hartmann luggage out on the range was right out of *Private Benjamin* ("does this come in anything other than green?").

"Do you think Frette makes sleeping bags?" he pondered, whipping out his cell phone as if he were about to make an urgent call.

"Too bad they don't make toilet paper." This trip had fast become a scatological obsession for me.

Richard was operating under the delusion that I would fly to San Francisco (our first point of arrival before driving the rental to Monterey) and then part ways with the motorcyclists. "Let them go be among the bikes," he proposed, "and you go check into the Fairmont and spend the weekend shopping at Gump's."

Believe me, I had already come up with the same avoidance plan. Even as I purchased a Swiss Army ballistic duffel bag and Nike neoprene sneakers, I was toying with the idea of just not going. It was like the more sporting goods I acquired, the more I started to panic.

To make matters worse, the morning before my departure, Jeanne and I went for a walk. As we paused midway to stretch our calves on a section of a fence, she looked at me very seriously and said, "Cathy, this trip will either make or break your relationship with Karl."

She was right. It was such a hugely obvious fear; why hadn't I already put it into my head—and onto my IOD list—to begin with? So far, my relationship with him was unfolding under ideal conditions—hand-in-hand walks around the Hirshhorn, candlelit dinners at cloth-napkin restaurants, Tempur-Pedic pillow talks into the wee hours. What if I became overtired and got weepy? What if his friends annoyed the shit out of me and I got bitchy? What if it rained the entire time and I got trench foot?

Who knew what kind of prima donna meltdown I was capable of?

The first thing I did when I returned home from the walk was email my friend Jane in San Francisco. "Are you going to be around this weekend?" I wrote. "I'm about to chicken out of a camping trip and hoped I could stay with you." It would have been shameful to let a pair of nonrefundable tickets go to waste.

When Karl came over that evening, I sat him down, gave him a beer, and took a deep breath. "I think when we get to San Francisco, I'm going to stay and visit my friend and meet you at the airport for the return trip home."

He tilted the neck of his beer bottle toward him, gauged he didn't have enough to adequately slug down, and said quietly, "I didn't see that one coming." It was like I had just announced my desire to become a circus clown. "But why don't you want to go?" he asked, finally looking at me. "What's changed?"

ACTIVITY	IOD
Show Karl the real me.	10^{400}

"Nothing's changed," I told him. "I was never wild about the idea of going. I was just so focused on the idea of going away with you, I tried not to think about where we were going. But now that I'm thinking about it, I'm thinking I made a mistake."

"But why?" he asked again.

"I'm not as hearty as you think," I replied before jumping off the deep end. "I'm scared you're going to see a side of me you won't like," I told him. "Or what if I get tired and mean? What if I only want to drink two beers and go to bed early and everyone else makes fun of me and I start to cry? And what if you think that I'm asking you to choose between me and your friends and you start to resent me and leave me all alone in the tent?"

Karl didn't say anything for a while. Maybe he thought I still had more run-on sentences to go. Or maybe he had just never seen hormones on parade before and was struck mute. As inappropriate as it was to be thinking this, an idea for an article suddenly popped into my head. I'd call it, "You Really Fucked Up. Now What?"

Finally, Karl put his beer down and took my hand into his own, which was cool and dry. "It would mean a lot to me if you were there, and I'll do everything I can to make you comfortable and happy."

I was crying by now, realizing that I had fulfilled my own prophecy of presenting to Karl the most undesirable version of myself. "But what if you can't?"

"Then I'll take you home."

That was all I needed to hear. In admitting my irrational fears, the internal Index of Dread, to Karl, I had gotten the worst part of the trip over. And in asking for comfort, because that was what I was really asking for here, I was taking another kind of risk—one of total exposure. It was a relief and a small triumph to lay myself out like this. In doing so, I had clicked another piece of my own puzzle into place.

I didn't know what pieces were missing from Karl's puzzle, but sitting there on my couch, I had the calm certainty that the blue piece I had been carrying around for so long, the oddly shaped piece that I always thought was meant for the water, actually fit perfectly in Karl's sky.

Now I was ready for anything. I threw my Index of Dread notebook in my backpack, along with the carry-on items listed in *Glamour*'s "Getaway Beauty!": a giant bottle of water, great sunglasses, hand disinfectant, fragrance, and face spray. I supplemented their suggested inventory with cigar-sized rolls of toilet paper, toilet seat covers (both purchased in the sporting goods aisle of Wal-Mart), and a recently filled prescription of Ambien.

The campgrounds turned out to be a fire hazard of brown brush, clouds of perpetually settling dust, and a row of four tilted Porta-Johns that I knew, upon entering, would turn me into a Johnny Knoxville skit where I'd tumble end over end until I came to a soggy landing, at which point the door would fly open and there I'd be, with my nylon pants around my knees, a camping spectacular for all to see.

We arrived just after lunch, fatally late in the world of campers in search of desirable plots, so we were relegated to a depressingly uneven patch of dirt. There was no avoiding being tightly packed against our neighbors, one of whom was the orgy tent. Ever since Karl and I learned that Amy, Larry, Tim, and Ellen were friends in the same way that Bob & Carol & Ted & Alice were friends, we had started pairing the word *orgy* with anything that had to do with them. For example, they flew on the orgy plane to get here, stopped at the orgy Starbucks for some latte, and were sleeping uncomfortably close to us in the orgy tent.

It suddenly occurred to me that the only thing Karl and these people had in common was a shared interest in motorcycles and that maybe he invited me along to help mitigate his own Index of Dread. Maybe we were in this mess together.

As Karl set about hammering stakes into the dry earth, I noticed a few bare-chested kids running around. For a moment I was greatly relieved, since I thought the sight of small children somehow indicated an early bedtime for the settlement. But then I noticed the trailer directly behind us. It had an eight-piece drum kit set up under its tarp.

"Rock and roll!" yelled Crazy Larry, who had just discovered our proximity to the band. With the intensity and square jaw of Henry Rollins, he received his nickname for being, well, a little crazy. I was worried about Larry, who on the outbound trip started calling me Yoko (when he wasn't referring to me in third-person pronoun, as in "Tell her to sit in back," or "She'll go get our coffee"). It was the war cry of a jealous friend. Don't come between us, Yoko. And I was worried about Karl, who, aided by a few campfire beers, might actually defend this guy.

I made a show of pulling out my green notebook, which immediately put Larry on guard. "Are you writing about this for a magazine?" he asked, eyeing the notebook. Larry was under the impression that I was preparing some Hunter S. Thompson exposé on men and their motorcycles. I was under the impression that if I waved around my notebook enough, Larry and everyone else would be on their best behavior for the duration of the trip. (Coincidentally, Monterey, California, featured prominently in Thompson's book *Hell's Angels*. It was in Monterey that a small group of Angels allegedly gang-raped two teenage girls, a crime that immediately catapulted the motorcycle club to outlaw status.)

While Larry, Tim, and Ellen took the orgy car to buy groceries and a portable grill, Karl, Amy, and I cut our way through the campgrounds and caught the shuttle bus up the winding road to the racetrack. The landscape looked like a Road Runner and Wile E. Coyote cartoon. As we approached the track, Karl began to visibly shake with excitement. He grabbed my wrist and brimmed, "I'm going to scream like a teenage girl!" Seeing Karl in such an unguarded, spazzed-out state, I forgot about my own campy melodramas. I saw that we were beginning to create a shared history, too: "Hey, remember that time on the bus when you screamed like a little girl?" For the first time since arriving at this wasteland, I felt certain I had made the right choice in coming.

There was a practice run in session, and Karl sprinted off the bus and made a beeline for the chain-link fence that wove around the track like a giant dragon's tail.

"There's Hayden!" Karl yelled, pushing his nose through one open link. "And Gibernau!"

"Rossi, Rossi!" shrieked Amy. An Italian mop-top with a baby face and absolutely no guile, Rossi was the easy favorite among women. Even I knew his name. But with the riders bulleting by us like a smudged line, I had no idea how she could isolate Rossi from the rest of the blurs. I was momentarily impressed and wondered if Amy, who hadn't held down a steady job since I'd known her, could parlay this fantastic ocular talent into employment with the military—spotting enemy jets, for example.

After the session ended, we wandered around for a few more hours, drinking warm cups of beer and pushing our way through a tented midway filled with gumball-colored helmets, stiff leather jackets, and rows of glistening horsepower, before boarding the bus for home. I had successfully avoided using the facilities all day at the track, but when we arrived back at camp, it was time to face my fears. My strategy was to pick one Porta-John and stay loyal to it all weekend. I chose one on the end, closest to our tent, mostly because I remember reading somewhere that in public restrooms, the stalls on the end proved to be the cleanest.

My technique was to back in, because then I could focus on the door in front of me, rather than think of what was behind or beneath me. Other than the blinding chemical atmosphere of the interior, the visit wasn't so traumatic.

With this small victory, I rejoined the group. Ellen had placed an assortment of hot dogs, hamburger patties, and veggie burgers on a briefcase-size grill. From my duffel bag, I pulled out four wooden Popsicle sticks onto which I had pre-written "Meat," "Veggie," "Rare," and "Well Done," a suggestion from *Real Simple* on how to serve up a summertime meal.

"Here," I offered, "I made these markers to help you distinguish the meat from the veggie burgers."

Ellen looked at me like I had just handed her a pile of used syringes. "The veggie ones have green in them," she no-duhed me. "And I'm making them all medium."

Everyone else sat Indian-style along the perimeter of a tarp, which was also doubling as a mat for Amy's sleeping bag. As usual, Amy had brought nothing to the party and was mooching for anything she could get her hands on—extra socks, deodorant, dollar bills, Karl's Camel Lights.

"A cigarette tastes so good when you've worked for it," she noted.

The hours ahead of me seemed endless. I used the "Rare" Popsicle stick to clean under my fingernails. Pretty soon, Ellen and Amy were doing the same thing with the "Veggie" and "Well Done" sticks. The noise from the surrounding tents sounded like an entire suburb had left their doors and windows open and all decided to play their televisions at full volume. Mercifully, either due to technical difficulties or an act of God, the band behind us hadn't yet materialized.

There was nothing left to do but drink. A lot, even for me, and I was drinking one beer to their three. When Tim broke out a deck of cards, things went downhill fast. We played Asshole, a fairly simple game perfectly suited to the escalating inebriation—which explained why I easily won the first hand and became, as per the rules, "the President." With the position came power, at least for the next hand, and I got to enact a law that the other players had to follow.

"Larry, you may no longer use pronouns when referring to me."

The light thrown by a small lantern caught Larry's thin snarl. "Fuck off." He pointed his finger at me but looked at Karl. "Tell her to shut up."

I thought back to my Index of Dread. Now that I was in the middle of it all, suffering the pubescent rage of Larry and being basically ignored by self-satisfied dummies like Amy and Ellen, I found that my initial fear had been replaced by a wonderful indifference. I felt as if I had conquered the high school cafeteria.

Before Larry could bait Karl further (he was obviously disrespecting me as a way to incite Karl), I touched Karl's arm and said, "Can we go to sleep now?"

"Let's all go to bed," he hissed, looking at Larry.

With only two of us in a four-man tent, and a roof that unzipped into a skylight, being inside a tent was not as claustrophobic as I expected. Karl had brought along a full-size air mattress, and once we zipped our two sleeping bags together, I was surprised by how much I liked the accommodations.

"Is this five-star enough for you?" Karl whispered.

I rolled toward him so our noses were touching. "It's really not so bad," I admitted.

I had another Hollywood montage moment—me making coffee in a tin pot, me washing my hair under a waterfall, me whittling a walking stick. All to a John Denver soundtrack.

"How are you holding up?" he asked.

"Okay," I responded. My fidgety feet made *shhft-shhft* sounds in our sleeping bag.

"Are you sure?"

We were both avoiding the elephant in the other tent.

I *shhft-shhft*ed some more until Karl finally scissored his warm legs around mine and said, "Is Larry getting to you?"

I surprised myself by getting a little teary. Maybe I hadn't faced down my lunchroom tormentors after all. Or maybe I was just being manipulative. "I'm tired of being nice to someone who's not nice to me," I finally said.

Karl cupped the back of my head. "Then stop being nice."

He slid his hands inside the waistband of my Patagonia base layer. Just as I realized I was about to have sex in a tent for the first time in my life, the orgy tent came to life. It didn't take long before it felt like Karl and I were in there with them. Together in one giant sleeping bag.

"Let's do shots of vodka!" Ellen cried. Amy let out some impressive ear-piercing shrieks.

"Knock it off!" growled Karl, switching on a small lantern.

"We're on vacation. Vaaaaacaaaaashun!" Ellen taunted, drawing the word out into eight syllables.

Karl reached out and jabbed the tent wall, which was pretty much flush up against the orgy tent wall. "I'm not kidding." He jab-jabbed. "I'm so tired my ass is twitching."

"Aw, is the baby tired?" singsonged Larry. Then came his fist, shrouded in our tent wall.

"Drop it, man," said Karl, "Now." He grabbed Larry's puppet fist and give it a twist.

"Drop what?" mocked Larry, pausing for effect before adding, "Man?"

"Fuck you," said Karl.

"Fuck YOU," said Larry.

"No, fuck you."

"No, fuck *you*."

"You."

"No, *you*," said Larry, changing the rhythm slightly by adding a "pussy" at the end.

Karl handed me a pair of earplugs and asked me to put them in.

"You have five seconds to shut the fuck up," he yelled over to Larry.

ACTIVITY	IOD
See Karl unleash his anger	I'd rather go to the Porta-John

I had been so worried about Karl seeing me in a bad light, I hadn't figured on Karl being the one to degenerate first. "I'll be right back," I said, unzipping the tent door.

With my earplugs still in, I experienced an eerie calm

inside the Porta-John—until I detected a muffled scream of, "No, Karl, no!"

Yanking out one earplug, I heard Karl yelling, Larry yelling, and a group of unfamiliar voices yelling. In the time it had taken me to make my silent bathroom walk, Karl had obviously punched Larry, a dustup had ensued, and some of our neighbors had busted up the brawl.

When I climbed back in the tent, my flashlight caught Karl laying spread-eagled on top of his sleeping bag, his eyes fixed on the apex of our tent's ceiling. He was breathing hard, I could see that, but with one earplug still in, my senses were warped and I confused the sound of breathing with one of sobbing. So I leaned over and, with the back of my hand, felt his cheek for tears.

Crazy Larry was still mouthing off in his tent. "It's over, Karl," he mooned. "Find your own way back to the airport. No one likes you anymore—except her."

"What did you do?" I whispered frantically.

"Nothing."

"What did you do?"

"Nothing."

My hand went from his cheek to his chest. His heart was beating like a rabbit.

"I don't believe you."

"I'm sorry," he said, rolling away from my hand.

But I knew what he did. He defended my honor by putting his friend in a headlock. And I knew what I did. I had turned into an episode of *The Real World*, playing the victim, squirting some tears, and manipulating Karl with my crazy girl emotions. In less than a day, I had taken Karl from rapturous teenage girl to Irish street fighter. What if he thought I was too much of a mess? What if I had just ruined the whole trip? My Index of Dread list suddenly looked like a joke. Toughening up went way beyond peeing in a Porta-John.

I reached inside the tent's convenient little inside pocket and felt around for my bottle of Ambien. Even though Dr. Oskar had warned me not to take a sleeping pill if I had been drinking, I swallowed one anyway.

I awoke to a smooth jazz version of "Go Ask Alice," and the unmistakable sounds of motorcycles being started. It was 7:00 AM, and I still had two more days to go.

Outside, the sky was scrubbed an unblemished blue. I stood in the cool sun and brushed my teeth, rinsing with an unopened bottle of Poland Spring, which I found underneath one of our foldout chairs. Inside my duffel was a Ziploc bag filled with *Glamour*'s "What to Pack" skin items, cleanser, moisturizer, body/foot lotion, emergency pimple lotion, and deodorant. I hadn't washed my face in twenty-four hours because the nearest sink, which looked like a pig's trough, was located about half a mile away, at the top of a small brown hill. The showers, located in a small trailer, were even farther away. Luckily, Amy had left a Mylar bag of Pond's facial pads (her only contribution to the trip) by the door to the orgy tent.

While Karl slept, I sat in a foldout chair and consulted

Marie Claire's "10 Best Ways to Look Hot Despite the Heat."
I was specifically concerned with number 4, "Nix a sweaty
neckline with two ponytails (one slightly higher than the
other), a great trick for layered hair." The model demonstrating this technique was adorable, her twin tails looked fun
and carefree.

"How about a hat?" Karl suggested, confirming what I
had already suspected—I looked like an ass. With two tails.
He crawled out of our tent and handed me a yellow painter's
cap with Valentino Rossi's number 46 across the brim, free
swag from the Yamaha tent.

We spent the day perched on top of a massive peak,
watching the riders come shooting down a small portion of
the track, like kids on a waterslide. We passed a pair of binoculars back and forth, and Karl tried to make the monotony of
bike, bike, bike, nothing, nothing, nothing, bike, bike, nothing
more appealing by imparting the racing history of every
single MotoGP competitor since the dawn of time. It was a
diversion tactic, of course, a way for him to avoid talking
about last night's pugilistic spectacular.

But I was desperate to know that everything was okay
between us. So desperate, in fact, that I committed verbal
plagiarism.

"Thanks for making me feel so safe," I said, lifting verbatim from this month's *Cosmo*, "Four Ways to Stroke His
Ego."

It was really amazing how much magazine-speak had
seeped into my language center. I was immune to nothing,
no matter how cliché!

"This trip has been a true test of your mettle," he noted, taking my hand for the first time all day. "I'm really glad you decided to come."

Maybe *Cosmo* was on to something.

That evening played out like the previous one, minus the brouhaha and plus the camper band playing a four-hour set of ZZ Top and Lynyrd Skynyrd. (When the crowd started to boo the fifth reprisal of "Legs," the singer apologized with, "Just remember, we're free.") The following day, too, was a repeat, except for a racetrack appearance by Brad Pitt and Adrien Brody, whom I viewed through my binoculars.

"This deserves a hug," said Larry to Karl, who extended his olive branch after two Americans, their favorite racers, took first and second place.

After the final race, we broke down our camp and drove to Santa Cruz, where we spent our last night in the comfort of a hotel with turquoise-colored walls and pink and green starfish on the bedspreads. For the first time in three days, I sat down on the toilet. Suddenly, every entire thing felt like a reawakening, from taking a shower, which left an impressive ring of dirt around the tub, to seeing my reflection in the mirror. I hardly recognized myself. It looked like I had summered in Saint-Tropez. I couldn't get over the whites of my eyes, which looked like they'd been Photoshopped. Amazingly, the first word that popped into my head was *healthy*.

Sitting on the starfish bed with my hair clean and softly air drying, watching *The Sopranos*, I felt a deep contentment.

My whole life, I've carried the reputation in my family for being delicate and hypersensitive. Their words, not mine—but words I had always pinned to my chest. Less than a week had transpired since I had composed my Index of Dread. I pulled out the chart and considered the Enjoyment Evaluation. (Remember, the lower the EE number, the lower the pleasure I had derived.)

ACTIVITY	IOD	EE
Sleep in a tent	8	8
Not bathe/wash hair	9	10
Use Porta-John	10	0
Watch motorcycles whiz by	4	7
Pretend to like others	11	4

I came, I saw, I camped. The only thing that remained a constant was my absolute dread/total lack of enjoyment of the Porta-John. Not a surprise. What was notable, however, was how much I enjoyed leaving my vanity packed in a duffel bag for a few days, how nice it was not to care if the part in my hair was straight—or if I even had a part. I didn't need a mirror to know that I was still there. And when I finally did see my reflection, in a hotel room that I once would have considered tacky, I didn't comb it for flaws.

Karl was sleeping on the other bed, his right arm bent at the elbow, his hand poised like Adam in a Sistine Chapel finger point. In the scheme of things, maybe a fear of camping was a relatively manageable one, but that didn't diminish the pride I felt lying there next to Karl on that pink and green bed. I honestly couldn't remember the last time I felt so good about such a simple accomplishment.

I slipped outside and phoned Jeanne. "I survived the Porta-John!" I announced by way of a greeting.

"Oh, Cathy!" I could feel her genuine pleasure as she exhaled deeply. "You and Karl made it!"

AUGUST

Jean Therapy

the more magazines that arrived in my mailbox, the
more overwhelmed I became. Under the foolish impression that I somehow didn't have enough content
to draw from, I filled out subscription cards to *Jane* and
Harper's Bazaar. Their arrival this month was enough to put
me right over the edge. I had so many dirndl skirts, lip glazes,
and sizzling summer sex tips in my head, I felt like I was
cramming for an exam. (*InStyle* actually had a feature entitled "Fashion 101.")

I realized I was going a bit batty when, at a party one
weekend, I overheard someone talking about Valencia, Spain.
I had just read an article about Valencia's "Hidden Gems,"
but for the life of me, I couldn't remember where. Was it in
Bazaar? Or was *Bazaar*'s travel piece on Positano and not
Valencia? Wait, maybe I read it in O magazine. Didn't Gayle

go there on her honeymoon? No, that's not right. Before long, I was driving everyone at the party crazy with my train of thought. My madman's itch to get to the bottom of the Valencia mystery was agonizing. Once home, I toppled stacks of magazines onto the carpet and tore through each one, page after violent page, until I found the article. It was in a three-year-old issue of GQ that I had swiped from Karl's apartment.

Another side effect of having an amalgam of magazine articles in my head at all times was that I was paying way more attention to fashion than I ought to. This month, the whole peasant look had me really stressed out. Intellectually, I knew that if I wanted to successfully dress like Eliza Doolittle, I would have to layer, wildly. But when I saw the three-tiered paisley skirt modeled across a two-page spread in *Self* magazine, what to pair it with baffled me—a cable-knit sweater and a smocked blouse? Slouchy boots? Or a crazy-quilt concoction of a Donegal tweed vest, mandarin-collar smock, and high-heeled loafers? I saw myself walking down Twenty-third Street on my way to work in one of the getups featured in *Allure*'s "Peasantville"—a billowing paisley silk shirt and skirt, a velvet corset, eelskin lace-up boots, and what looked like a tasseled curtain pull as a necklace—and easily recognized there was no way in hell I was going to pull off that look. The skill required to peacefully introduce so many textures and textiles together—velvet, wool, silk, eel—was too advanced. Plus, it was about 90 million degrees in D.C., so the last thing I wanted to do was dress like an extra from *Doctor Zhivago*.

Which was why, weeks after my camping trip, I was still

wearing what my friend Richard had lovingly nicknamed the *Survivor* sandals (when he wasn't referring to them as "those unfortunate bull dyke sandals"). If Jesus had played for the NBA, he would have worn these beauties. All hopped up on brown leather and Velcro, still covered in a layer of fine dust from the motorcycle track, they made Birkenstocks look dainty. I had also been sneaking around in my nylon-and-polyester hiking pants, which were cropped and a confused shade of blue. Like the sandals, the pants employed Velcro, the official fastening device of all outdoor gear. Worn together, the look was so unflattering and unfashionable, I wouldn't have been surprised to open up *Glamour* and find a photograph of me, front and center in "Dos & Don'ts," with a black bar across my eyes.

Like someone who continues to wear their personalized Mickey Mouse ears long after they've left the Magic Kingdom, I was the walking embodiment of a bad souvenir. Or, even worse, I was this month's centerfold from *Field & Stream*. I decided my mission was to get my wardrobe back to big-city standards.

Practically all the magazines had something major to say about dungarees this month. *Glamour* clocked in with a ten-page feature called "Your New Jeans," with a special "Flattery Top 10!" section showcasing denim for every kind of body shape. *Cosmo* also had a similar concept with "Blues for Your Bod." But, as Rudyard Kipling once wrote, "Never the twain shall meet."

BODY TYPE	*GLAMOUR* SAYS	*COSMO* SAYS
Boy shape	Gap, straight fit	Tommy Jeans
Petite	Joe's Jeans	Levi's
Full thighs	American Eagle	Gap
Long torso	Tommy Hilfiger	Diesel
Long legs	Rock & Republic	Polo Jeans Co.

Cosmo also had a solution for "Flat Butt," my particular problem. "Built-in butt lifting pads give a barely-there booty a little boost." At $198, the FRx Clothing brand jeans (does this stand for "Fanny Rx"?) weren't a joke, even though they sounded like the sequel to *Saturday Night Live*'s "Mom Jeans" parody.

I had never heard of the FRx brand before, and I wasn't about to waltz into Neiman Marcus and ask where I might find their butt-pad jeans. So I walked to the Georgetown outpost of Miss Sixty to look for what *InStyle* called "the cream of the cropped." The photo spread showed the pair of just-below-the-knee jeans worn four different ways:

- **Downtown Bound,** paired with a pink and black empire top and gold flats;
- **Country Escape,** tucked into tall boots with a sweater coat opened to reveal a wife beater;
- **Flash Dance,** teamed with a baby-doll top and stilettos; and
- **Class Action,** matched with a ladylike blouse, fitted jacket, and peep-toe pumps.

I did the math. For $159, I was really getting four different jeans and spending only $39.75 for each.

I got about two feet into the store and immediately experienced what I call the Urban Outfitter Effect. There's a period in your life where you delight in shopping at Urban Outfitters—all the ironic message-print T-shirts, kooky calico-print skirts, and zany shower curtains. And then you walk in one day and think, *Am I the oldest person in here?* That's what it felt like to be standing in Miss Sixty, wondering if the men's clothing was on the right side or the left.

I grabbed at the first salesperson I saw, a lanky guy with closely cropped cornrows and silver pants, and gave him an apologetic silly-me look. "Am I in the right section?" As if to illustrate my confusion, I pointed to the rack in front of me, which consisted of orange nylon genie pants and stretched-out tank tops with 1980s spin-art designs.

"What did you need help with?" I waited a beat before he added, "Ma'am."

I showed Silver Pants the page I tore from *InStyle* with the cropped jeans. "Do you have these?"

He studied the picture for a while and seemed to actually be reading the whole article. "I'm going to have to look around," he said, taking the page with him.

I followed Silver Pants around the store while he eyeballed the racks for any short-legged pants. Occasionally he'd stop on a pair, hold it up to himself, look at the *InStyle* picture, and then silently place it back on the rack.

"I know we had this style a few months ago," he said,

sounding like someone who forgot where they put their reading glasses. Except he was about twenty years away from needing them.

Thankfully, there were very few customers around to witness the clueless foreigner being led around by the supercool native. Everything about this experience was mortifying to me—from the Day-Glo homage to 1980s fashion that I had actually worn in the '80s to the beeping and whirring electronica being pumped out at ear-bleeding decibels, to, when Silver Pants eventually found the jeans (on the sale rack for half price!) the dressing room curtain that provided about as much privacy as a hospital gown.

The jeans fit perfectly, which didn't really surprise me, since my body is still pretty much prepubescent (no boobs, hips, or ass). Even if I wasn't a schoolgirl, I could still fit into schoolgirl clothing, which is not necessarily a good thing. I didn't want to end up looking like one of those desperate housewives who try too hard to be hip and young. (Like Lindsay Lohan's mother, for example.)

"Do you have a question?" asked the cashier, even though I was standing in front of her with my jeans in one hand and my wallet in the other. Was she as confused by my presence in the store as I was?

"Yes," I said. "I have a question. Can I buy these?"

Next to me, twin girls were jointly buying a shredded T-shirt. As the cashier rang them up, they faced each other and silently mirrored each other's movements. The one in the micro mini would slowly circle her arm and the one in the skintight low riders would begin to slowly circle her arm.

They reminded me of those creepy "Play with us" twins from *The Shining*. The woman ringing me up wasn't giving them the time of day, but I couldn't stop staring—at their identical Bettie Page hairdos, their undead pallor, their telepathic game of Simon Says.

After the sisters left, I wanted to bring the cashier into my intimate view of them and say something like, "What do you think was up with those girls?" But I was afraid that would make me sound like my mother. When I lived in NYC, I brought my parents to the East Village, and my mother went into fashion-police overdrive, making loud comments about all the pink hair and apron dresses on Eighth Street. I remember feeling sorry for her then, like she was fundamentally unable to appreciate the carefree fun and experimental wit that the young so naturally possess, especially in downtown Manhattan.

And now, standing adrift in Miss Sixty, I at last understood my mother's haughty disdain. I didn't like young people anymore. Especially the gangs of college girls who walked around Georgetown dressed in their layered tank tops and micro kilts. I hated their long Victoria's Secret hair and the way they pushed by me without ever saying, "Excuse me." Feeling invisible was not, as I had recently read in *Allure*, the sole domain of over-forty actresses in Hollywood. We are all competing for something, and the fact that we will inevitably lose our ingenue status is heartbreaking in its simple truth.

I wasn't ready to blame the inordinate amount of time I was spending with women's magazines for creating this Victoria's Secret insecurity—but the magazines were definitely pollinating my preexisting condition. The more I looked at pictures of clear-complexioned, strong-jawed women, the uglier and more out of place I felt in stores like Miss Sixty.

Walking home, I hit on my true challenge. August wasn't about a pair of new jeans. It was about a set of old genes. In order to feel comfortable in Miss Sixty, I had to feel comfortable in Miss Thirty-nine.

It wasn't just the Miss Sixty experience that had me feeling so focused on my age (a cold, hard fact that I still hadn't revealed to Karl). There had been a confluence of events over the past few days that left me particularly vulnerable.

For one, there was the phone call that Karl received from his most recent ex-girlfriend, Jackie, a twenty-four-year-old model. I had seen a picture of her once, when Karl was opening some files on his desktop, searching for a photo of his old Triumph bike to show me. When he accidentally landed on the photo of Jackie, who was wearing a bright yellow bikini and leaning forward to show off her impossible cleavage, he closed the image with the trigger finger of a Wild West outlaw and said with a mix of pride and shame, "I had to try the cliché at least once."

So I wasn't very inclined to like this girl, even though Karl had told me she was crazy and superficial and too high-maintenance (don't all guys describe their exes that way?). When she called, Karl was sitting next to me, talking about bugs.

"Did you know that cicadas don't have a mouth or an anus?" he informed me, just before his cell phone rang.

Jackie was calling to ask if Karl had any extra tickets to see Thievery Corporation, a local band who was playing a sold-out show the following night. Why she thought he was suddenly a ticket scalper was beyond me, but that's not what I focused on. No. I was stuck on the fact that even though I looked pretty cute in my new jeans, I was never going to look like a twenty-four-year-old bikini model.

"She still thinks we're friends," explained Karl, thinking the threatened look on my face was one of jealousy and not one of envy. "She doesn't understand that it's over."

It may have been over for him, but for me, things were just beginning. Jackie's phone call went hand in hand with an article I had just read in *Glamour* that confirmed, in 1,500 words, all the fears I had about where I lay along the continuum of bikini model and old bag.

In an article entitled "Men's Upgrade Addiction," Rory Evans asked, "Why is it that guys can't seem to resist trading in everything—from their iPods to their girlfriends—for a new version?" A harshly lit photo of Brad and Jen, their lips pressed into tight smiles and staring vacantly in opposite directions, was placed side by side with a color-drenched one of Brad and Angelina. Angelina looked smug and completely full of herself. Brad, his hand casually tucked into his front pocket, looked like he just had the best lay of his life. Along the bottom margin of the page, in a CNN-like crawl, was this breaking news item: "Infidelity starts in the mind: 30% of committed partners have fantasized about cheating."

Now, the smart thing to do would have been to quickly move along to the next article, "Make Over Your Hair without Cutting It." (Besides jeans, hair was also big news this month.) But I had already pulled up to the car wreck. The need to rubberneck was too irresistible.

If I weren't already the "older model," Evans's article would have been great fun to read. In it, she came up with hilarious nomenclature to describe the ways men cheat, from "'expiration dating' (cycling through girlfriends more quickly than it takes the milk in the refrigerator to sour)" to "'nesting-doll wives' (marrying younger, newer versions of essentially the same woman)." She recounted the tale of a high-profile Hollywood husband who cheated on his wife, one of "Los Angeles' best-looking women," by slumming it with "ultra-*average* looking women."

Evans quoted notorious celebrity cads like Bill Maher: "It's never about big or little or short or tall or blond or brunette. It's only about old and new." And she cited an interesting study of a male lab rat who "will copulate early and often with a cohabitating lady rat, and then his libido apparently tapers off . . . until a different lady rat is put in the cage and he gets busy with her all over again."

It was impossible for me to glean anything good from all of this. Evans didn't even offer any constructive advice, other than to satiate men's constant need for novelty by constantly evolving ourselves. "We have to do our part and invest in change," she concluded. I suddenly remembered that scene from *Fried Green Tomatoes* where Kathy Bates, attempting to jazz up her marriage, greeted her husband at the front door swaddled in Saran Wrap (a skill that I had thankfully mastered back in June).

Was this my destiny? Would Karl trade me in unless I answered the door wearing nothing but a Brazilian wax and a platinum blond wig? (My brother and I once found a ratty Marilyn wig in our attic, and when my black-haired mother saw us playing with it, she had said, "Oh, your father bought that for me and asked me to wear it out to dinner one night." Which she did. Just once.)

But my mother was nine years younger than my father. She was also so entirely comfortable sitting up on my father's pedestal, so entirely convinced that she looked just like Catherine Deneuve, so entirely content with where her life had landed her, that I couldn't imagine her ever worrying about being retired for even a second out of her thirty-five-year-marriage. When my dad wanted something different, he bought a new pair of Ferragamos.

And even though she had zero concerns about her own relationship, that didn't stop my mother from bothering with mine. After two months of dating Karl, I finally decided to tell my parents I was seeing someone new.

"Is he Jewish?" was my father's first question.

"He's half Jewish," I replied, "and half Chinese."

"Oh. He's a Chew," he quipped and passed the phone to my mother.

"How old is he?" was her first question.

"He's twenty-nine."

"Be prepared for disappointment" was all she said.

After having recurring nightmares where Karl, appearing as a club bouncer, carded me and then refused to let me past the red velvet rope, I made sure I had my driver's license on me at all times. When I slept over at his place, I put my pocketbook on the floor next to my side of the bed, and when he was over at my place, I stored it in the bottom of my desk drawer. I was constantly preoccupied by my dirty secret and fretfully wondered how long I could keep it comfortably underground.

"No, no, I don't like this for you at all," pronounced Dr. Oskar when I admitted I still hadn't revealed my grand age to Karl. "He will not mind," he prophesized. "He wants to only celebrate you as the beautiful woman you are." Dr. Oskar was big into celebrating me. He had heard enough about my mother to know that she hadn't partied enough in my honor (when I told him that my mother had once sat me down, at twelve years old, and in defense of always wearing makeup, informed me I was no Christie Brinkley, he choked up and said, "I need a moment to get over my sadness for you").

I promised Dr. Oskar I'd come clean to Karl before our next session, which was a week away. "That way, if he dumps me," I reasoned, "I won't have to wait that long to cry on your couch."

"Karl will not leave you over this," he assured me. "But please listen to your dreams. They are very anxious for you."

So, between the phone call from Karl's boob-infested ex, the piece in *Glamour* about a man's biological compulsion to trade up, my mother's spectacularly unsupportive remark about steeling myself for disappointment, and the nightly outings of myself in dream form, I'd say there was a lot of anxiety in bed with me.

And yet for help, I had no choice but to turn to the same sources that were contributing to my suffering. After all, shouldn't these magazines also dispense equal amounts of optimism to balance out the stinging despair of articles like "Men's Upgrade Addiction"?

So I began to look for the good. Maybe Diane Lane could offer some encouragement. Here she was in *Self*, talking about how she was finally comfortable in her own skin. "Luckily," she reflected, "40 is the new 30." Which was great news, because that would make Karl and me the same age. Lane also joked that she gave herself a husband (the studly Josh Brolin) for her fortieth birthday and credited more sleep for her good looks.

In "Dating *You* at 20, 30, 40," Jake, *Glamour*'s thirty-two-year-old male columnist, offered his "man's opinion" on what he had learned after wining and dining three women from three generations. "All turned out to be flings," wrote Jake, "but in that brief period of comparison shopping, I learned a lot about what's great, and not so, about dating women of every age."

Jake, who was pictorially represented by Jude Law in *Alfie*, and the spanning decades by Sienna Miller, Marisa Tomei, and Susan Sarandon, opined on everything from . . .

HER SEXIEST BODY PART

20s: Anything chubby. Chubbiness is unbelievably attractive in women in their twenties because it's springy, curvy and healthy looking. Does it subconsciously signal their fertility? Is that the draw? Who knows—maybe it's just cute.

30s: The butt. It's sexy at *any* age, but women in their thirties are old enough to love and flaunt what they've got.

40s: The calves. Or any other part that shows strength. Sarah [Jake's "Sarandon"] has such beautiful, defined calves, I used to beg her to wear skirts.

to . . .

WHAT'LL IMPRESS HER

20s: I gave Stephanie [his Sienna] a favorite book of mine, one that came out maybe 10 years ago. She was thrilled to be introduced to Martin Amis. In 1995, after all, she was busy reading the Torah at her bat mitzvah.

30s: Unlike Nora's [or Marisa's] previous boyfriend, who was 27, I knew enough to pick a vacation spot that hadn't been featured on a *Girls Gone Wild* video.

40s: Sarah appreciated my ability to begin foreplay without the aid of a little blue pill and dismount without having chest pains. Note: She'd just divorced a 53-year-old.

I reread the article, substituting my ribbon legs for Susan Sarandon's sexy calves, and wondered if Karl would have been so faux-charitable in his own categorizations. Did he find his ex–bikini model's "night out" ensemble of "stilettos and sparkly dress" sexier than my "designer suit," which, according to Jake, is the fuck-me outfit for women in their forties? (I had already put myself in the forties slot, since I would be, in four short months.) What if Karl preferred the kind of conversations he could have with Jackie, who "hadn't gotten to the point where arguing about Led Zeppelin versus The Rolling Stones, God versus Nietzsche, and Snickers versus Milky Way seemed cliché" to the special kind of chit-chat he could have with me—where, like Jake's older woman, I'd use my seasoned perspective to assure him that his "big life quandaries," from his beliefs about marriage to his questionable career choices, "would work themselves out just fine." ("Sometimes," revealed Jake, "just feeling understood is the best aphrodisiac.")

I looked at the photo of Sienna Miller with her head thrown back in open-mouthed laughter, a flute of champagne in her hand and compared it to the one of Susan Sarandon, who was eye-locked with Jude Law. He was leaning forward conspiratorially and painting her fingernails a Russian red. I didn't know whom Jude wound up with in the movie version, but postproduction, he had continued to romance Sienna, who didn't look like the kind of girl who would squander precious party time waiting for her polish to dry.

I flipped back to *Self* and had another look at Diane Lane,

who made a much better mirror for me. She was too good
for the likes of Jake/Jude. Sure, she was beautiful in an unfussy, unmadeup way that probably took three hours and
four stylists to stage, but there was still something about
Lane that was entirely transcendent. To paraphrase the
famed line from *When Harry Met Sally*, how could I have
what she was having?

I found the answer in *Real Simple*, where three female
writers, all confounded by traditional standards of beauty,
discovered that "true or real beauty can best be found by creating standards of one's own." In her essay, Lily Tuck examined how she was shaped by her mother, to whom
appearance, and its meticulous upkeep, was everything. Lisa
Teasley's definition of beauty was informed by black men,
who rejected her for darker skin and "regular black girl" features. And in the final essay, Ann Patchett discovered that her
attractiveness was influenced by her geography. Because she
didn't have big hair or blue eye shadow, she was dowdy in
Kentucky; because she wasn't a gay man, she was invisible in
Provincetown. She finally felt at home in Montana, where
her freshly scrubbed face and lip-balmed lifestyle fit in with
the rest of the residents, male and female.

Of the three women, I identified most with Lily Tuck,
who wrote about her changing attitude toward going gray,
which she had recently embraced, but had combated for fifteen years with hair dye. She contrasted her un-dye-ing,
quite literally, with her mother's dying: "My mother, until
the day she died in her eighties, was blond." The desire to
preserve her youth, her gilded artifice, ranked higher than

anything else—even her health. Tuck's mother, we learned midway through the story, refused chemotherapy to treat her cancer. "She claimed that if she were to go bald she would no longer be able to look at herself in the mirror," wrote Tuck.

I don't have gray hair, and my mother does not have cancer, but still, when I read that line, I instantly wormholed back to a conversation I had with her years ago. I was spending the weekend with my parents in Connecticut, on hiatus from my totally chic life as an executive trainee at Bloomingdale's, and as I usually did when I was home with nothing much to do, I came down to breakfast unshowered and with very little intention of even putting on a bra until suppertime.

"How can you stand to look at yourself in the mirror like that?" complained my mother.

Like Tuck's mother, mine also derived her sense of self through what she reflected back to the world, her adoring audience. Like Tuck's mother, mine also felt duty-bound to maintain her good looks. If you were born pretty, as my mother was, you stayed pretty, no matter what.

Back then, when I was doing my own Goldilocks search for style (*These stirrup pants are just right!*), my mother was always regarding me, cataloging what I had on my feet ("I knew a girl who used to wear shoes like that," she'd comment, "until she fixed her club foot") or appraising the efficacy of my hairdo ("When you don't fluff the back," she'd note, "you look like you have cradle cap"). Whenever I did assent to wear makeup, she'd stand at the bathroom door and watch me like a cat. "You look pretty," she'd allow, after I had put on my face.

And so I spent a great deal of the vulnerable years between girlhood and womanhood (and beyond, quite honestly) thinking my mother's interest in me was purely cosmetic. When she sat me down and announced that I was no Christie Brinkley, she was telling me that I was not a natural beauty and I should get used to having a makeup bag as a constant companion. Not surprisingly, my mother's standards of beauty (which included a slavish devotion to Revlon's Love That Red lipstick and her treasured black Armani pantsuit) developed out of her own painful past. She often referred to her preteen years as her "chubby baby" phase and admitted to still seeing a fat face every time she looked in the mirror.

I knew then, as I know now, that my mother only wanted for me what she had wanted for herself—to be accepted, to be popular, and to have a happy life. But back then, her way of expressing this ambitious wish for me really did a number on my self-confidence. Instead of landing in that soft spot of unconditional love, I often felt that the only way to win her acceptance was to model myself after her. Whenever I was home for a visit, I'd walk around my house in a What-Would-Mommy-Do haze, wondering if I'd ever find the perfect shade of me. But the barefaced truth was (and still is) I looked horrible in red lipstick.

Struggling against my mother's beauty paradigm had the unintentional benefit of generating my own standards. I may have turned my back on her red army, but I was in no way retreating. No. I was still fighting for something; I just was using a more gently hued arsenal.

As if reflecting on my mother and her makeup bag wasn't enough, Karl invited me to meet his mother, Joy, for dim sum. This presented a few problems, least of which was the actual meeting of his mother. For instance, dim sum contained unidentifiable food that could kill me—like kung pao shrimp dressed in moo-shu-chicken clothing. Worse, we were going to a traditional Chinese restaurant out in the suburbs, and that could only mean one thing: our table would be set with those paper placemats depicting the Chinese zodiac. I was 100 percent sure that at some point during lunch Joy was going to look down at her placemat and innocently ask me when I was born.

"Why don't you find out what animal will make you thirty-two?" schemed my mother.

"Because I don't want to lie," I said.

"I would."

But as far as I was concerned, I had already cracked open my fortune cookie and learned my fate. There was no escaping it. So when we got to the restaurant and I saw those placemats, the same placemats of my imagination, with the twelve zodiac animals positioned around a *Wheel of Fortune*–like circle and the words "What's Your Sign?" done up in fancy calligraphy across the top, I felt psychically vindicated. The only thing I couldn't have predicted was how long I could dodge the bullet. I sat down next to Karl, and immediately reached up my skirt and began to dig my fingernails into my thighs.

Joy knew half the staff, whom she brightly greeted in Cantonese. An ancient woman in a shiny red cheongsam immediately swooped down on us and set heavily chipped dinner chargers directly over our placemat's zodiac wheels. As long as we continued to eat, I figured, the stimulus for my undoing would remain hidden under plates of greasy dumplings. Karl told me that dim sum typically lasted for three hours. I wondered if I'd have any flesh on my thighs by the end of the day.

Joy continued to hold court with the waitresses, each of whom she held by both wrists while trilling like an exotic bird. I was so thankful for the whole flock, since they also served to distract her from the placemats. After the last one flitted off, she shifted back around in her seat and looked terribly amused.

"Do you want to know what they were asking me?" she giggled. "They all wanted to know if you are my daughter-in-law."

I found a nice meaty piece of flesh and dug in deep.

"In Cantonese, there is no word for girlfriend," she explained before continuing on her delightful roll. "So I guess Karl is just going to have to marry you."

I couldn't tell if she was fucking with me, fucking with her son, or just fucking around in general. So I decided to play along.

"Well, I guess I'll soon find out if you really like me or not," I teased.

"How?" asked Joy, suddenly intrigued.

"If I suddenly start puking," I cautioned, "I'll know you secretly told the waitresses to give me shrimp balls."

Since Joy had done all our ordering in Cantonese, it was a real—albeit absurd—possibility. I think Joy fully appreciated the comedy I was suggesting for her. "Don't worry." She laughed. "You'll live."

I spent the rest of the meal feeling half like the life of the party and half like dead man walking. When the busboys finally cleared our table, I was desperately praying the placemats would go, too. But there they sat, stained with duck sauce and spilled tea.

I became more and more frantic, filling up every inch of dead air with increasingly ridiculous questions. "Where did you grow up in China? How long have you been a nurse? Have you ever seen a dead body? Do you like cats?" I knew it was coming, and finally, it did.

"Cathy," Joy began excitedly. "I'm year of the monkey. What animal year are you?"

I flashed back to an article in *Real Simple* about how to handle nosy questions. "How old are you?" got five noses out of ten on their nosiness rating scale. But none of the suggested responses ("I'm aging rapidly just thinking about it" or "Age means nothing to me—I'm a character actress") worked when animals were thrown into the mix. Unless I tried answering in dog years.

I quickly scanned for my animal. The snake. There I was, 1965, carousing among those born in 1905, 1929, 1941, and 1989.

"I think I'm the year of the snake."

There was a moment of silence as Joy consulted her placemat.

"No, you can't be." She clucked. "Look again."

I continued staring at my placemat. I had yet to look over to Karl.

"Yes, that's right," I said with more confidence. "I'm year of the snake."

"You can't be," Joy insisted.

"I can."

This went on, seriously, for a few more rounds. Finally, Joy pounded her small fist on the table and said, "But that means you would have been born in 1965."

"I *was* born in 1965."

Things could have gone a few different ways at this point. Joy might have responded with something flattering like, "Wow. You look so much younger." Or with a neutral, "How nice for you." I even would have accepted, "Oh, Karl and his Mrs. Robinson fantasies."

The reaction I wasn't expecting was a fifteen-second: "NOOOOOOOOOOOOOOOOOOOOOOOOOOOOOOOOO OOOOOOO!"

As Joy continued to cry out like she was falling off a cliff, waitresses came out of the woodwork to offer their help. As they formed a shield around Joy, I turned to Karl, who was staring at his knees, and said, "Did you know how old I was?"

Without taking the focus off his lap, Karl began to slowly shake his head back and forth in small, silent *no, no, no*'s.

Cosmo had an article this month called "6 Signals His Face Is Sending You." With his lips pressed into a thin line and his face remaining in profile, Karl was giving me the dreaded combo of "He's having doubts" and "He needs some space."

The back of my neck felt wet, and my hands were buzzing. I couldn't imagine what was going to come out of Joy's mouth next. When she finally stopped shrieking to the heavens, she said matter-of-factly, "In 1965, I was in my second year of nursing school."

We spent a few more agonizing moments waiting for the check, which Joy paid as foot-in-mouth penance. Getting up from the table, I played a horrible game of "If he doesn't hold my hand/put his arm around me/come within two feet of me, he's going to dump me." And when Karl didn't reach for my hand as we walked from the restaurant to the car, I was certain he was disgusted with the idea of touching my rotting flesh. I imagined he was replaying all the times we'd been naked together and how he couldn't wait to take a shower and wash off my decrepit germs.

As we drove back to D.C., I planned out the rest of my afternoon. When Karl dropped me off at my apartment, I would walk to the 7-Eleven and buy a bag of Doritos and a few giant Snickers bars. Back home, I'd fling myself on the bed, cry my eyes out for a few hours, and then call my mother and tell her she was right.

I imagined my good-byes to Karl. *It's been a nice time,* I would tell him. *I liked you very much. I'm sorry I'm old.*

From the backseat, Joy said, "So, Cathy, what brought you to Washington?"

Great. Now she's going to find out about my divorce. Is this what they mean by Chinese torture?

"I moved here to be with my boyfriend at the time," I told her. "But we broke up." Which was mostly true.

I caught Karl's eye, finally, and whispered, "Should I tell her about my prison record?"

He took his right hand and placed it on top of my left and patted a few times. Then, he slid his hand next to mine and let our pinkies touch. When we drove right past my apartment building, I felt the bottomless relief of waking up from a bad dream.

We all arrived at Karl's apartment and before Joy continued home to Virginia, she hugged me around the waist and said, "Next time, you pick the restaurant."

After Karl and I had sucked the life out of a few cigarettes, we lay down on his futon with our noses touching.

"How do you feel about what my mom said at lunch?" he asked bashfully.

"I feel like throwing up," I answered, closing my eyes.

"What?" Karl sat up on one elbow and laughed. "Why?"

"Because all this time I've been afraid that you'd think I was too old for you."

"That's funny," he said. "Because all this time I was worried you'd think I was too young for you."

It was like we were in some perverse "Gift of the Magi" story. *But I sold my Game Boy to buy you a gold-plated walker!"*

"You mean you knew?!" This was stunning news to me.

"Yeah," he replied casually. "But not exactly how much older. I figured you might be a Rabbit . . . maybe an Ox."

"And you don't care?"

Then, just as I had seen his mother do with the Cantonese waitresses, Karl took both of my hands in his and said, "I love everything about you."

And I realized that I had been reading these magazines hoping for the same kind of tender care. But instead of helping me feel good about myself, the sisterhood had merely provided the nod for what was already in my head, tickling my neuroses by manufacturing problems that weren't even part of my world—but would be, if I continued to read the magazines as parables for my own journey.

In what should have been the biggest no-shit moment of all time, I was only now just recognizing that just because I read an article about men trading up or making "I need space" faces, that didn't mean that Karl was going to, for lack of a better phrase, "pull a Jake" on me. At that moment, I realized the very real possibility that instead of helping me get a better life, these magazines might just bring about my downfall. All heroes have a tragic flaw—what if believing in *Cosmo* was mine?

I seriously thought about canceling all my subscriptions.

SEPTEMBER

Bust a Move

for the past week, Karl had been dropping hints about moving in together, commenting, for example, on how well our belongings would merge and how compatible our decorating tastes seemed. Now, considering that Karl's aesthetics ran toward the postapocalyptic—a collection of inside-out socks strewn over all available surfaces; a trail of dirty dishes leading straight to the bedroom (and ending with a plate of half-eaten scrambled eggs under the duvet); and a twisted motorcycle carcass hanging on a bathroom wall—I wasn't really sure if he saw his approach to design truly blending with my more Aunt-Fanny-Drops-Acid-at-a-Fleamarket whimsy.

Then, on the phone, each of us in our separate beds, Karl had said, "You'd be easy to live with."

This comment was like 2 in the 3-2-1 countdown to cohabitation. Overanalyzing as usual, I heard Karl's round-abouts as a preamble to a much more official conversation.

And I was ready. After nearly four months of dating, we were practically living together anyway. If Karl wasn't sleeping in my bed, I was clearing the dishes off of his. We had already survived some rough patches (for me, at least)—the camping trip, his mother-traumas, the aching details of my divorce—that had added metaphoric years to our nascent relationship. It was like that scene in *The Jerk*, when Steve Martin documents the rapid course of his relationship with Bernadette Peters. "I know we've only known each other for four weeks and three days," he whispers to her as she sleeps next to him, "but to me, it seems like nine weeks and five days."

Once again, I didn't want to lean on my own understanding. Which is why I was able to slide so easily back to the comfort of magazines, the way a junkie succumbs to the warmth of the pipe. I was addicted to the quick fix.

And so I found myself once again at the same bookstore where just a few months earlier I had stood for hours in front of a wall of screaming women's glossies. But I was not in front of that wall quite yet when as I was heading toward it, something on a different set of shelves completely stopped me along the way. Something that was screaming even louder:

The Cohabitation Trap
When "Just Living Together" Sabotages Love

A sun-kissed blonde in an orange halter dress and ponderous expression stared sideways at me from the cover of

Psychology Today. She held a chrome floor lamp with a purple-striped shade, its chord lassoed around her and her boyfriend, who was nuzzled against her, smiling like he had just seen God, his eyes closed in divine bliss.

Upon closer inspection, I realized the cover date was July/August, and I saw this as a personal sign from the publishing gods. The outdated magazine had somehow climbed back on the shelf just so I could learn from its magic. There was nothing on the subject of shacking up in any of my September issues; I had already been through them twice looking for exactly that, madly ripping through each one looking for the good stuff in the same way a twelve-year-old boy devours a *Playboy*.

I needed this information right away, and who knew when my ladies would get around to revealing the goods? Intent on finding out if I was literally making the right move, I didn't want to wait unknown months to find out about what *Psychology Today* was offering me right now—like the characteristics of "The cohabitating type," or "What to do before you cross the threshold."

So I scored me some *Psychology Today*. I had never read the magazine before, but because of its title, I had always assumed it was on a par with the *New England Journal of Medicine* and read primarily by academics or members of the trade. I felt lucky that these professionals were providing expert guidance for just $3.99 plus tax. Once inside, though, it was obvious I had been majorly mistaken. Maybe it was the photo of a lion tamer in a top hat next to a feature about a man who cured angry people with a little whipping of compassion. Or perhaps it was a story under the Insights column that promised to reveal what the length of your fingers said about your sex life. Was this *Cosmo* for the math and science crowd?

Despite the colorful typeface used in the story title, "The Perils of Playing House" was a grim piece of writing. In fact, the story began with a giant orange letter *F,* which composed the first word of the story: *Forget.* Were those bastards at *Psychology Today* trying to send me a subliminal message? I read on. "Couples who move in together before marriage have up to two times the odds of divorce, as compared with couples who marry before living together."

Well, yes. I had lived with my ex-husband for a year before getting married, and clearly that hadn't worked out. But still, in my mind, living together went hand in hand with marriage. Moving in meant marriage. And because this was the sequence of my first marriage, I was deeply conflicted about wanting this same progression with Karl. I feared that I was destined to repeat my same miserable history.

The editorial supported my doomed expectations. "We move in together, we get comfortable, and pretty soon marriage starts to seem like the path of least resistance. Even if the relationship is only tolerable, the next stage starts to seem inevitable."

This was really depressing stuff. The article went on to analyze all the wrong ways people move in together: slowly, one toothbrush and bra at a time, until they're de facto roommates; experimentally, choosing to take a trial run rather than commit; stupidly, under pressure to move the relationship forward.

It was hard not to read this with one foot in the past, one cast in midair. With my ex, I was guilty of all of the above. But with Karl, I was guilty of nothing. How could I forgive myself for things I hadn't done yet?

■

After I was done reading, I did something that, depending on how you looked at it, was either stupidly brilliant or brilliantly stupid. I left the magazine out on my coffee table. Sure, there was probably something subconsciously premeditated to my carelessness, like I left it there on purpose for Karl to find. Like I left it there because even though I had long ago decided to let Karl be the pacer of our relationship, I was tired of dancing around and wanted to force the issue. Like I left it there because I had gotten quite comfortable with letting magazines do the talking for me.

Whatever the mental underpinnings, I set the magazine on my coffee table (cover side up, no less), turned on *Judge Judy*, and forgot about it. Forgot about it until Karl unexpectedly dropped by later that evening.

"Oh, ho, ho," he singsonged, picking up the evidence. "Doing a little research?"

I had already come clean to Karl about my self-improvement project, so he had a vague sense of what I was doing with all these magazines in my apartment, but I'm not sure if it had actually dawned on him that he would be a major player in the story.

"What does the magazine have to say about living together?" he asked, gingerly resting it in both palms like it was the Magna Carta.

"I'm pretty sure the word *trap* used in conjunction with *cohabitation* is not a good sign," I answered.

"I'll be the judge of that," he said, walking toward the bedroom with the magazine.

With Karl off in the bedroom, I felt nervous and off balance. After all, I had just willingly handed over my playbook and showed Karl all my moves. Then again, I wondered how much stock he would actually put in what he was reading. Ever since reading O magazine's *Ah, Men!* June issue, Karl had a blanket hatred for all my magazines and for Oprah in particular. When I had asked him why, he responded like a freshman who had just signed up for her first women's studies class.

"Because Oprah is a perpetrator," he had insisted. "She preys on any insecurity a woman might have, and confirms these insecurities with bullshit articles dressed up as expert testimony. What a great way to sell magazines," he had sniffed. "Yellow journalism for women."

"Is this what they're teaching you in *Maxim*?" I had joked, realizing that poking fun at his magazine of choice was easier than trying to defend my gendered love of Oprah.

I had only seen Karl react this way once before, when he unleashed a torrent of insults concerning the appeal of Sarah Jessica Parker, the very definition of *belle laide*, a personified middle finger to conventional beauty. Men hate her for the same reasons women love her. I had thought SJP was an anomaly, but then I started reading *Oprah* and realized she held an equally powerful dividing rod.

When Karl emerged from the bedroom, I had already done some preemptive wine guzzling. A bit numbed by the booze, I was ready for "the talk." One, I now worried, that I had deviously preordained by leaving the magazine out in the first place. One that could completely backfire on me.

"Did you learn anything interesting?" I asked, taking the magazine, which Karl had rolled into a tight tube, the way a relay racer grabs a baton—and then runs away as fast as possible.

"Nothing that I didn't already know," he answered ambiguously. "What did you get out of it?"

"The main takeaway for me was the importance of discussing our expectations about living together right up front, before even one box is packed."

I refilled my wine and poured him about nine fingers' worth of whiskey. Karl took a healthy pull and took another tiptoe through the topic. "Well," he slowly edged, "what are your expectations?"

I was too chicken to tell him that my expectations led straight to a proposal. So I danced around the topic. "I think we need to just make sure each of us is getting what we'd like from the arrangement."

I sounded like I was making some sort of deal with Sammy "The Bull" Gravano. *I think this would be mutually beneficial for the both of us. Badda bing!* But I also realized that I was talking like we had already had the discussion to live together, like it was already understood that, of course, this is what happened next.

Karl brought up the massage chair to illustrate his expectations. A week after our camping trip, Karl had showed up at my door with a globular black armchair that, once plugged in with its garden hose of a cord, pounded, kneaded, or vibrated its way into every imaginable nook and cranny. It was a merit badge of sorts, a reward for surviving the rigorous demands of the outdoors. It was also the ugliest piece of furniture ever to cross the threshold of my apartment. At the time, I didn't want to criticize his largesse, afraid I'd turn him off from future gift giving. But at the same time, I worried that the vibrating chair was just the tip of the déclassé iceberg. What would be next—a velvet Elvis? Even worse, what if Karl was an unromantic gift giver— did he even know his way around a jewelry counter?

Pointing to the chair, which I had shoved as far into the corner of my living room as geometrically possible, he said, "If I told you a month ago I was planning on getting you this chair, it wouldn't have been as good as my just showing up at your apartment and surprising you with it. It's the same thing with living together. To analyze and discuss and pick apart what it all means takes all the fun out of it."

"But look at what it says right here," I said, opening up the magazine and pointing to the "Talk Talk Talk" section of the article. I tried not to whine, but I could feel that familiar tone of quiet hysteria enter my voice. "'It's helpful for partners to talk about topics ranging from the sublime to the mundane,'" I read. "'Marriage, kids, life goals—and who will take out the garbage or feed the cat.'"

"Listen to me," he said, prying the magazine out of my hands. "I know that I just want to come home to you every day. Beyond that is left for discovery."

Did he understand what I was really asking? It was true that he was answering me fully, just not fully answering the question I was *really* asking: Will this all lead to marriage? I racked my brain trying to recall any of the tips from O magazine's June feature, "Getting Him to Open Up." I remembered, for example, that it was vital to "Choose the right time" when embarking on important subjects. And that it was strategically smart to have any life-changing conversations on his turf. Luckily, since the first two tips were moot by this point in the evening, I also remembered an actual line from the article:

"That's so interesting," I said coolly. "I wouldn't have thought of it that way—please go on."

Karl gave me a look like lava had erupted from the top of my head.

"Let's say you move in with me," I inched, copping another of Oprah's tactics. "Can you tell me what needs to happen in order to take the next step?"

"I'll try and make all my crap fit in with your crap."

"No"—I inched again—"what do you think would happen next?"

"We'll spend some time bumping around, trying to make room for all my motorcycle parts."

"And next?"

"Oh, baby, are you worried?"

Karl was taking a totally different read on this conversation. He was correctly sensing my insecurity, but his timing was all wrong. He understood my "nexts" as being about immediate concerns when I was really talking about the future.

"The article says that couples who cohabitate are less satisfied, argue more, and have lower levels of commitment," I recited, realizing I had this part practically memorized. "Doesn't that worry you?"

"I don't think we have any of those problems," he said, taking the magazine away from me and tossing it facedown on the floor. "We just kick ass."

Karl would find a young student to take over his lease at the end of the month, and then would move into my apartment. (Because really, that was the only option, considering Karl lived in a subterranean cave—where if moving from room to room I forgot to duck, as I always did, I'd slam my forehead against the top of every door frame.)

With one major set of logistics resolved, new ones presented themselves. Now, I had to make room for Karl. Metaphorically speaking, I had made tons of space for him. But that didn't do me much good when considering, for example, the state of my closets. A parade of mismatched shoes cluttered the floor and made it impossible to get inside for a good look, as did the sagging racks, anachronistically organized with 1980s pleated-front khakis traffic piled into low-rider jeans, sandwiched next to, tragically, a pair of OshKosh B'Gosh overalls.

Clearly, I needed to divest myself of at least five hundred pounds of clothing. A writer's words are her babies, but to me, so was my beloved and trusty wardrobe. I didn't know how—let alone want—to edit it.

Once again, I was back on the pipe, jonesing for my magazines, hoping for a hit of competence. Basically, I needed to demolish and then rebuild a wardrobe with half the closet space.

To celebrate its eight hundredth issue, *Glamour* offered eight hundred beauty and style ideas in what they called their "Bible of Insider Scoops, Solutions and Secrets." However, once inside, I noticed that their holy book was a bit misleading. Instead of eight hundred separate and distinct tips, I quickly deduced that the editors counted a column like "11 Reasons We'll Always Love Black" as eleven ideas, which was sort of cheating the reader a bit. (And actually, the eleven reasons should have been ten, since number 1 and number 11 were the exact same reason: it's slimming.)

But despite their hinky math, I was still able to find plenty of inspiration from *Glamour*'s scriptures. To help pare down my wardrobe, I focused on the "84 Things You Need for the Perfect Wardrobe."

- 14 pairs of no-visible-panty-line undies
- 7 bras (2 black, 3 nude, 1 pretty color, 1 convertible)
- 1 warm coat
- 1 good suit (pant or skirt)
- 2 work blazers
- 1 casual weekend jacket/parka
- 8 knit tops (a mix of cardigans, pullovers, and heavier sweaters)
- 5 shirts and blouses

- 10 good tees/tanks
- 3 little-bit-sexy, dressier tops
- 4 pairs of work pants (1 black, 1 khaki, 2 others)
- 2 pairs of jeans
- 1 pair of other-fabric casual pants
- 3 dresses (1 you can dress way up)
- 3 go-to-work skirts
- 2 pairs of shorts (or casual skirts)
- 2 good-fitting swimsuits
- 4 pairs of flat shoes/sneakers (1 work-appropriate, 3 others)
- 5 pairs of heels (2 work, 2 fun, 1 dressy)
- 1 pair knee-high boots
- 4 bags (1 work, 2 casual and 1 night)
- 1 set hat/scarf/gloves

An encouraging note accompanied the list: "Don't panic about the number—think of it as a goal!" (Which made me wonder—was *Glamour* trying to calm the readers who needed to pare down to this number, like me, or to work up to it?)

What followed was an exhausting trip down memory lane. I encountered the first coat I ever bought with my own money, a Calvin Klein navy duffel coat that I acquired in 1989 at Barneys New York for $600. With the hood on, swallowing my head and instantly robbing me of my peripheral vision, I looked liked the Grim Reaper. If I could only have one warm coat, this was not it.

I found the Anna Sui pin-striped dress I wore to my five-year high school reunion. While all the other women wore some boring variation on the little black dress, there I was, fresh from NYC (I'd show these plebeians!) in my larger-than-life lapelled, faux-double-breasted, Wall Street-meets-Jessica Rabbit glory. I had even managed to find pin-striped stockings to confound the whole look. And just to ensure NYC-sophisticate overkill, I had tied the whole ensemble together with a stiff leather motorcycle jacket and a perpetually lit cigarette. Considering my nickname in high school was Brownnose, I was aiming for the whole Olivia-Newton-John-as-Sandy transformation. In reality, I probably looked more like a drag queen on a smoke break, but at the time I thought I was hot shit, which explained why I had saved the dress all these years. But again, if I could only have three dresses, I was not willing to sacrifice current style for outdated memories.

A dress I did keep was an orange velvet empire-waist number that belonged to my mother. When she gave it to me, she had said, "I paid a lot of money for this in the sixties." It's true that if you keep something long enough, it's bound to come back in style. With its high-seamed bodice and romantic mix of velvet and paisley, my mother's old pride and joy looked like it had just walked off the sketch pad of Marc Jacobs. Plus, the cut gave me excellent cleavage.

I also hung on to a 1940s brightly painted and outrageously sequined Mexican skirt, a popular souvenir that women brought back from their honeymoons. I purchased it ten years ago at Manhattan's Twenty-sixth Street flea market and have worn it continuously (though it makes me look like a walking piñata). This season, finally, designers had caught up to my fashion acumen, and everyone from Cynthia Rowley to French Connection to Donna Karan was doing a version of my skirt. Naturally, I was convinced that I was responsible for the whole craze.

By the time I was done with my closet, the majority of it lay heaped on the floor. Among the casualties bound for Good Will were anything made out of velour (unfortunately, this would be more than you might think), a disturbing number of belts, and an office's worth of suits (happily forgotten as soon as I abandoned my position as a Bloomingdale's executive trainee and opted for a career in the dress-code-free world of advertising).

I also discarded enough shoes to rival my local DSW. Jeanne once mentioned she read an article that estimated the average woman owned forty pairs of shoes. "Per season?" I innocently asked.

In the end, a rough count confirmed that I had twice the wardrobe that *Glamour* advised (remember, it was just a goal!), but I had still successfully freed up more than half of my closet—including, once I pitched my bulky L.L.Bean ragg wool, reindeer-print, and Nordic ski sweaters, an entire shelf!

The things we do for love.

Moving on to the bathroom, I used *Glamour*'s "19 Beauty Items Every Woman Should Own" as a guide to dump an entire medicine cabinet of gummy nail polish, any suspicious-smelling lipstick, and about a decade's worth of sample perfume vials. Surprisingly, for a pretty clueless beauty shopper (that was a challenge for an upcoming month), I had everything on *Glamour's* must-have list:

1. Foundation
2. Tinted moisturizer
3. Concealer
4. Mascara
5. Black or brown eyeliner
6. Neutral eyeshadow
7. Fun-colored eyeshadow
8. A rosy bronze blush
9. A lipstick that works day and evening
10. Clear nail polish
11. A lash curler
12. Slanted tweezers
13. An 1,800-watt blow-dryer
14. A wide-tooth comb
15. A round brush
16. A shampoo for my hair type
17. A daily conditioner
18. A deep conditioner
19. Anti-frizz crème for curly hair

I had already looked in the cupboard under Karl's bathroom sink, and knew that we were headed for trouble. He bought in bulk, and from the looks of things, had cornered the market on Yardley's Natural Oatmeal & Almond Soap. I had a similar soap problem, just on a slightly smaller scale. Deaccessioning my collection of hotel soaps, especially the bite-size Hermès samples, was a personal defeat of sorts. I had been hanging on to these morsels for years, imagining how they'd play out in my future guest bathroom, contained in their fancy logoed green boxes, coolly waiting to cleanse and impress the scores of visiting hands. The soaps marked me as an expensive traveler, even though Jeanne, an authentic five-star guest, gave most to me as souvenirs.

I realized I was using the space under my sink as a hope chest. But if I cleared space for Karl's soap stash, I was actually fulfilling a less invented future for myself. One that wasn't valued by illusion.

When my brother David was potty training, he availed himself of any open receptacle that remotely looked like a toilet. My mother found him variously in the garage, crouching over unused flowerpots, in his bedroom, squatting, most fittingly, over his Tonka dump truck, and on our front lawn, aiming into the hole left by an old tree stump.

Karl packed his belongings in a similar fashion. Anything that was suitable for stuffing was suitably stuffed. While he lugged over the latest carload from his end, I unpacked it at mine. During one exchange, I unfurled a lumpy sleeping bag and found it filled with an entire library of Ian Fleming paperbacks. Lifting the lid off a surprisingly heavy saucepan, I discovered about fifty million at-large BB pellets. And, in a spectacularly unpleasant morning wake-up call, a box of cereal contained heaps of dirty nickels, not, as promised, bunches of honey and/or oats.

As long as I was in charge of dispersal, everything had a place, either hidden in a drawer, tucked into a bookshelf, or, like the set of sticky shot glasses I found in a pair of tube socks, chucked in the garbage.

Unfortunately, there were some items that defied placement. One night, while Karl worked late at his new job (he was now a marketing director for a national retail chain), I busied myself with the contents of a mesh laundry bag. Loosening the drawstring, I shook the bag open and poured out a dozen boxes of lightly scented tea lights. Along with the candles came a leather presentation box. Lifting the lid, I expected to find some vintage wristwatches or maybe Karl's bar mitzvah cuff links. What I wasn't prepared to encounter was a roll of twenty-eight condoms, all expired. He had never lit candles for me, and we did not use rubbers. I had a vision of Karl, splayed out on his futon with the bikini model, aglow in a thousand tea lights, going through Trojan after Trojan.

I immediately phoned Jeanne and reported my findings. "The only thing missing was a Barry White CD."

"At least the condoms were expired," she offered, trying hard not to laugh.

"Should I feel relieved or concerned?"

"I think you should quit while you're ahead."

When Karl got home later that night, the incriminating pile was right where I had left it.

"Did you light those candles for all your girlfriends?" I wanted to sound playful, but I succeeded in coming off like an insecure twit.

"And how was your day?" he asked mockingly.

Pointing to the snake of condoms, I said, "It was going fine until I decided to help you unpack."

"I guess my pimping days are over." He sighed.

It wasn't that I had found the condoms. It was that I had opened a leather presentation box into his past. "I don't like to imagine you with other women."

"You think it doesn't kill me to know you've been with other men?"

"Didn't you know I dropped out of the sky a virgin?" I gently teased.

"And just so you know," he offered sheepishly, "those candles were just for me. After a certain hour, bright lights bother my eyes."

This was such an unsexy statement, how could I not believe him?

Occasionally, there was a design challenge. My hundred-strong collection of bride-and-groom cake toppers, for example. I had been collecting them since my early twenties, after I had seen hundreds of them marching around the store window of a Rhode Island antiques store. Whether an adult way to play with dolls or evidence of a burgeoning fetish, I loved my miniature couplings and made a point of proudly displaying them. When I lived in New York, my collection congregated on a bureau in my bedroom. Whenever a new conquest would walk past them on his way to the bathroom, he'd always return with the same strained look on his face.

"What are you, obsessed with getting married or something?" he'd always ask.

My army of brides and grooms were my best barometer for men. And luckily, Karl wasn't threatened by what they represented. He was simply bothered by their existence.

"One cake topper is the equivalent of ten doilies," he insisted. He also complained about their placement in the bedroom. "I don't like them watching me sleep." I compromised by wrapping all but my favorite ten couples in tissue paper and storing them on the top shelf of the linen closet. Karl cooperated further by adding a pair of plastic motorcycles to the processional.

Karl had been living with me for a week, maybe more. It's a shame I didn't remember the exact date, but it just sort of happened. Like boobs. It's not like you can point to a day on the calendar and say, *There, that's the day I got boobs.* In the same magical way, I went from a state of not having to one of having.

But I knew we were really living together when our new bed came. I remember that date. It was the last Tuesday in September (I made sure to mark the event in my Day-Timer). Karl and I had decided we didn't want to sleep with the ghosts of our respective pasts, so this bed represented a true clean slate, pristine and unsullied.

"We've made our bed," I told Karl as he unloaded an armful of suits into the closet.

"Now let's get busy in it," he quipped, swan-diving right in.

That night, I had a dream. In it, Karl had moved the last of his belongings, and we were about to go to bed. As we got under the covers, I looked at Karl and thought, *didn't he used to be a lot cuter?* Then, when he reached over and cupped my breast, I told myself, *it will all be over in a few minutes.*

"I know what this dream was about," I announced brightly to Dr. Oskar. I had conveniently dreamed it the night before a session.

"You do?" asked Dr. Oskar incredulously. I had never analyzed my subconscious before. Dr. Oskar scribbled something in his notebook and shifted forward in his seat.

"It's about my ex-husband."

Any lust I had felt for my ex was quelled as soon as I left my life in New York and moved into the moldy-smelling apartment we shared in Arlington, Virginia. We began fighting immediately, usually verbally, more than once physically.

The front he held up while we were both living, separately, in New York, the one where he presented himself as a responsible citizen who kept normal hours and didn't lose his marbles every time he felt even the tiniest bit challenged, was dismantled the moment we began living together. At least once a week, I threatened to pack my bags and move out. And once, after one of those threats cast me outside of our apartment barefoot and hysterically clutching the bra that I was about to pack in my suitcase, I phoned my parents and told them I was moving back home to live with them and that I was "going to need a lot of therapy."

Of course, none of that happened. I had given up too much in New York—my beloved brother, a job in advertising where, miraculously, I was appreciated and valued, and a fabulous rent-controlled apartment on East Eighty-third Street—because I had believed this was the right person to give everything up for. And so I stayed and convinced myself that relationships were supposed to be hard work.

But really, there was no saving us. I told Dr. Oskar about the breaking point, the actual moment in time when I stopped desiring my ex.

"I woke up in the middle of the night and heard lip smacking coming from his side of the bed, like he was eating something," I explained, and then paused for effect. "When I looked over to see what he was snacking on, I saw him picking his nose and eating it."

Dr. Oskar's face turned from its usual pink to an angry red, like a Looney Tunes character who had just hit his thumb.

"You have ruined my lunch," he complained and quickly covered his face with his freckled hands. "I just enjoyed a nice halibut with a friend. But you have made me very nauseous."

Considering I once showed up early for an appointment and overheard the patient before me yell, "I don't know what the fuck I was doing but all of a sudden I was fucking kicking his fucking head in," I figured telling him about my ex-husband's nose-picking was fairly tame stuff.

I began to laugh. "Oh, yah," he said through his fingers. "I'm glad you find this funny. Yah, ha ha hah."

"I'm sorry," I told him. "I didn't think you had such a delicate stomach."

It took the rest of the hour—*my* hour—for Dr. Oskar to recover. "I'll never get that image out of my head," he whined, ushering me out of his office and quickly closing the door. I felt bad about Dr. Oskar almost losing his lunch, but I was proud of myself for having that dream. I had already made physical room for Karl, but I realized that the dream about my ex was about making some emotional room as well. I was telling my sleeping self that it was okay to be concerned about my future with Karl.

When I was going through a pile of old books, deciding which ones to leave out in the lobby for the betterment of my neighbors, a piece of paper slipped out from one of those gift books found at checkout counters around Valentine's Day, *I Like You Because*. I recognized this small white sheet immediately. It was a list of pros and cons I had made during my marriage. The pros column was completely blank. And all I had written down the cons side was:

this
this
this
this.

Would I one day make a similar list for Karl and hide it among the pages of an impulse buy?

That evening, as Karl banged around in the bedroom, I opened the bottom of my armoire and reached deep in the back, where I had been keeping a secret stash of photos—of my old boyfriends, of my ex-husband, of my past lives. There was one of me, as a wife, with my ex holding our cat, who was trying to escape his arms. There was one of me, as a girl-friend, celebrating my twenty-fifth birthday in a red leather miniskirt. My legs are splayed, encased in Donna Karan opaque tights, and I am looking hopefully over at the dark-haired boy who would break my heart less than a month later. And there was one of me, as a fool, posed next to Bruno, just after I had surprised him with a ride in a blimp. My shoulders are turned toward him and I'm smiling like I'm at my senior prom. He is gazing downward, most likely checking his cell phone to see all the calls he missed while up and away.

For an hour, I pulled photo after photo from their frames and put the pile of loose pictures into a legal-size white en-velope. It didn't feel right to throw them away. Not yet. I piled the empty frames into a corner and thought about all the new memories I was about to create.

When I joined Karl, I saw that he had also succeeded in making some room. He had Velcroed everything from his nightstand—the phone, his clock, an eyeglass case—to the wall.

"What do you think?" he asked, clearly satisfied with his decorating touch.

He was reclining on our bed with his arms folded behind his head. I sat down next to him and tentatively touched the clock.

"I just hope it sticks."

Promote from Within

Lately, I had been walking to work with the sound track of *Song of the South* playing in my head. There I was, practically skipping down Twenty-third Street in my well-edited fall outfit (under which I still wore the warm cloak of waking up next to Karl), swinging my Neimans bagged lunch, and feeling that there was, finally, plenty of sunshine headed my way. It wouldn't have surprised me if a cartoon bluebird landed on my shoulder and started whistling "Dixie."

Absolutely everything seemed more animated—even my coworkers. As I made my way through the marketing department, I was reminded that, like me, most of my coworkers carried on second, less profitable lives as photographers, winemakers, and, in the case of one shy environmental editor, shamanist. I imagined their cubicles as booths at a flea market—each one displaying the vendor's true passion. As I made my way to my own stall, I passed by Kym's Asian art emporium, Rob's world of puzzles, and Rena's mind-blowing collection of cow-related paraphernalia, which was highlighted by an udder-shaped vase that sat next to her iMac. Even my manager Todd, a feckless leader whose man-agerial style was to let his department run amok, gave more wall space to his framed drawings of ferrets than to our award-winning direct mail, samples of which sat piled on the floor.

I wondered what my own cubicle, which had more kitsch than a VH1 marathon, said about me. Every cornerstone of camp was represented in the form of Pee-wee Herman, *Baywatch*, and a huge psychedelic paint-by-number of a bouquet-bearing Uncle Sam (who is trying to win back his amputated left leg, which is being carried off by a naked angel with an afro). The sheer busy-ness of my workspace acted as a sort of camouflage. There was so much going on, I suppose I was trying to distract people from what (and not so long ago, who) I was doing.

Because my back was to the entrance, I used to have a large, motion-sensitive plastic frog near the opening to my cubicle as a warning device. Whenever anyone rounded the corner, the frog emitted four metallic-sounding *ribbit*s. It also drove my coworkers crazy, and one morning I found the frog flipped on its back, batteries removed, with a ballpoint pen speared through its eye. Ever since, I worked on my freelance pieces, chatted on the phone, and basically goofed off at my own peril.

I was doing just that when my phone rang.

"This is Cathy," I answered, with my embarrassing first-grader's greeting.

"This is Chew." Karl had taken to calling himself by my father's nickname for him.

"This is Girlie," I replied on cue, using the name his mother had reserved for me.

His call marked the safe start of his workday. I was nervous about Karl riding his motorcycle on the Beltway, a route that was filled with road rage, unpredictable construction, and SUVs driven by people from Virginia.

We chatted about nothing for a while, and I guess I just got lost in another *Song of the South* moment, floating around my color-tastic cubicle, with Karl in one ear and the happy clacking sound of Rena stringing beads in the other, when, zip-a-dee-doo-dah, the music came to a grinding halt as a hand plunged down the front of my blouse and seized hold.

"Jesus Christ," I blurted, grabbing Bruno around the wrist and yanking his hand out of my shirt with such force, his knuckles rapped me on the chin.

"What's the matter?" Karl asked, pausing the story he was telling me about robot arms.

As soon as I had extracted one hand, Bruno dove in with the other. "Nothing," I said, rolling my chair across my cubicle to get away. "Just reading an annoying email from one of the editors."

When he approached again, I kicked him in the shins and

mouthed an exaggerated "Go away." When he didn't, I cradled the phone under my chin and batted at Bruno with both hands. "Stop it," I mouthed again, slapping away his dancing fingers.

Bruno was clearly enjoying this game, laughing and pretending to shadow box with my boobs. Once, when I was talking to one of my editors at the *Washington Post*, Bruno slipped into my cubicle and, before I could finish my sentence, placed his mouth over mine and kissed me so deeply, I began to gag. At the time, I thought he was being playful. But now I realized his sport was one of control and needy aggression, and I was done playing by his rules.

After saying good-bye to Karl, who had become so enthusiastic in telling his robot story he didn't notice how out of breath I was from all my arm flapping, I grabbed a red marker and a printout of a catalog we'd been working on and escorted Bruno back into his own cubicle. Spreading the pages across his desk and pretend-pointing to them with my marker, I gave him my meanest gunslinger look and hissed, "Don't ever touch me again."

He closed his eyes and shook his head slightly from side to side. "Ssst, ssst, sssst," he snickered.

I had been ignoring Bruno's advances ever since getting together with Karl. I hadn't yet informed Karl of my past with Bruno because, as with revealing my age, when, really, was an appropriate time to admit this staggering truth? So rather than tell Bruno about Karl—which wouldn't have stopped him anyway—I chose to say nothing. I wanted Bruno to know that I was done with him. I wanted him to believe that there was no special reason or excuse other than I had simply lost interest. In not providing grounds for my shutting down shop, I finally held a bit of power.

Unfortunately, Bruno didn't seem too wounded by my rejection. For weeks, he had been convinced that I doth protest too much, that *no* meant *yes*—and it had turned him on. If he had merely been a bad employee, I could have gone to my manager. Bruno's shoddy output, grossly abbreviated workday, and misuse of company property for his own extracurricular propaganda (I had recently found a stack of his flyers, "A True Patriot Should Know the Truth," clogging up our printer) was grounds enough for complaint. But I couldn't exactly walk into my manager's office, stand in front of his wall of ferrets, and announce, "I've recently ended an affair with Bruno, and he's still trying to feel me up in my cubicle."

I not only needed advice on how to deal with a crummy coworker, I also needed to know what to do if I just happened to have fucked that crummy coworker.

This was a job for *Cosmo*. Helen Gurley Brown practically wrote the book on office affairs. In her 1962 book *Sex and the Single Girl*, she breezily noted that a job "has everything to do with men anyway," and filled her early magazine columns with strategies for how to impress the boss—and marry him as well.

It didn't take me long to find what I was after. In "Take the Sting Out of a Breakup," *Cosmo* editors had culled through

Greg Behrendt's latest book, *It's Called a Breakup Because It's Broken: The Smart Girl's Breakup Buddy*, and reprinted his six commandments of surviving a painful split. I have to admit, I was predisposed to disliking whatever Behrendt had to say. Last year for my birthday, a former coworker had given me his first book, *He's Just Not That Into You*, after endlessly eavesdropping on my one-sided phone conversations about why so-and-so didn't call me/buy me/do me anymore. At the time, I huffed about her overbearing gift and questioned why she hadn't attached a string so I could wear it around my neck like a scarlet letter. Fearing I'd see myself all over every page, I had never even cracked open the binding.

But things were different now, and I was ready to admit that even though Bruno had always just not been that into me, the pain was still hanging around. The stress of working side by side, of fending him off, of not forgiving him or myself for the joylessness that went on in our cubicles, was only going to get worse unless I did something about it.

This time around, I eagerly embraced Behrendt's wisdom.

COMMANDMENT 1:
DON'T SEE OR TALK TO HIM FOR 60 DAYS

Even though I couldn't totally "he-tox" from Bruno since I had to see him almost daily (the days he chose not to call in sick, that is), I could easily get away with not talking to him. Email is a wonderful invention, after all. Any communication that couldn't be shot out into the ether could be contained on a Post-it or relayed by my manager (who was secretly, tragically in love with Bruno and took any opportunity to pull Bruno into his office for a meeting).

COMMANDMENT 2:
TOSS STUFF THAT REMINDS YOU OF HIM

"It's crucial that you transform your place into recovery central," wrote Behrendt. I had already packed away the blimp photo, but I still had one souvenir from my time with Bruno.

During one of his trips to Argentina, probably before boarding the plane to come home, Bruno must have had the anomalous desire to buy me a gift. I say this because, from the looks of it, he bought it at the airport. It's a metal cup covered in white leather, with the Argentine flag embroidered across the center. With the cup came a long metal straw with a perforated hollow spoon bulb at the end. I had unwrapped the straw/spoon first, and my initial reaction was to think it was some kind of drug paraphernalia. Later when Bruno visited my cubicle, he explained that it was for drinking maté, a traditional Argentine drink that looks and tastes like cut grass. Afraid to leave this token of our relationship on my desk at work, I brought it home and used it as a pencil holder.

Now, looking at the flowerlike arrangement of pens, markers, and multiple scissors bursting from the cup, I felt stupid for hanging on to this hideous desk accoutrement for so long. Behrendt was right—this last-minute impulse buy was still acting, according to him, as an "altar to your failed relationship." Not anymore. I found a brightly painted vase from Czechoslovakia for my pencils and tossed the maté set into the garbage.

COMMANDMENT 3:
ENLIST A BREAKUP BUDDY (BUB)

This commandment was also easy to follow. Dave, my gay work boyfriend, already knew all about my fast times with Bruno. Dave missed hearing my bawdy tales of cubicle sex and had transferred this resentment into an even deeper hatred than mine for Bruno. For Dave, who managed our company's human resources publications, Bruno was only good for one thing, and it certainly wasn't creating cover art for Dave's products. Bruno was a great punch line with a funny accent.

"Your BUB's new job?" asked Behrendt rhetorically. "To talk you down when you're struck by an uncontrollable urge to call your ex or stalk him or boil his pet bunny."

Dave's new job? To make me feel better about myself by making fun of someone else.

The next day, I got my "ass in motion" by practically sprinting to work (COMMANDMENT 4), and didn't let "my appearance slide" by wearing a tight pencil skirt and sheer blouse (COMMANDMENT 5). Then I followed the third commandment and picked up the phone and made Dave the job offer.

"Cat, Cat," said Dave in his best Bruno voice, "I accept in the name of my country!" Making fun of Bruno's national pride was already standard shtick for us.

"Oh comrade Dave," I replied like a Telemundo soap star, "If only Che were alive to see you now."

Having an ally like Dave would be key. Not only was it comforting to have someone to bear witness to, it was also a small measure of protection, since I didn't know how Bruno would react to the silent treatment. What little I did know of Bruno's early days was that his father had died when Bruno was only a few weeks old and that his mother, who slept in the same room as her son when she visited from Argentina, thought Bruno was Jesus incarnate. Bruno was used to the warmth of being in his own spotlight. What would happen when I killed the lights?

Showtime!

Like clockwork, Bruno arrived for work at eleven, strolling down the hall like he was window-shopping along the Champs-Elysées. He paused by my desk and greeted me as usual. "Hi, Cat."

I regarded my computer screen as if it were revealing the eighth wonder of the world. Bruno hesitated for a moment before slinking off, whistling something low and tuneless.

Later that day, Bruno showed up with a flyer for me to proofread. I gestured for him to leave it on the end of my desk. Taking the pages out of his hands was too much communication for me and would have felt like I was accepting an offering. Thinking I was going to attend to the many typos I would inevitably find in his layout, Bruno stood there expectantly. When he realized I was not going to jump to, he pushed the flyer a few inches in my direction. "Cat?" he said quietly.

I stood up so fast he jumped. Then I slid by him, turning my body so that I was showing him my back, and took the elevator up to Dave's floor.

"This is going to be fun," I told him and then sat down and reported every gleeful detail.

It actually was fun. I marveled at how efficiently I could conduct business with Bruno without uttering a single word. If I had to check on the status of one of our projects, I'd send him an email that did the asking for me.

During the course of the week, Operation Freeze Out backfired only once. While Bruno was taking one of his obscenely long lunches, Todd brought me a marked-up document, one of Bruno's handiworks.

"I'm about to go into a meeting," he explained. "So when Bruno comes back from lunch, I'll need you to go over all these changes with him."

As Todd went through the revisions, I jotted each fix down on a jumbo Post-it, drew an arrow, and stuck it next to the mistake. When my manager left for his meeting, I laid the Post-it-laden folder across Bruno's keyboard and took my own obscenely long lunch.

The next morning, there was a Post-it note smacked on my computer screen. It read, in red, "See me now!"

Out of all the people in my department, I knew Todd felt most comfortable dealing with me. We had become a little friendly out of the office, I think owing to his partner Jim's affection for me. In the office, Todd relied on my reputation for being well liked along the hierarchical ladder to help mitigate his reputation for being a bit of a joke. He was only a year older than me and often seemed both surprised and annoyed to find himself in the position of authority.

"Did you go over those changes with Bruno?" he asked, handing me the same folder that had been on Bruno's desk the day before. It was untouched, my Post-it notes still secured in the exact same place.

"Yes," I half-lied.

"He said you never talked to him." Todd bore a striking resemblance to a better-dressed Pee-wee Herman, and I always had the urge to say something stupid like, "I know you are but what am I?" whenever I felt him challenging me.

"He hadn't come back by the time I left for lunch," I began, thinking up the excuse as I went along. "I didn't want to waste any time, so I just left the folder on his desk with enough direction for him to do the job without my supervision." Then, just to divert the focus even further, I added, "I didn't think I was supposed to be his manager."

I'm sure normal bosses wouldn't have put up with this kind of nonsense. But Todd was different. He was a pushover. Not only would I slip out of today's deserved admonishment, Bruno would continue to escape them as well. The last time Todd tried to discipline Bruno for his late arrival time, Bruno had yelled, "Manage yourself!" and threw an apple at Todd's computer.

Until things soured with Bruno, I never really paid attention to the screwy corporate culture around me—I was too busy getting laid and working on my freelance writing. I was also benefiting greatly from a compressed workweek, supposedly putting in longer hours in order to get every Wednesday off. My boss left every day at 4:50 to catch his train home to Baltimore; I left at 4:51.

Walking back to my desk, it occurred to me that Bruno wasn't the only thing wrong with my job. I recalled an article I had read in *Marie Claire* the night before called "Your Weirdest Boss Dilemmas Solved!" In it, Kristen Kemp highlighted six uncomfortable office scenarios and offered sample scripts, "face-saves," for maneuvering through each one.

The mortification was all fairly standard business:

You're trapped in an elevator with the company's CEO. And she says hi.

> **MAKE IT THROUGH:** Respond to her hello with something basic: Hi, how are you today? said with assurance.

> **MAKE A SPLASH:** If she smiles or keeps the conversation going, drop your name. Tell her, I'm Becky Smith, and I've always admired you. I really enjoy working here.

Here's how this situation would have played out at my company:

I'm on the elevator with my company's president and he says hi.

> **MAKE IT THROUGH:** I say hello and ask him how

his ex-wife is doing. (My friend and former co-worker knew her, and we had all spent a Saturday wandering around a crafts show. She was a lovely, loose-lipped woman who didn't mind dishing about her no-good ex.)

MAKE A SPLASH: I say hello and ask if he appreciated the irony in a recent lawsuit where our company paid out one million dollars in damages after being sued for sexual harassment, even though our company publishes *Sexual Harassment Report*, a weekly journal whose sole mission is to help companies not get sued in the first place. "Don't you read your own work?" I say, stepping off the elevator.

The more I thought about my fellow employees, the more I realized the fucked-up-ness rained down all the way from the top. For every one of Kemp's sticky situations, I had one of my own.

1. The coworker directly behind you has had a disgustingly productive cough for six months straight. She refuses your gentle suggestions that she should see a doctor or at least call in sick and allow you to get through one day without listening to her death rattle.

2. The coworker next to the coughing queen has been planning a trip to Australia for over a month. As part

of her research, she has spent days printing out the entire Internet, using up all the toner when she knows full well that no one in our department knows how to correctly load new toner into the machine.

3. The coworker down the hall passes by your desk at least ten times a day on his way to the bathroom and wants so desperately to say hello and announce his I'm-here-ness, but is so socially awkward, all he does is sigh like the weight of the world rests upon his ability to edit books with titles like *The Sedona Principles: Best Practices, Recommendations & Principles for Addressing Electronic Document Production, Annotated Version.*

4. Your friend in the legal division, after gleefully discovering that your company's HR handbook has no formal policy about drinking on the job, keeps a bottle of whiskey in the bottom drawer of his desk. Every day at 4:00 PM, he and his cubicle mate pour themselves a stiff one and flagrantly toast their manager.

5. Another Argentine coworker who is not Bruno but is as equally in love with the idea of getting something for nothing frequently calls in late because he has scraped up roadkill—most recently, an opossum—and needs to head back home before coming to work so he can clean it up and refrigerate it for tonight's supper.

6. And, unbelievable as it may sound, a coworker down the hall takes nude sponge baths from the middle sink in the restroom. Her washing is random and unpredictable, so one day you might find her standing naked in front of the mirror, her clothes casually draped over a bathroom stall, and the next day, you might find her applying lipstick, fully dressed in head-to-toe floral.

Naturally, as a writer, I knew my nutty coworkers would eventually wind up on the page (and so they have). But even fruitcakes have a shelf life. As I became more and more attuned to areas in my personal life that weren't working, I realized there was another sector that needed fixing, or scrapping entirely.

Bruno was definitely reacting to my silent treatment—just not in the way I had intended. My inattention had caused him to desperately seek the reverse, in an escalating manner. At first, when I'd drop off work for him, he'd take a finger and lightly draw circles around the crotch of his pants. When this didn't elicit the desired response, he began to strum his crotch like a banjo. When this display failed to pique my interest, he resorted to exposing himself, an act that had once worked so marvelously for him.

COMMANDMENT 6.
NO BACKSLIDING

"Sure, it's tempting to hook up one last time," read Behrendt's sixth commandment. "Maybe you convince yourself that you need carnal closure. But that kind of relapse doesn't just put the brakes on your progress; it sends you reeling to the bottom of that hellish pit of pain you've been working so hard to claw your way out of."

This was the easiest commandment of all to honor. The kind of closure I needed was not carnal and would never come from Bruno. It was the storybook ending that explained why I had allowed myself to be mistreated for so long by such a loathsome creature. And I was the only one who could write that conclusion.

About two weeks into my vow of silence, I entered Bruno's cubicle and found him staring at his computer screen, jerking off like a monkey. At first I thought he had downloaded some porn, but then I realized I could see my own reflection in his blank screen. As my plastic frog had once warned me to stop my cubicle wrongdoings, the image of me playing across his darkened monitor had alerted Bruno to begin his. He had been lying in wait, gun in hand.

"Cat, take a look at this," said Bruno.

"No, thanks," I said coolly. "I've already seen it."

I had broken the first commandment after only sixteen days. But did I have any other choice? What if Bruno continued turning more and more twisted and mad, like the Latin version of Howard Hughes? What if he went from masturbating in his cubicle to showing up at the front door of our apartment wearing nothing but shoes made out of our Dear Subscriber letters? What if he told Karl everything?

It was time to consult with my Breakup Buddy. "This isn't working," I told Dave.

"Of course it's not," he said. "You can't insult a narcissist. Bruno is taking your silent treatment as a challenge. Rebuffing him is just feeding his ego, not shrinking it," he explained. "This is all light banter for him."

"What should I do?"

Dave gave me one of his I'm-glad-you've-finally-asked-me looks and laughed like a mad scientist.

"Turn into the entire cast of *Dynasty* and become the biggest bitch Bruno has ever seen."

Dave was right. Being ambivalent was too soft-shoed a strategy. Bruno only allowed for intense emotions. I could either fuck him or fuck him over. As it happened, I had an article on this exact topic. "Evil chick behavior is on the rise," began the title deck to *Cosmo*'s "How to Handle a Bitch." Luckily, Freya Williams offered a plan of attack. "In order not to get torn to shreds," she wrote, "you need to know what to do when one of them bares her fangs."

Actually, I was more interested in picking up a few tips on how to *be* the flesh-shredding canine. I planned on turning this article on its head, reading it as a roadmap to becoming a bitch instead. A pull quote on the article's first page gave the following statistic: "Female bullies choose female targets 87% of the time." I planned on being part of the smaller percentage, taking aim at Bruno with both barrels loaded.

First, I had to figure out how to be one. I mean, I knew how to be bitchy—just ask my mother—but my style was predictable and one-dimensional and consisted of me sounding like a teenage girl who has just been told to get off the phone. But maybe all this time, my inability to be a full-on bitch has been dependent on a reason to behave like one. Williams's article shed even more light. "These days, you can't buy a coffee, exchange some clothes, or get through a day at work without running into a vicious chick with a chip on her shoulder." That was the key to the bitch kingdom—I had never had a chip on my shoulder. Until now.

I read on. Williams first identified two kinds of bitches: "The obvious in-your-face bitch (like a demanding, snarling, screaming boss) and the underhanded bitch (like that sweet-as-pie pal who says, 'Stress makes you break out, too?')." I was definitely attracted more to the idea of becoming the second kind of bitch because, as Williams explained in her "Know Thy Enemy" analysis, "an underhanded bitch favors sabotage. She'll undermine you by spreading rumors ('I heard she's hungover'), making 'harmless' comments that sting ('Your outfit is so . . . interesting'), and incriminating you when *she* messes up ('That's *her* job')."

This bitch was cunning, diabolical, and a whole lot of passive-aggressive. She was also a chicken. But I could live with that. "She attacks through cruel jokes and backhanded compliments because they're easy to laugh off or deny, which makes it hard to catch her," revealed Janet Alberts, a PhD whom Williams interviewed.

There was one bitch tip in particular that stood out. Williams warned about revealing too much personal information to a conniver like myself, which could be twisted against you or used as ammunition. I had never considered the kind of talking Dave and I did behind Bruno's back as being bitchy. Done over a glass of wine, our accents getting heavier and more outrageous with each sip, it was more like dinner theater. But what if I staged a command performance for my boss and other coworkers?

The plot would center on a creative presentation Bruno and I were giving to our boss Todd and his boss, Mary (an in-your-facer) the next afternoon. My portion of the work had been finished for so long it was collecting dust on Bruno's desk. Even though he had chosen the date and the time of our presentation (casting his decision in an email, which I had been prescient enough to save), I knew Bruno had totally forgotten about our meeting and when the time came, it would be curtains for him.

For a brief moment, I had some qualms about the havoc I was about to wreak. But then I reminded myself about the type of guy Bruno really was. Here was someone whose goal in life was to get something for nothing, me included. I spent the morning preparing some bombshells for the second act: He called in sick for almost two weeks from a beach in Mexico! His portfolio contained work that wasn't his! He was loose with his expense reports!

These were just some of the whoppers I was privy to

while Bruno and I were still communing. And just as the *Cosmo* article had cautioned its gentle readers, I was about to use this intelligence to crush Bruno like a stiletto heel.

Ten minutes before our presentation, Bruno appeared at my desk, wearing a coat and a ridiculous newsboy cap.

"I have a doctor's appointment," he said, handing me a folder.

"How could you have scheduled a doctor's appointment for the same time as our meeting?" I asked sharply.

He stared at me blankly.

"You were the one who picked the time," I continued, raising my voice so the people in the back rows could hear. "And now you suddenly have a doctor's appointment?!"

He shrugged his shoulders. "This just came up," he said and walked off before I could respond.

Opening the folder, I realized that he had done just one of the six ads we needed to show our bosses. I used the remaining minutes before the meeting to become the biggest electronic tattletale of all time.

I forwarded his original email where he had picked the day and time of our presentation to my boss and other key players (cc-ing Bruno, which made me come off as a conscientious worker with nothing to hide as well as the underhanded bitch I was fast becoming). "To All," I wrote, "Bruno has scheduled a doctor's appointment for the same time as our presentation. He has left me with a folder containing his share of the work, but I am concerned about the art being incomplete and I don't feel comfortable presenting it in his stead."

I blind-copied Dave and called him as soon as I hit the send button.

He picked up the phone on the first ring. "Stand back," he said. "The shit is really going to hit the fan."

I didn't expect a response from Todd, who always folded his cards when an action was required. But Mary loved a good blame game. Aware that Todd was a spineless wimp, she had once pulled Rena and I into her office and asked us why we thought Todd was such an enabler.

I dialed Mary's extension. "Can I come talk to you about this?" I asked sweetly. Then, in her office, I opened up the folder of Bruno's crap. "I find this so upsetting," I said, taking a seat. "I was so prepared for our presentation and I thought Bruno was, too. I don't understand how he could schedule a doctor's appointment for the same time—especially when he was just at the doctor's for most of yesterday." (Another bombshell.)

"Why don't you phone me as soon as he's back, and I'll deal with him."

"Are you sure? I would hate for you to think of me as an informant." I was giving an Academy Award performance now. "I'm just concerned this will all reflect poorly on our department."

Could it really be this simple? Not only did being an underhanded shifty bitch feel vindicating, it might actually get him fired as well. I remembered that old Robert Fulghum book and changed the title to *All I Really Need to Know I Learned in* Cosmo.

When Bruno hadn't returned by 5:30 PM, I phoned Mary.

"Just thought you should know," I happily reported, "he still hasn't returned from the doctor's."

"Gee," said Mary. "I'd hate to fire him. He seems like such a nice guy."

"He's not that nice," I told her.

Karl had only seen Bruno once, when he picked me up on his scooter to go to lunch. We had passed by the restaurant near my office where Bruno was seated at an outside table, cloth napkin folded grandly across his lap, enjoying what looked like a five-course meal.

"Is that the lazy idiot you work with?" he asked as we motored by.

"How can you tell?" I asked, shocked and slightly worried there was somehow a second blimp photo.

"Only someone who thought he had all the time in the world would treat himself to a meal like that in the middle of the day."

So I let Karl believe that Bruno was that lazy idiot. I told him all about his overweening behavior, his broken moral compass, his lies and deceits—just not in relation to me. I was definitely making things worse for when I eventually revealed the truth about our "work" relationship (*You fucked the lazy idiot?!*), but I just couldn't bring myself to come clean. Not now. Not yet.

When Karl came home from work that night, the only thing I revealed was that Bruno would soon become a thing of the past. "His days are numbered," I said confidently.

"It's about time," he said, kicking off the weekend by cracking open a beer. "If he was working for me, I would have busted his fat head by now."

On Monday, the first thing I did was stop by Bruno's cubicle to see if it was stripped of his personal belongings. But there they were—his photos of his childhood dog, his books about the grandmothers of the Plaza de Mayo, his piles of unfinished work, and finally, at 11:00, his self.

Maybe Mary was waiting to deliver his coup de pink slip during our Monday staff meeting. I had dressed especially for the occasion, kissing ass in the same power colors that Mary usually wore (although Dave and I joked that her wardrobe consisted entirely of Kmart's Jaclyn Smith Collection).

As usual, Todd had to phone Bruno from the conference room and tell him we were all waiting for him to join us. "Yes, it's Monday again," he'd say every single week, as the rest of us snickered and shook our heads in expected disbelief.

Bruno sauntered in a few minutes later, like he half expected to see a cake and people in party hats. "Good morning," he said, nodding in Mary's direction. He took a seat all alone at the end of the conference table and leisurely began to pick stray hairs from his sweater.

"I have an announcement to make," said Todd, glancing nervously at Mary. "We have decided to do away with our flexible workweeks."

Before I could stop myself, a "WHAT?!" had escaped my mouth.

"Mary feels that it's essential for all of us to be here, working at our desks, five days a week."

Bruno and I were the only ones in our department who took advantage of the compressed workweek. He remained calm, assured in his fantasy that Todd had meant everyone *except* him had to work five days a week.

I was so dizzy, I thought if I opened my mouth again to object, I'd throw up. I recognized that management was trying to punish Bruno by taking away his liberty, but why did I get lumped into the deal? If nice guys finished last, weren't bitches supposed to wind up on top?

On my way to Dave's office, I thought about the impact of losing my Wednesdays and what that would do to my career. My *other* career. In my mind, Wednesday was my day to be a real writer. It was the day when I rented a car and drove out to Virginia to interview the owners of The Inn at Little Washington. It was the day I spent at the Library of Congress researching sideshow freaks in the Prints and Photos department. It was the day I sat home, with unwashed hair and a half a dozen samples of lube, lustily pounding away on a story about better sex prep. What was the purpose of working a soulless job, only to have my soul-saving day kicked to hell?

"This is even more messed up than the nude sponge bather and the lushes in the legal department," I shouted to Dave.

"Cathy," he said pulling me in for a bear hug, "this company is fucked."

"What do we do?"

"We ride it for as long as we can," he said, releasing me from his embrace and looking me in the eye, "and then we quit."

I knew Dave was shopping around a book proposal as well as doing some consulting work on the side with a friend of ours. "Are you serious?" I said, suddenly giddy. "I'll never know if I can make it as a freelance writer unless I quit my day job and try to find out."

"I'll go from being your Breakup Buddy to your Breakout Buddy," he said.

I ran around the side of his desk to where a calendar hung. "We need an 'out' date," I decided.

"I thought I already was out," he joked.

"How about Friday, July 1?" I suggested. "We can celebrate our Independence Day together."

I pulled my Day-Timer out of my pocketbook and wrote "OUT" diagonally across the day. July was just nine months away, the same amount of time it took to have a baby.

That evening, I tore out a page from *Allure*'s Insider's Guide called "How to Quit Your Job Gracefully," and gave myself another year-end goal. Not only would I be hosting the perfect dinner party and getting rid of upper-arm jiggle, by the time my year of magazines was up, I'd also be handing in a letter of resignation.

Party Favors

my clever attempt to use an article about handling a bitch as a tutorial in becoming one had backfired, landing a big bitch slap across my own rutilant cheek. Not only did I feel the sting of moral shame, I realized my machinations had taken me down as well. In being underhanded with Bruno, I had merely undercut myself.

Dr. Oskar had given my involvement and lingering preoccupation with Bruno a clinical name: repetition compulsion. Basically, I psychologically got off on repeating a traumatic event over and over again (in my case, rejection and abandonment), thinking if I could somehow do something different *this* time around, I'd finally change the odds. Like *Groundhog Day* as imagined by Freud. "You stay with the pain until you can get it right," Dr. Oskar explained.

I had to consider that Bruno was simply too big and too complex a problem to solve in two thousand words or less. That no matter what articles and advice I enlisted, Bruno was a lost cause. He was never going to quit his job, never going to repent, and never going to see me as anything other than an all-access pass.

As I began to accept the mistakes of my ruinous past, I consciously chose to move more and more away from them. Even though I hadn't succeeded in destroying my tormentor, I had removed a layer of numbness that had once allowed me to walk through my days—my daze—demanding so little for myself.

I saw that now. And over the past few months, as the shape of my decisions changed, I truly began to feel things shift internally as well. If living well is the best revenge, then I had already settled the score with Bruno. The realization that I was getting things right startled me on a daily basis. How else to explain the man who was now sitting on my living room floor, *our* floor, happily tinkering away on something that looked like a tripod.

"Did you ever think you'd be living with a robot a year ago?" asked Karl, fidgeting with a giant eyeball. "Hello Karl," the tripod said suddenly. "How are you?"

Karl looked directly into the eyeball and asked, "What is Raymond?"

"Raymond is a small cat," responded the tripod.

"No," I said after their exchange. "I can honestly say, in my entire life, I never thought I'd be living with a robot."

But I was, and it was well beyond what I could have

imagined for myself. I couldn't listen to certain song lyrics or watch a particularly soulful *American Idol* contestant without crying fat tears of gratitude. Life was a proverbial Hallmark commercial. I wanted to tell the world what real love—my love—felt like and then worried that if I did, I would sound smug and vainglorious and no one would want to hang out with me anymore.

But I announced it anyway, broadcasting the news like I had just won a Pulitzer. In a diabetes-inducing email to a friend, I dripped, "Karl and I are living together and it's unbelievably amazing! No fighting, no arguing—nothing but love."

"Let's be clear," she wrote back, "you two have something that poets write about. It's why people went to the moon. It was something they glimpsed from afar and wanted to touch for themselves. Living it is inconceivable."

Reading this sort of review of my relationship—and actually believing it—was pretty heady stuff. Karl and I had our own shorthand to describe the lucky state in which we found ourselves.

"It's disgusting," he joked one night.

I was sitting Indian-style, barricaded behind a wall of magazines. I had recently added *Lucky* to the gang. I didn't mean to, since that brought the tally up to twelve fat glossies a month, but I had become so easily lured by outer come-ons and inner promises.

"I think we should start our own magazine," he continued, picking up the latest issue of O. "We could call it *Ewww.*"

Looking at him standing there, clutching his nemesis to

his chest, the cover line "Hope!" practically silk-screened across his heart, I knew I needed to celebrate this kind of devotion. It marked my progress as well.

Karl's thirtieth birthday was a week away, which didn't give me a lot of time to throw together a surprise party. Not that I knew how to throw one anyway. But after the challenges of the past months (I was still having nightmares involving tents), how hard could it be? Plus, I already had a dozen magazines on my planning committee. With the holiday high season about to hit, I knew I'd have an easy time finding party-related advice, from how to feed the masses on a budget to scoring the perfect hostess ensemble. It was time to shine—even if that meant slicking on some metallic eye shadow. Even though it was Karl's birthday, I still wanted to be the girl with the most cake.

I have never been the life of the party, at least not without a little help beforehand. In college, any pre-frat prep involved drinking massive amounts of liquor or smoking so many bowls I would famously misidentify people, confusing people I knew in high school with total strangers in college. I once chased someone around the Theta Phi taproom screaming, "Michael! Michael!" thinking I had just seen my best friend from ninth grade, only to find that, upon closer inspection, it was the girl who sat in front of me in sociology class.

An article in *Self* called "The Stress Mess" explained why I may have needed to shotgun three Old Milwaukees before heading out to the boy's dorm for a night of quarters. A survey by *Self* and the Anxiety Disorders Association of America found that, "Fifteen percent of women who say they're frequently stressed turn to booze to regain calm." Ironically, I was reading this with a glass of wine in one hand and the beginnings of a guest list in the other. It had dawned on me that before I could play hostess, I actually had to invite people to host. Which meant that unless Karl wanted to party down with a roomful of my friends (mostly gay men and, now that I thought about it, women over forty), I was going to have to bite the bullet and include some of his.

Most I liked, including his best friend Rob, a father of two who was married to a warm and wonderful woman from Puerto Rico named Mariel. I knew Karl thought of Rob as his brother, since they had helped each other through disappointing childhoods. Now, since Rob worked two jobs to support his family and lived a good hour away from D.C., we hardly ever saw him. I knew if I could cajole Rob and Mariel to hire a sitter and make the trip in, I'd win major points with Karl.

Besides Rob, Karl's sister Val, and a few other names I swiped from a mass email our friend Daz sent out to announce his upcoming photography show, the only other people I knew how to get hold of were the jerks from our camping trip. Naturally, I didn't want to ever see them again. Since July, they had been giving me the cold shoulder whenever we bumped into them at parties. There had been rumblings on the playground that I had stolen Karl away.

Supposedly, Crazy Larry was running around saying that I kept Karl's balls in my pocketbook. I was worried they wouldn't come to Karl's birthday just to spite me. Which would have been fine, but this camping crowd was at the epicenter of a larger crowd of jovial, up-for-anything people I actually wanted in attendance. I was afraid they'd bully the other guests into not coming, or worse, schedule a competing event.

"They are total *fainéants*," said my friend Andrew when I phoned him for help with the guest list. In the Fabergé Organics shampoo commercial of D.C., Andrew had a friend who had a friend who knew this gang.

"What's that mean?" I asked.

"It means they're a bunch of do-nothings," he said.

Maybe so, but the thought of dealing with them again was definitely doing something to me. I flashed back to my Index of Dread list. At least I was planning to hold the party at a place with flushing toilets.

I returned to the stress article in *Self.* "To grow as a person, it's important to challenge yourself with things that aren't always easy or familiar," remarked Jack Gorman, an M.D. and professor of psychiatry who was quoted in the story.

Since the whole experiment was about growth and improvement, I wondered if my anxiety was evidence that I hadn't progressed further along. Even though I felt like I was taking all the right steps, it was still hard for me to leave my comfortable world and enter one that might be dangerous and unknown. But then it dawned on me that Bruno had been the troll under the bridge, and I had already paid that toll and moved on. Compared to him, Crazy Larry et al were just some pebbles in my shoes, annoyances to shake out on the side of the road.

But not just yet. I composed a breezy email invitation to a list of sixty people. To ensure the John Barleycorns of the camping world wouldn't sabotage the surprise, I sent them a separate follow-up email. "I hope you come!" I bullshitted. "It wouldn't be the same without you."

Next, I made a shopping list. In a special *After-Dark* issue, *Glamour* devoted almost half the real estate on its cover to a feature called "Look & Feel Like the Sexiest Woman in the Room: The Clothes, the Makeup, the Hair, the Confidence." The other half of the cover starred Natalie Portman, hand on hip, wearing a filmy Matthew Williamson goddess dress. The *M* and *O* of the magazine's title were hidden behind Natalie's unusually fluffed-up hairdo, and I wondered if "Glaur," who was a minor female character in Norse mythology and a synonym for *mud* or *slime*, was some kind of subliminal message to readers.

Inside, I found a story called "Party Prep," where writer Stephanie Huszar got Nicky Hilton to reveal "how she always manages to look so right." Four evil-queen mirrors right out of *Snow White* framed a glimmering tidbit of Hilton's wisdom.

1. HER HAIR STRATEGY: A LITTLE EXTRA VOLUME

Usually, Hilton just grabbed a bobby pin to pull her bangs back and "make a tiny bump." But when she wanted to make a splash, Huszar divulged, "she's also game for tossing in a few hot rollers." There was a photo of Hilton, perched on a gleaming vanity dressed in a lilac slip, rolling a section of brunette hair around a pink sponge curler.

I didn't have long enough hair to roll and, thank God, no bangs with which to make tiny bumps. (Seriously, what does this even look like?) So I looked into the next mirror on the page.

2. HER MAKEUP M.O.: IT'S ALL ABOUT THE EYES

Hilton's preferred method, at least in this photograph, was to slick on purple metallic eye shadow in a shade also favored by most hair bands of the 1980s. Then came the black eyeliner. Lots of it (around the insides, too).

I had to admit, the color combination made Hilton's eyes really pop. Maybe she was onto something with this purple. Because of my green eyes, women who worked the makeup counters were always trying to steer me into some shade of violet. "I don't wear color on my eyes," I always told them, which was something I once heard my mother say when a woman at the Clinique counter came at her lid with a burgundy pencil.

Hilton's remaining two mirrors displayed what you could expect to find in Hilton's evening bag (her Sidekick!) and how many hours of beauty sleep she required (eight!). If the accompanying photo was any indication, Hilton caught those z's in full makeup.

Hilton had inspired me, at least with her eye makeup. I decided to go all out and supplement her advice with *Allure* magazine's *Best of Beauty* issue from last month. (I had saved the master list of 152 products, knowing that I'd eventually figure out an excuse to buy a shitload of makeup.)

I scrolled down the list of the ten best eye shadows and circled the colors that looked the most purple. Then I tore the entire five-page directory out of the magazine and marched straight to Sephora.

"Ooooooh, you have a list!" gasped a male employee with ambitiously streaked blond hair. Sidling up to me, he pulled a pair of nerdy art glasses from the pocket of his black lab coat. "What should we do first?" asked the Streaker excitedly.

"I need to get Chanel Illuminating Eyeshadow in Riviera," I announced, reading verbatim from my list.

"Oooooh," Streaker cooed, looking at my face. "That's going to be gorgeous."

We spent some time at the Chanel kiosk—the Streaker, pulling out various boxes, reading the label, and then returning them to their cubbyholes; me, studying my list and thinking of what goose chase to send him on next.

"I guess we don't have it," Streaker said, illustrating his disappointment with a lip-jut. "How about if I put you in a color that's close enough?"

"No," I said seriously. "I need this color."

"Have you worn it before?" Streaker asked, stepping closer to me.

"No."

"Then how do you know you won't like another color?" he asked pleasantly.

"I have to have *this* color," I explained. "*Allure* said so."

By now, I was in full character, playing a woman who treated *Allure* like the beauty bible it was. The Streaker didn't even flinch. "I see," he said, completely unfazed. "What else do you have on that list?" As we flitted through the store, I wondered how many other women came to the Streaker clutching their own torn pages.

I escaped with just over $101 in merchandise, a haul that included only two items from my original list: Stila eye shadow in Kitten (a sort of pinky mauve, which was purple enough for me) and Fresh Sugar Lip Treatment, because an old gay boyfriend of mine used this stuff religiously, and every time he kissed me hello, I vowed to get my own tube. (I also replenished my supply of Shu Uemura mascara, which is always on every magazine's Best list.)

In "The Stress Mess," *Self* suggested I calm any preparty jitters by wearing "something interesting, like funky jewelry," an instant conversation starter that "makes it easier for people to find something to say to *you*." I was in Filene's Basement, the mecca of attention-grabbing fashion (designer garb way too outré to sell at retail, especially in suntan-pantyhose-wearing D.C.), trying on a dressing room full of sparkly, deeply discounted leftovers from Barneys New York. I had just slipped on this season's mandatory cropped-sleeve chunky turtleneck sweater by Chaiken, a steal at only $49.99. Its colors, a mottled mix of blues and pinks, were a lucky find, compared to the universally unflattering shades that typically filled the racks at places like Filene's.

When I stepped closer to the mirror, I spotted something I had never noticed before. Maybe it was the specific spot where the turtleneck hit my neck, maybe it was the severe dressing room lighting casting phantom shadows on me, but there it was, staring me right in the face. Or neck. A turkey gorgle, flip-flapping back and forth. I studied myself from different angles, tugging at the hanging, crepey skin in scientific wonder and womanly derision. Instinctively, I started doing a facial exercise I remembered my mother doing (probably around the same age as I was now). "Pretend you are kissing the sky." She had demonstrated by keeping her eyes forward and pursing her lips upward, like a mackerel gasping for its last breath.

I traded the turkeyneck sweater for a body-hugging Nicole Farhi panne velvet gown the color of a desert cactus. *Glamour*'s "After-Dark Special!" was bursting with sexy, strappy eveningwear like this. Pulling the dress over my head, I thought of how hot Natalie Portman looked in her Dior sequined slip. This was how I wanted to make an entrance.

The Farhi dress, however, needed to be quickly evacuated off my body. It hung off me in unrepentant ways, just like the skin on my neck. It was time to come up from the Basement and admit the truth. I could no longer pull off dressing like I was twenty-five. Karl was turning thirty, and a month later, I would be forty. Was this why they had seats in dressing rooms? Parking myself on a sheet of particleboard, I recalled number 3 on *Self*'s "Seven Days to Less Stress."

LISTEN TO YOUR BODY

Close your eyes and notice where you're feeling tension. Is your jaw tight? Are your fists clenched? Concentrate on the trouble spots and think about releasing.

I focused on my neck flap and took a deep breath. Then I thought about Barbara Bush and wondered if Filene's sold a triple strand of pearls.

"That's a wattle," said Jeanne after I phoned to tell her what I found in the dressing room. "W-A-T-T-L-E," she spelled helpfully, in case I was taking notes on the other end. For me, it would have been more useful if she had denied its existence instead of confirming it with an actual word from the dictionary.

While brushing our teeth in our yellow-tiled bathroom, I showed Karl my wattle.

"Someone from work told me I was a lucky bitch and wanted to know how I managed to get such a young boyfriend," I said.

"She's the bitch," Karl answered, spitting toothpaste into the sink. "What did you tell her?"

"I told her that I had used a stun gun and kept you under heavy sedation." Actually, I had told her that I was insulted to be cast as the predator. Demi Moore had recently married Ashton Kutcher, and I was sick of the whole Cougar story. "What makes you so sure I was the one who 'got' Karl?" I had asked her in a tone that let her know I thought she was an asshole.

Karl knew I was worried about what other people might be saying about our age difference. "Fuck her and fuck the people," he said. "I've never followed convention and neither have you, which is why we're together and why we'll die together."

"What will you do when I'm old and wrinkled and you're still young and Buddha-faced?" It may have sounded like an extreme question, but it was the burning, febrile core of my insecurity.

"I'll kiss your liver spots."

In bed, we played our favorite game. "Would you still love me if I had a tail? If I had hair all over me? If I was a dwarf? If I had robot legs?"

"Would you still love me if you had amnesia?" I asked.

"That would be great." He pulled my head to his chest and combed through the wispy hair at my temple with his fingers. "Then I'd get to fall in love with you all over again."

I roped Zelly, our little motorcycle-riding friend from JDate, into being a surprise party accomplice. Zelly had recently moved to California to teach economics at Berkeley, and his visit home that weekend was the excuse I needed to get Karl out of the house for what he thought would be a cheap Italian dinner for three.

"Sounds fun," Karl had said gamely, even though I could tell he was disappointed at the thought of turning thirty over a plate of pasta.

The night before the party, I had taken two Ambiens, so I spent the majority of the next day too doped out to be anxious, an unintentional and unexpected benefit. Luckily, I had already preselected my outfit, based on *Glamour's* "12 Ways to Be the Most Irresistible Woman at the Party." Under the heading

3. LOOK COOL, ACT WARM.

writers Kimberly Bonnell and Pamela Redmond Satran recommended wearing "your favorite curve-hugging jeans and your sexier-than-thou pumps, then treat everyone like your favorite cousin."

At almost six feet tall, I have never needed to augment that fact by wearing heels, so for the pumps I substituted a touchable eggplant-colored velvet top trimmed with gold rope along the neck, a sort of mini-goddess version of Natalie Portman's cover look.

Karl remained oblivious to my added ministering, even when I presented my black-rimmed purple eyes to him.

"You're very pretty," he said, patting my back pocket. His compliment did more to energize me than *Glamour's* most improbable suggestions:

1. DANCE IN YOUR UNDERWEAR.
AT HOME. *BEFORE* THE PARTY.

No. Way. Ever.

While Karl walked to the car, I lagged behind and called Zelly.

"We're on our way," I said just loud enough for Karl to hear. I didn't want him getting suspicious so close to the surprise.

"So am I," said Zelly.

"But you're already supposed to be there." Zelly's only job was to get to the restaurant early and usher the guests into the back room that I had reserved for the night.

"I'll be there in twenty minutes." Since Zelly was the one who gave me the Ambien, I wondered if maybe he had taken one too many himself. It was a good time to repeat the mantra that *Self* had suggested for times like this. *Peace*, I told my brain.

When we got to the restaurant, I saw half of the party standing at the front bar. I immediately spotted Zelly, who was yukking it up with a whiskey in his hand. When he saw me, he sprinted toward the back of the restaurant.

"Why is Zelly running away?" said Karl, who luckily hadn't noticed that most of his friends were about three inches away.

"SURPRISE!" everyone yelled from various corners of the restaurant. I looked at Karl, who was standing there with the face that most babies get when they figure out they've been tricked into getting a vaccination. *Peace*, I told myself.

Crazy Larry was the first guest out of the gate. He ran over to us like Karl was a returning hero and Larry was his war bride. "We did it!" he said, giving Karl a bear hug and acting like he had something to do with the party. I was glad to note that Larry had already broken one of *Glamour*'s cardinal party rules in "Do's & Don'ts of Ruling the Night." According to Amy Sacco, NYC nightlife queen, "If you see people you know walk into the party, let them get a drink, take off their coats, and settle in before you approach them. No one likes to be bombarded."

I was about to break another.

7. BE THE ONLY ONE AT THE PARTY *NOT* DRINKING.

From the bar, I watched Karl on his own journey of discovery. Every time he'd spot someone else he wasn't expecting to see, his hands would fly up and he'd laugh and yell, "Holy shit!"

He was basking in the spotlight. And other than making a brief announcement about gathering for birthday cake ("11. Speak Up!"), I was happy to remain off in the wings.

At the end of the night, which had venue-switched to a seedy bar with a woefully bad cover band, Karl's best friend Rob pulled me aside. He was a man of few words, usually parsed one at a time, over a period of weeks. "You are so fucking in," he yelled over the din.

I spent the next couple of weeks feeling like a superstar. Karl told everyone about the party—from the checkout cashier at

the supermarket to the couple next to us in the movie theater. When my parents phoned to confirm the arrival time of
our flight home for Thanksgiving, he told them, "It was the
best birthday of my life."

It was then that I began to have the entirely irrational yet
wholly possible idea that Karl might propose to me on my
birthday. I was turning forty a month away, on Christmas
Day. What if Karl one-upped the Baby Jesus by getting down
on one knee and presenting me with the best birthday of my
life?

Of course, now, looking back, I admit I was getting a little
ahead of myself. But who could blame me? I was riding high
on the success of the surprise party. It didn't happen often,
but when it did, my confidence level knew no boundaries.

My parents had met Karl only recently, on a whirlwind
trip to D.C., where my father was rendered speechless after
Karl stealthily picked up the tab for an expensive dinner. "I
hate to tell you," said my father the next morning, "that is
one handsome guy." My mother was also a huge fan. She had
forgotten her initial warnings about steeling for disappointment and looked upon Karl as the daughter she never had.
Both shared a retail background, and Karl had spent hours
talking with my mother about the benefits of private-label
clothing.

If Karl wanted their blessing before proposing next
month, now was his chance to get it. I began to plot ways to
throw my father and Karl together for "the talk." At the same
time, I was hoping that my mother and I would also have our
own reasons to engage.

Before leaving for Connecticut, I spoke with Dr. Oskar about how guilty I felt about shutting down whenever I went home. For reasons I still didn't understand, every time I was around my mother, I reverted back to my sullen high school self. Basically, I went mute, a condition that caused my mother to default into oratory overdrive. In other words, I got constipated, she developed verbal diarrhea.

"It's so cruel to do to her," I told him, reaching for a tissue. "Why do I do it?"

As I said before, Dr. Oskar wasn't a big fan of my mother. His memory was sharp, and the scene of her explaining why I'd always need to wear makeup had not sat well with him. Even though I constantly defended my mother with plenty of examples of her kindness, openness, forgiveness, and intense love—all directed at me—he still wasn't quick to forgive her for being so emotionally blind to her daughter's voracious need to be seen and accepted, as is.

"It's very violating," he explained, "to have your mother define who you are."

"That word is a little strong," I challenged. It bothered me to hear him talking about my mother like this.

"Maybe *violating* isn't the right word," he apologized. "Let me try again." He looked down at his hands for a moment, maybe running his thoughts through the Swedish-to-English language engine in his brain.

"Okay, we try this again," he began. "Because your mother

has defined you in the past—as klutzy, or shy, or sensitive—
you have learned to shut down to protect yourself."

I thought about what he said for a while.

"It's not that my mother doesn't know me as a person," I
said finally. "She knows who I am. She just doesn't know
what to do with me."

"Yah, okay," agreed Dr. Oskar, "that's another way of
saying it."

"So what do I do when I'm home with her?"

"You need to figure out a way to be vulnerable with each
other."

All weekend, I watched my parents' faces to see if they were
trying to swallow their big secret. But I saw no big smiles, no
meaningful eye shifting. If they knew, they gave nothing away.
But I still couldn't stand keeping quiet, even if they could.

"Why don't you go watch some television with my father
while I shower?" I said to Karl one morning.

"Because he's watching golf," he responded.

"Well, now's your chance to learn a little about the sport,"
I suggested brightly. Karl looked at me like I was sending him
off to the SATs.

When I wasn't trying to orchestrate "the talk," I was
taking a stab at creating a mother/daughter bond. Early
Thanksgiving morning, while Karl and my father lugged a
dozen extra folding chairs from our basement (ample time
for a talk!), my mother opened her boutique to me for some
private shopping.

"What do you need?" she asked, using what sounded to me like forced chipperness.

No matter how much time had elapsed between shopping trips, I always dreaded the way my mother followed me around her store like an overzealous publicist.

"Maybe some jeans?" I weakly suggested, pulling out a pair with heavily embroidered legs.

I saw her visibly exhale, happy that I was at least feigning interest. It always took me a while to warm up to the fact that she was eager to give me whatever I wanted.

"What size are you now?" she asked.

This was a test. My mother constantly accused me of losing weight. Except for the months directly preceding my divorce, when stress and grief had taken off pounds like an illness, I had remained at the exact same weight since college.

"I'm still a size six."

Just to make her point, she added in the size four. When I emerged from the dressing room in the size six, which fit perfectly, she looked at me very seriously and said, "Your legs look like sticks."

I said nothing.

"Are you eating?"

"Yes."

"You look unhealthy."

"I'm fine."

Dr. Oskar had urged me to have an authentic, genuine exchange with my mother while I was home. Obviously, this was not it. But why was the thought of having a meaningful conversation with my mother so hard for me to digest? I knew that this was her way of expressing concern, however misguided. Why couldn't I grasp the meaning and embrace the messenger?

We drove back to the house in silence, walled off further by my new pair of size 6 jeans. In the hours leading up to Thanksgiving dinner, I sat quietly in the guest bedroom, psyching myself up for the party. The fact that I began the month playing the hostess and ended it being a guest did not escape me.

As relatives started to arrive, I watched my mother go into high gear. Surrounded by our family, she was in her element fixing drinks, hanging coats, manning the stereo. She was barefoot, and the *whisk-whisk* sounds of her soles across the floor sounded like rustling silk taffeta. I looked at her and thought, *my mother is the most beautiful woman in the world*.

I felt like I had come to the Thanksgiving table with a whole new appreciation for my mother and her skills as a true entertainer. Unlike me, she loved to be in the limelight and often directed the conversation to some escapade in which she had the starring role. Her storytelling reminded me of *Glamour*'s final tip for being irresistible at parties.

12. PUT YOUR SOUL OUT THERE.
Go ahead and risk self-exposure with that story about your run-in with your boss. Confess embarrassment. Tell a joke you love even if you're really bad at it. Be-

cause off-the-charts charm comes from letting them
know the real you.

Usually, her stories involved dating the star quarterback of
her high school, Richard (she called him Dick) Romanos,
who more recently had a bit part on *The Sopranos*. Or the
time in the 1970s when she grew marijuana in little flowerpots that she kept on the windowsill of our dining room.
With their mischievous theme and slightly delinquent subject matter, her stories were usually crowd pleasers.

Tonight, however, after a few glasses of champagne, my
mother began to regale the crowd, which consisted of, in
part, my father's sister Gladys, her hard-of-hearing husband
Bill, and a young couple invited by my brother and his wife,
with a version of number 12 gone horribly awry.

"Elliott [my father] and I once made a home movie with
our friends," she began teasingly. "Our scene was closed set
only." When no one bit, she added, "I agreed to go topless."

Another story began with her sewing her own maternity
minidress ("Hey! This was the sixties!") and ended with her
taking it off and going skinny-dipping. "With the neighbors!"

Whether she was trying to feel relevant, reminding the
younger people at the table that once she too was a hottie, or
just had one too many glasses of champagne and felt like
boasting (which, again, I guess, is a sadder way of being relevant), I was completely unnerved by her ribald tales. They
embarrassed and scared me.

Later, I asked Karl if he'd noticed anything odd about the
topic of my mother's dinner conversation. By then, I was re-

ferring to it as the "And Then I Was Naked" story collection by Time-Life.

"I didn't hear her saying anything weird." He looked at me with concern. Neither of us said anything for a while.

"I guess I never noticed it before," I said finally. "But so many of my mother's stories are about herself. I don't know how to connect with her."

Karl gave me one of his default replies, the one he used when he had no immediate plans of dealing with (cue ominous music): A Conversation.

"We'll figure it out," he said. When he saw that his (typical male) response had no effect, that I was still standing in front of him awaiting better marching orders, he added, "Don't worry. I love your mother. She's awesome. I love your whole family."

At least he knew what he was getting into.

■

Still searching for a way to make my time with my mother more meaningful before we left for D.C., I asked her if she'd file my nails. When my grandmother was still alive, though barely, my mother would file and polish her nails as my grandmother lay in her hospital bed. Like she was getting her ready for a cocktail party. Whenever I'd visit my grandmother, I was always so touched to see the bottle of Revlon's Love That Red on her nightstand. It was the same color my mother wore.

Was I subconsciously trying to create the same caretaker bond that my mother and her mother shared? My mother definitely was the better manicurist. But more than that, allowing her to take charge of my ten fingers reinforced the silent contract we had with each other. I would always need her help.

"You always did file your nails into funny little points." She laughed, taking my hand into hers. I remembered that line from the movie *Beaches*; when Barbara Hershey's little girl holds her plump hand next to her dying mother's, she says, "Look, we have the same hands." No matter how many times I see that movie, and it's been a lot, that scene always makes me bawl.

I also had my mother's hands; small palms, long piano player's fingers, thin wrists that wore watchbands on the last hole. But hers were always hot, and mine were always cold.

She started with my thumb, and as she went along, my nail filings formed tiny mountains of white powder on my jeans. She worked quickly, using the previous finger's handiwork as a visual guide before beginning on the next. "You have to make the shape of your nail match the shape of your cuticle," she explained, starting on my index finger. This was perfectly acceptable conversation, of course. But sitting there, hand in hand, I had the familiar pang of wanting another kind of connection, one that was easy and honest and where we could both be ourselves. I wanted to say something, anything, everything. But I was still mute as she started on my left hand.

It was time to pull out the serious guns. I remembered an article from *Real Simple* called "Getting to Know You," a four-page list of Barbara Walters–esque questions intended to help readers begin meaningful conversations with relatives and friends, preferably after a few eggnogs. The questions were divvied up into categories, such as "Childhood" and "Love and Family." Reading it, I had been particularly moved by the questions under the "You and Me" heading, especially, "Is there anything you wish had been different between us?" That one was too painful to imagine asking my mother. Even writer Erik Jackson admitted, "such topics can seem scary (or face it, best avoided)."

I started with a few softballs from under "The Kind of Life You've Lived." For some reason, I felt like a pimply-faced boy about to ask the most popular girl in school to dance.

"Mommy," I said, half expecting my voice to crack, "what do you like best about yourself?"

My question broke her filing rhythm. "I don't know." Her tone of voice was surprised, amused, and a bit flirtatious. I could tell she was flattered to be asked. And so I asked her again.

"I'm funny and loving and caring," she ticked off. I used the journalistic trick of staying quiet and nodding my head in encouragement. She continued. "And I rarely get angry."

It seemed more like she was writing her own personals ad. I had dealt with tough interview subjects before—I just had never considered my mother to be one, but I had never exactly sat down with her before in this capacity.

I kept on her. "Do you have any other positive traits?" I asked.

"I'm very generous," she said, suddenly more firm in her answers. "And I'm protective of the people I love."

"How are you protective? Can you say more?"

It didn't take any further probing. She finally got what I was after.

"If anyone was ever mean to you," she said, squeezing my hand for emphasis, "I would make sure that it didn't happen again."

It was interesting that she was talking about future cruelties as opposed to all the nastiness I had endured, motherless, in the past.

"Is there something about yourself you'd like to change?" I asked gently.

"I'm happy with myself." The quickness of her response sent a red flag to my reporter's ear.

"Come on," I prodded, suddenly more assured. "There must be something. Everyone has something."

"I'm too impulsive."

"How?"

"I open my big yap too much."

And there it was, and it was everything. For so long, I had wondered if my mother possessed even a smidgen of self-awareness—and if she did, would she be willing to reveal the dirtier parts to herself? Finally, she had seen for herself what had long been hanging off the clothesline for me.

"You're not so bad," I said. She held both of my hands in hers and examined her neat artistry. "Neither are you," she said, turning from my hands to my face. For the first time since sitting down, I looked directly at my mother and saw that her eyes were wet and shiny.

And I realized that all along, I knew exactly how to get more out of her; I had just never asked.

As my father drove us to the airport, I wondered if Karl had done any asking of his own.

Gift Wracked

*e*ver since returning from Thanksgiving, I had a newfound obsession with engagement rings. The impendence of a significant birthday, coupled with a half-baked belief that Karl would use this milestone to propose, was turning me into a total caricature of a woman in desperate need of a diamond.

All of a sudden, I found myself ripping out ring ads from *InStyle* and scrutinizing them like I was studying for the bar. Most designs operated under the more-is-more aesthetic, but that didn't stop me from debating the merits of each maker. Most dramatic was the ring by Scott Kay, which rose from the page like Venus on the half shell and had diamonds bursting out in every direction, like the ring had vomited mini engagement rings all over itself. Then there was the ring offered by Simon G, a headlight-size solitaire surrounded by an octagon of pink diamonds on a three-rowed band of white diamonds. It looked like something Willy Wonka might have masterminded, had he operated a jewelry store instead of a candy factory. A trilogy ring by Diavante (which I had initially misread as *Deviant*) was my least favorite, mostly because it combined both yellow gold and platinum, which only highlighted the diamond's poor taste in neighbors.

An equally new and regrettable development was my selective hearing. Every time Karl began a sentence with, "Will you . . . ," my heart raced. And every time that sentence ended with, "get me a glass of water, hand me a towel, wash my brown pants," I felt simultaneously ashamed and enraged at myself. I had fallen prey to the worst these magazines had to offer, becoming a living, breathing *Cosmo* article.

Actually, I was even worse. In October's "10 Ways Not to Get Him to Propose," I was **Cosmo Commandment Number 2**. In a watch list that included "Gain 35 pounds to show him how sexy you'll look pregnant," and "Oh so casually request 'Babe, can you scratch my ring finger? It's kind of itchy'" was this big don't: "Freak out whenever he utters 'Will you . . . ,' then act all depressed when the words '. . . marry me' don't follow. Practice on these: 'Will you . . . pass the remote?' or 'Will you . . . stop staring at me like that?'"

I knew women like this. I just never fancied I'd become one. I thought about a college friend who believed her boyfriend would propose over Christmas break. When she came back to school in January, she was absolutely livid after she unwrapped a blue box from Tiffany's to find a pair of what she described bitterly as "mother-fucking pearl earrings."

I wondered if I'd exhibit the same grand disappointment and foiled sense of entitlement if my birthday came and went with no knee dropping, no quavering speech, and no velvet box. Would my heart end up crushed under all my foot stamping? To make matters worse, Hanukkah began the evening after my birthday, which provided eight more opportunities for letdown.

I needed to do some damage control. Pronto. In the days leading up to my birthday, I had to emotionally prepare in the event of a nonevent. This month, every one of the magazines offered plenty of nifty ideas for what to get your boss, your sister, your globetrotting friend. But what about an article that dealt with the gifting aftermath? The fact of the matter was I needed an article that addressed what to do if I *didn't* receive my heart's desire, an article complete with scripted dialogue and a photo showing how to appear gracious that I could take with me to the bathroom and practice striking in the mirror.

The makings of a colossal disappointment were already there. For instance, while on an overnight getaway to New York City, Karl and I were shopping along Madison Avenue, pretending we were rich and pointing at the astronomical things we'd get for each other. "Just wait here," I instructed outside Prada, "I want to pop in and buy you the whole store."

We wandered into a shop with beautiful leather coats from Canada, and Karl wanted to buy me a knee-length trench that was the color of a dull nickel. It was slim and fitted to my body like it was custom made for me, and it was the most gorgeous thing I had ever seen. It was also on sale for $700, which, had he got it for me, would have been a pretty amazing souvenir from our trip. It also would have been the first real gift Karl had ever bought for me.

But, and here comes the crazy, I was nervous about Karl spending that much money on me. Not because he couldn't afford it or that we had already spent too much money on our train fare to New York. So I asked myself, *what was really going on here? What did this jacket really represent to me? Why, when what I really wanted to say was "Yes, please buy me this jacket," what I said instead was "No, I already have plenty of jackets"?* The answer that came was this: *if Karl was spending $700 on a coat, then that was $700 he wasn't going to be spending on a ring.* Looking at my reflection in the store's mirror, I continued to make more troubling if/then statements. *If he bought me the coat, then he wouldn't be buying me a ring. Which also meant if he was prepared to buy me the coat, then he hadn't already bought me a ring.*

"You are turning into such a girl," teased Steph, my first cousin and the person I felt closest to in my family. She and her husband Drew ran a porn website out of their farmhouse in Maine. They were also in town, having flown into Manhattan to meet with one of their site's contributors, a gay hardcore star from the 1980s.

Over dinner, while Karl and Drew chatted about deer meat, Steph and I sat with our shoulders touching, and I relayed some of the side effects I was suffering from my now-seven-month immersion into women's magazines.

"Who cares about a ring?" Steph asked in all seriousness. She held out her hand to show me hers. I remembered when she picked it out, under duress from her mother, my aunt Hava and my mother's sister. It was white gold with a dull, dark stone that was set flush with the plain band. "I hate things that sparkle," she explained. "I'd take it off right now if it wasn't stuck on my finger."

"Sometimes I feel like *Cosmo*'s Bedside Astrologer has taken over my brain," I said, switching the topic to something she was more familiar with. Even though she was almost nine years younger than me, it was Steph who had first told me about the birds and the bees.

"If you were a magazine article," she posed, her cheeks bright from too much wine, "which one would you be?" She began to lampoon my reading material by offering me some helpful title suggestions.

"How about 'I Love Me Now,'" she said, draining the rest of her wine. "Or, '12 Ways to Fuck Yourself and Other Things I Learned from Reading Magazines.'" By the time she came up with my personal favorite, "Our Parts Fit: A Love Story," we both had tears streaming down our cheeks.

Outside the restaurant, I hugged her. Moving her heavy red hair, I whispered in her ear, "Once I make it through my birthday, I'll be back to normal."

"I hope so," she whispered back. "Otherwise I'm going to get you a subscription to *Leg Sex* and that will *really* fuck you up."

Seeing Steph again was a good antidote for how nuts I was feeling. But now that she was on a plane home to sell porn to high-
tech workers (her biggest client base), and Karl and I were
sitting on a D.C.-bound Acela, I had settled into my seat with a
broad sense of disappointment and *Marie Claire* on my lap.

As our train pulled out of Penn Station, Karl turned to
me and said, "Every time Drew and I looked over, you and
Steph had your heads together and were laughing like you
were up to no good."

I gave him a weak smile. The kicker to the whole trip was
Karl had ended up buying himself a jacket from that store.
He was wearing it now, and the leather smelled faintly of tobacco and turtle wax. I would say it also smelled of broken
dreams, but that would be too pathetic. Even for me. As he
buried himself in the new *Maxim* (unlike mine, his reading
experience was one of pure pleasure), I opened up *Marie
Claire* and began reading an article in the "Couples" section.
"The Dangerous New Infidelity You Need to Know About,"
blared the headline. "HEAD SEX!" The art showed a string
of Lotus Notes emails between Derrick, a married father of
one, and Lucy, a contributor to a feminist webzine, whom he
met at a bar. "Even if we never do anything," began one from
Lucy, "I have to say that this whole drawn-out text/voice/
tactile foreplay with you is very exciting. I would like to continue to explore."

"Though they may never have had sex on the set," writer
Sandra Barron began, "Brad and Angelina were technically
cheating. Emotionally." The term *head sex*, according to
Barron, "springs from a feeling that you're on the same wave-

length with a guy." Which, she noted, is way more intense than a physical connection. And, Barron included in a bright pink box-out, head sex is way more popular than ever. "Major societal changes have affected even the way we form crushes." Barron provided three new enablers of the new head sex explosion: longer hours at work, more time spent online, and BlackBerries.

As Lucy and Derrick's emails continued to be sprinkled throughout the six-page feature, other women stepped forward to attest to this phenomenon. "The night I met Michael," revealed Mia, 24, "I swear the song 'Magic,' by The Cars, started playing in my head." Mia went on to explain that even though Michael was the boyfriend of her good friend, she still maintained a consistent email relationship with him. "We even shared a bed one evening and spooned all night without taking it further." Eventually, what a surprise, Mia and Michael ended up "making out on a hill under the stars, for so long that I had grass burns." Two days later, Michael broke up with his girlfriend to be with Mia; two months later, Michael's ass was grass. "I called it quits via email," Mia confessed.

After reading the seven telltale signs that a guy is heading for trouble ("Your guy is paying more attention to his appearance, whether it's new clothes, new cologne, or increased time at the gym"), I looked over at Karl in his new jacket. "Karl," I baby-talked, showing him the title page to the article, "are you having head sex?"

He refused to take the bait. "You don't have much to worry about," he said distractedly.

"That kind of response, to me, means I may have something to worry about."

"It's just an expression."

"So is 'You have nothing to worry about.'"

Why in the world did I feel the need to show him this article? Why did I endlessly need his reassurance? *Peace*, I told myself, seeing if my mantra from last month still worked. I closed my eyes, took a deep breath, and realized I was still a piece of work.

The truth of the matter was, I was regressing. My impending birthday, which by now I had built up into an event as monumental as a virgin's deflowering, had caused me to backslide into a playground of insecurity and bullying self-doubt.

Work was the last place I wanted to feel vulnerable. Lately, I was spending at least an hour a day holing up in Dave's office, "in different meetings," I told my manager.

"I know Karl is going to get me a digital camera for my birthday," I whined, flopping myself dramatically across his desk. A few months ago, I had mentioned how nice it would be to have a camera like Jeanne's, a miniature apparatus that she always carried during our walks in case we spotted what she referred to as "nature shots." I had no choice but to think, in hindsight and with much regret, that Karl had taken my photographic desires a bit too seriously.

"Do I take a picture of myself giving him the finger and then throw the camera across the room in a fit of Veda rage?"

Dave found my *Mildred Pierce* reference hilarious and launched into his own routine.

"You son of a bitch," he cried, pantomiming like he was throwing the camera like a football.

"I don't get it," I said, switching into the character of a ditz. "How am I supposed to wear this?" I mimicked, trying to put the camera strap around my ring finger.

To cheer me up, Dave offered to throw a small post-birthday party on the twenty-seventh at my favorite restaurant. I was hesitant though, uncomfortable with the idea of asking people to add one more name to their holiday dance card, not to mention buy me a gift on top of it. But I agreed to let Dave organize it, mostly because he promised to make it low-key.

"Don't worry," he said, "I'll keep the emphasis off your birthday."

And then I got his Evite:

**Cathy Alter. Jimmy Buffett.
Jesus Christ. Anwar Sadat.**

What do they have in common? All great minds, of course. Spectacular fashion trendsetters. That's indisputable. Very creative, except for maybe Anwar, who would have been born on the 26th if the camel had slowed down.

Most importantly, they share a birthday!

And yes, it's a big birthday . . . so
let's celebrate in style with Cathy!

And may I say, as we all move forward in
the time continuum: let us not fear the
big birthdays. As the fabulous Sally
O'Malley once said, "Ladies and gentlemen, my name is Sally O'Malley. I'm
proud to say that I am 50 years old. I'm
not one of those gals who are afraid to
tell her real age, and I like to [demon-
strate] Kick! Stretch! and KICK! I'm 50!
50 years old! 50 years old. Not afraid
to hide my age, 50!"

So come out and let's KICK and STRETCH
and KICK and just generally have fun for
Cathy's 40th!

After assuring me he wouldn't stress my birthday or my
age, he goes and crafts something like this? What should
have been the appropriate reaction? Not only did he make
a not-so-subtle dig at women who are uncomfortable
broadcasting their real age, but he had to do it in the voice
of an old *Saturday Night Live* sketch. And come on, could
he have possibly squeezed in the number 50 a few more
times? Was he doing me a favor by using fifty to deflect
forty?

But I didn't want to look a gift horse in the mouth, even
if he was an ass. Besides, I still had to make it through my

birthday and a couple of nights of Hanukkah before I needed to deal with this party.

In order to survive the five days leading up to my birthday, I would have to pull myself together and perform a major attitude adjustment. Despite what I did or didn't get, I had to see the value in it, unconditionally—whether it was a digital camera or a birthday party thrown by a showboating friend.

And so I asked myself: what would Oprah do?

In her What I Know for Sure column, Oprah talked about "five-star pleasures," and opened up her own pleasure map to reveal some of the things that made her happy. "For me just waking up 'clothed in my right mind,' being able to put my feet on the floor, walk to the bathroom, and do what needs to be done there is a five-starrer."

There was a joke in here somewhere (like, she scores her bowel movements?), but I was really trying to cast aside my judgment and bias (although, call me cynical, it was hard to imagine that Oprah did all of the above unassisted). I looked at Oprah's photo. She was leaning back in laughter, one heel kicked up in the air, her left index finger pointed to the heavens. Was she inferring that she got her greatest pleasure from God?

As part of a feature called "Take Pleasure," there was a bliss list called "What Makes Us Purr." God was not on it. Yoga was. So was Scrabble, homemade whipped cream, and "a great scalp massage from the shampoo lady at the hairdresser." I had to agree with that last one. After the fortieth (symbolic?) item on the list ("Wearing a wide-brim hat just because you want to") were five blank lines with the instructions, "Please feel free to add, adapt, borrow."

Similar to the wish list I made for myself at the beginning of my year, it took me a while to eke out my own five-starrers.

The first thing that came to mind was: counting eleven deer on my last walk with Jeanne.

Then: watching Karl spritz cologne in his armpits.

And: seeing my byline, cupping the heads of babies, the Sunday flea market.

I'm not going to tell you that Oprah cured me of my materialistic impulses and my desire to hurry up and get engaged now, please. But goddamn if that list didn't put things into perspective. "What you put out comes back," wrote Oprah at the end of her column. "Your base level of pleasure is determined by how you view your whole life."

I decided I was going to love my new digital camera. Five days before my birthday, Karl came home from work and set down his motorcycle's saddlebag. "I know you," he said in lieu of a greeting. "And I know you'll go snooping around for your birthday and Hanukkah presents. So I'm keeping everything at my office."

"I already know what you got me for my birthday," I said.

"What does it begin with?" Karl asked, nervously eyeing his saddlebag. I knew whatever he got me was in there and not, as he just warned, at his office.

"It begins with a *D*."

"Well, you know," he said slyly, "they are forever."

"Oh yah. Karl is going to propose. He wants to marry you. Definitely."

I was sitting across from Dr. Oskar, milking my last appointment of the year for all it was worth. We had spent most of the session taking stock of my progress, even though I was insisting that my rush-to-the-altar machinations didn't feel much like giant steps forward.

"That is because you're ready," he said. Somewhere in the back of his mind, he was high-fiving himself for helping to get me this far.

"What if he's not? What if he likes things the way they are?" I had never heard Karl utter the word "marriage" before, even in reference to someone else. Maybe his hard palate was different from other men.

"I shouldn't stake my reputation on this," Dr. Oskar began, "but Karl will ask you to marry him before the end of the year."

"How do you know?" For a second, I thought maybe Karl had called Dr. Oskar to ask for my hand.

"It's just a feeling," he answered, leaning back into his tweed couch. "But I will bet you I'm right."

"Is this what you call trying to manage my expectations?" I asked, shaking his hand and taking the bet.

We had cake for breakfast. Karl had used an entire tube of pink icing to write, "Happy Birthday, Girlie." After I blew out my candles, one for every decade, he disappeared into the bedroom and I soon heard the unmistakable snow-crunching sound of a plastic bag being disturbed. My ear told me it was Best Buy.

"I didn't wrap it," he said. "Since you already knew what it was."

We spent the rest of the morning taking silly photos with my new camera. Earlier in the week, a coworker had given me a paper crown that read "Birthday Slut" across the front. We took turns posing for each other, wearing it at increasingly rakish angles.

The phrase *self-fulfilling prophecy* had flitted through my brain when I first saw the box, wounded for just a second that it wasn't black and velvet and palm-size. My ex-husband had given me tons of small shiny things that were now tucked away in the back of my sock drawer.

This month, *Cosmo* had a spread called "Unwrap the Meaning Behind His Gift." On each of the four pages, a different shirtless and waxed man posed next to something with a bow. The copy read, "Every offering is a statement of how your guy feels about you and your relationship. Here, find out what he's really trying to say when he surprises you with . . ."

A digital camera fell into their "Exactly What You Wanted" category. "Those 7,000 hints you dropped didn't fall on deaf ears," congratulated the text. And I guess, now that I replayed the previous nature shot conversation on fast forward, how could I be disappointed with Karl's level of attention? At least he hadn't gotten me "A Practical Present," which according to *Cosmo* could be anything from a flash-light to an umbrella. The accompanying photo showed a baby-faced guy with a completely hairless torso toting an emergency roadside kit with a big red bow stuck to the plastic handle.

I tried taking pleasure in the gift. Really, I did. But still, all day, I kept wanting to hear that question. So much so that when we were lying quietly in bed together, listening to the rain hit the air conditioner, and Karl said, "Doesn't the rain make you want to pee?" I heard, "Don't you want to marry me?"

Early that evening, we made our own menorah out of polymer clay, and Karl presented me with my first night's gift: two bears, one gray and one pink, that he had also made out of the polymer.

"I'm the gray one," he explained. "I made the pink one a little smaller, because it's you."

The bears represented a dream Karl had when we were first dating. He had woken up one morning and had told me about us being little bears, wandering through the forest and sniffing for berries.

"Every once in a while, you would grunt—but I somehow understood exactly what you were saying," he had said excitedly.

Soon after, I had recounted the dream to Dr. Oskar. "What an excellent dream!" he had remarked, clapping his hands. "Karl is telling you that even if you speak to each other in bear, he feels understood at the most primal level."

The next night, after lighting our clay menorah, Karl gave me more handmade clay gifts—a heart-shaped charm (so small I had to look at it under my jeweler's loupe to fully appreciate the level of work he put into it) and an intricate snowflake that looked like Belgian lace. He had attached the snowflake to a straightened paper clip, explaining that I could wear it like a stickpin. The following night, he gave me a plaid scarf flecked with gold, which he had actually bought at a store. "You can stick the snowflake into the material," he demonstrated, tying the scarf around his neck and stabbing it with the end of the paper clip.

Later that night, I showed off the scarf and stickpin at the birthday party Dave was throwing for me.

As soon as we walked through the door of the restaurant, my friend Chris swept me off to the bar. "What did he get you for your birthday?" she asked with way too much eagerness.

I unzipped my pocketbook and pulled out the digital camera.

"Oh, no!" she exclaimed, covering her eyes with both hands to block out the offensive sight. "I'm so sorry."

"For what?" I blinked to emphasize the naïveté I hoped I was pulling off. "It's exactly what I wanted."

Experiencing someone else's disappointment for me had an inverse effect. The fact that she thought I was suffering some sort of collapse because I received a piece of electronics for my birthday probably said more about her own life's discontent.

The truth was, I knew Karl was getting ready to propose. Everything was leading up to it. And once my birthday was over, so was the anxiety that went along with it. I became a whole lot calmer about the waiting process.

"It's good you're not stressing, C Dawg," emailed my friend Missy, using my rap star name. Hers was Money Mel. "You know it's going to happen sooner rather than later."

Missy was also invested in my getting engaged, but mostly because she lived in Boca Raton and a wedding meant that she and I could see each other again. I had last seen her at her own wedding, which was a year ago. Because she had gone through a similar impatience waiting for her husband Brad to propose, I had found myself calling and emailing her more than usual over the past weeks.

"Are you checking Karl for pocket bulges?" she emailed. "Before Brad proposed, every time we did something different, I thought tonight's the night. One time he suggested going to the beach on a random night and I kept checking his pockets for a ring box indent."

Missy eventually found the ring box hidden in the refrigerator a few weeks later. "When you least expect it, it will happen, so don't worry. Soon, we'll all be jetting off to Las Vegas!!!"

I had jokingly told her that I wanted to get married in front of Siegfried and Roy's white tigers dressed in a sequined jumpsuit with a fat Elvis officiating. Missy ended her email with hotel recommendations. "The Bellagio or The Venetian work for me, Dawg!"

With all the hoopla surrounding my birthday and coming up with eight nights of Hanukkah gifts (alas, mine were not homemade), I had completely forgotten about New Year's Eve. As far as I knew, Karl and I had no plans. Which wasn't a big deal. I knew one phone call to Crazy Larry would solve that dilemma. But I wasn't about to dial the number. After spending most of November ascending the twelve steps to sexy party girl consciousness, I didn't care if we spent New Year's Eve in our pajamas eating frozen pizza.

"So what are we going to do?" I finally asked Karl over breakfast.

"I rented a car for the afternoon," he said. "I thought we'd take a drive out to the mountains and tool around." I knew his definition of mountains was a particular stretch of Route 211, just west of Sperryville, Virginia, where the road twisted and turned like a piece of Silly String. It was Karl's favorite spot to ride his motorcycle because he could take each bend like an acrobat, leaning his bike so far over that his knee practically touched the ground. The few times he'd taken me on the ride, I had to sit out on the side of the road, nauseous from all the pitching around.

"Why don't we take the bike?" I asked, genuinely confused. This was Karl's favorite kind of weather to hop on a bike.

"I thought it would be nicer to dress in normal clothes, in case we decide to stop for a late lunch."

I don't remember what we talked about as we drove along the back roads of Virginia. I only remember looking up at the sky and watching the sun begin to set behind a bank of clouds. The effect of the pink rays coming through the haze and the clouds drifting toward their finger-tipped union reminded me of the ceiling in the Sistine Chapel.

Karl made a few turns, and all of a sudden, I recognized where we were.

"The Inn at Little Washington is right around this corner," I said helpfully. I had been out to the Inn a few years ago when I profiled the two owners for a feature in the *Washingtonian* magazine. At the time, I had asked Reinhardt and Patrick to adopt me, falling in love with them and their business of making guests feel, as Patrick had said, "like baby birds in a nest."

"Are you hungry?" asked Karl.

"A little." I hesitated.

"Let's see if we can grab a burger at the bar," he said, pulling into the Inn's small parking lot.

"Are you crazy?" I looked at him like he was about to greet the Queen of England with a corncob pipe between his teeth. "First of all, it's New Year's Eve. You can't just walk into the Inn without reservations. Second of all, the Inn doesn't have bar food."

"Let's just see." I had learned not to argue with Karl. Instead, I just stood in the doorway of the restaurant so I could make a quick exit. "They're going to laugh in your face," I said to Karl as he brushed by me.

Instead, a hostess appeared. "May I take your coat?" she asked warmly.

"What in the world?" I said to Karl, who was doubled over in hysterics.

"You should have seen your face!"

When Karl declined to check his coat, I thought of what Missy said and checked his pockets for any bulges. In my research of the Inn, I had read that the restaurant averaged one proposal a night.

"What do you have in your coat that's so important?" I teased.

"It's still Hanukkah," he answered, unrattled by my interrogation. "I still have to give you your surprise."

After that, I turned the what's-going-to-happen-next part of my brain off. If that's what it means to live in the moment, well, I was finally doing it.

Our dinner talk was so obscenely romantic we should have been slapped with a fine. Karl told me he loved the way I swung my knees back and forth when I drank my coffee. "Sometimes I look at you," he said, "and I see a little girl."

Karl asked if we could have our dessert outside in the garden, which was lit by hundreds of tiny lanterns. He had given me his coat to wear, and I absentmindedly put my hands in the pockets, which were both empty.

We sat down at a small wrought-iron table with our wine and a plate of miniature pastries. "Would you like to come back here next year?" he asked quietly.

I told him that if we came back, he'd have to let me pay. "This place is a fortune."

"If we come back," he continued, "you couldn't come back as my girlfriend."

For a fraction of a second, I had the delusional thought that he was breaking up with me. "What? I can't what?"

"You'd have to come back as my wife."

When we talked about that moment the next day, Karl had told me he had gotten down on one knee, but I hadn't seen a thing. I think I must have developed hysterical blindness. My eyes were behind a wall of tears. I couldn't make out the ring in the box, just a slight glitter coming out of a dark shape, like a tiny star from a million miles away. In the movie of my life, I saw Oprah as my bridesmaid, dressed in pale lilac and holding my bouquet under the chuppah. Next to her, my matron of honor, Helen Gurley Brown, was dabbing her eyes.

When I finally went to the bathroom, dragging my newly ringed hand down the blue suede wall to the inn's spectacularly gilded powder room, I sat down on the toilet, dried my eyes, and finally had a good look at what was on my finger. It looked nothing like the photos from *InStyle* and felt better than anything I had ever put on my body.

We called my parents from the restaurant. They were having their annual New Year's Eve cocktail party, and when my father picked up the phone, he sounded like he was in the middle of a conversation.

"Do you know whom you're talking to?" I quizzed him.

Mostly because I couldn't be sure if he was actually paying attention to my phone call.

"Of course I know," he insisted.

"Who is it?" I tested him.

"It's my daughter."

"No, it's not," I corrected. "It's the soon-to-be Mrs. Karl Feldman."

It turned out that Karl had sent my father a letter, announcing his intentions in writing. He had hoped to sync the letter's arrival with his proposal (so there would be no chance of my parents spoiling the surprise), but had mailed the letter to our home in West Hartford instead of to our weekend house in Stonington, where my parents were celebrating the long weekend.

"Hey!" I heard my dad tell the crowd. "My daughter's engaged!" The living room erupted in cheers and applause. I started crying all over again.

My mother grabbed the phone, and my father's laughter faded into the distance. "How do you feel about the backyard?" I knew that as she was talking to me, she was standing by the sliding door that led to the garden. "We could fit at least forty people back here."

"How about a congratulations first?" I laughed, lifting my chin to Karl in an it-figures look. "We can talk details tomorrow."

"I am so happy for you," she said before getting distracted by someone's request for more ice and hanging up.

I remembered seeing my sister-in-law Abby right before her wedding. I had come to the bridal suite to watch her sign the *ketubah*, a sort of Jewish marriage certificate. "I'm so happy," she had swooned. Even though I was married at the time, I remember thinking to myself, *I don't know what that feels like.*

But now I did. And it was a good thing I had my digital camera along to capture the moment.

Wrangle Your Wiggle

i began the New Year the same way I had for the past ten years—walking with Jeanne. With most of George-town sleeping off the previous night, the path along the canal was deserted, except for pockets of rummaging turtledoves. We paused at our regular turnaround point, a portion of an old fence, where we stretched and looked out over the Potomac, which glittered like a sheet of mica.

"It's amazing," said Jeanne, holding my hand and address-ing my ring. "I remember you last winter. Two winters ago. Three winters ago." She looked up at me and I saw that her eyes were brimming. "Cathy," she said, "your ship has come in."

She was right, of course. I thought about where my ship

was moored last year, nursing a serious hangover and trying to figure out how I had managed to wake up with a black eye. (Reliving the evening, I recalled my friend Sabrina performing an elaborate dance move and elbowing me in the face.)

In less than a year, I had turned my life around—mentally, emotionally, and romantically.

"I'm self-flagellating for everything I didn't accomplish in the past year," laughed Jeanne. "And you actually managed to make and keep a new set of resolutions every single month."

In all honesty, I felt like taking this month off. Not because I had finally reached my goal. Getting a man was never my endgame. Karl was just one part of my betterment plan (or perhaps he was the external reward for my internal ones).

The truth was, I still had more months of ameliorative work to contract. But I just didn't want to think anymore. Or read another word. I just wanted to ring in the New Year, to literally flash around my ring, without first checking to see if January had any articles about "The Rules of Engagement" or "How to Fast Track Him Down the Aisle."

All of a sudden, I had an epiphany. These magazines were like good politicians. Packaged for mass appeal on the shelves, once off, they still needed to shake hands with the widest audience possible. Maybe it was time that I started reading the magazines the way the rest of the female constituents did. Instead of using them to take and retake my psychological picture, why couldn't I enjoy the magazines for more trivial pursuits? I had spent entire months perfecting my insides—

wasn't it time for the rest of me to get in on the action? After all, I had a wedding dress in my not so distant future.

This month, with the goal of being the hottest bride in history, I was turning my internal plight outward—on my jiggly upper arms and stomach pooch. For the first time in recent memory, I wanted to feel the burn of multiple fire hydrants.

I have never owned any of the following: a yoga mat, dumbbells, an exercise ball, or any types of rubber bands, other than the kind that go in your hair. When I was in college, my friend and I famously worked out to Jane Fonda's 1982 video masterpiece with an open bag of Doritos and a six-pack on the floor next to us.

Which is not to say I never belonged to a gym or didn't own a Thigh Master. I'm just extremely lazy and would prefer not to break a sweat while attaining a perfect body. My current fitness routine, walking around, fit the criteria perfectly.

And that was why *Glamour*'s "The Year You'll Get a Great Body" appealed to me. Instead of designing an intimidating, equipment-heavy routine, *Glamour*'s plan, which was adapted from *Your Ultimate Pilates Body*® *Challenge*, consisted of "a 15-minute workout you can do in your pajamas!" Besides not needing a supersized beach ball or a set of dumbbells to complete any of the ten exercises featured in the article, I didn't even need to leave my bed for the first one, a move labeled "Footwork," which, curiously, toned the abs and inner thighs. The instructions called for a modified sit-up, where the legs worked independently, bending and un-bending with each sit-up or sit-down. The accompanying photo showed a pixie-haired model, smiling like a nut on a floral print bedspread, elbows at her ears and legs aimed toward a sheer-curtained window.

I've always been pretty good at sit-ups. In sixth grade, I did more sit-ups in a minute than my entire gym class and won an iron-on patch as part of the President's Fitness Campaign. This has been my only physical claim to fame, however.

As I lifted up and down on my bed (on which rests a Tempur-Pedic mattress that is super cushy and probably not conducive to good sit-upping), my cat Raymond got in on the action. Purring madly (something I rarely heard), he rubbed his cheek on my bent elbow as I got in position, and persisted in circling around and under my raised legs like a maypole for the entire eight repetitions. Thinking Raymond was simply attracted to the newness of the activity, I repeated the exercise, hoping he would lose interest. This only further intrigued him, and he spent the next eight repetitions standing on my chest, staring hard at me.

The rest of the nine exercises required getting on the floor. Here was where the cushy properties of a yoga mat would have proved beneficial. Before continuing, I had to take a break and hunt around for the ratty sheepskin throw that Karl had bought at Ikea so my coccyx didn't bore into the floor. Once in place, I was ready for the second exercise, "Breathing," which, as in "Footwork," was a misnomer and had nothing to do with exercising the body part suggested. For this move, I had to squeeze my butt cheeks together as I lifted my hips off the floor and formed a slide with my body. "Hold for five counts, squeezing butt, keeping abs tight and pressing the backs of your arms into the floor." The lady in the photo looked relaxed, and actually, so was I. I could see why Pilates was taking the country by storm.

Next, I performed some sort of leg lift/scissor kick combo (although its official name is "Single Straight-Leg Stretch"). Despite the misleading names, the directions were clearly written, and the matching photos were easy to pattern. The model looked high on life—who wouldn't want to give Pilates a whirl? (With all those high-achieving posers in their organic fold-top pants, yoga would always be a hard sell.)

But then I got to exercise number four: "Rowing." In one photo, the model reclined on a green square of carpet, in a Tutankhamen-rising-from-the-sarcophagus pose. Then, in a second photo, she had somehow left the carpet and was floating floorless in white space. She was now curled over her straightened legs with her arms thrust out behind her, palms up. How she went from one position to the next was a mystery, and the copy, instead of offering supplemental aid, just confused the situation even more:

> On the floor, sit tall with your legs extended, your feet
> in a V with heels together and toes slightly apart; place
> your hands in fists, and bend your elbows wide to the
> sides and bring your hands to your breastbone.

This was the King Tut pose from the first picture; it was as far as I could go before everything disintegrated into a game of S&M Twister:

> Pull your belly button toward your spine, inhale and slowly roll your lower back toward the floor, as shown, squeezing your butt and inner thighs together to keep your lower body anchored to the ground. (Only go as far as you can without tipping backward.) From this position, open your arms wide to the sides, palms facing back. Exhale and fold forward over your legs as you circle your arms behind you with palms up and fingertips touching the floor, as shown. Holding this position with your upper body, inhale, circle your arms around and reach toward your toes. (Throughout the move, do not let your shoulders ride up toward your ears.)

Also, do not let your fists rise up to God in unmitigated rage.

I made it to the seventh exercise, "Chest Expansion"—which, surprise, surprise, toned the opposite and worked the back—before I was forced to quit. I just couldn't face the "Mermaid," a bizarre pose where the model appeared to be legless, like a beautiful sideshow attraction.

Surprisingly, the next morning, although I couldn't recall any exercise that actually targeted this area, my inner thighs felt like I had just gotten off a horse.

"Why are you walking so funny?" asked Karl, banging his

chest like a gorilla. Apparently he thought my gait had something to do with his sexual prowess.

I was actually keeping Mission Hot Bod under wraps. My
cat had continued to mock my attempts at Pilates, and I
knew if Karl caught wind of my routine, he would have a
field day teasing me. Even though he knew I was sensitive
about my tummy bulge, he overjoyed in grabbing it and
speaking to it like a separate organism, a symbiotic bird on a
hippo. To ensure that he never witnessed a single sit-up, I
used the hour between work and his arrival home to exercise, changing from my office uniform to workout wear like
the jazzercise version of Mr. Rogers.

Even though I never mastered "Rowing," after the first
week I was able to perform most of the exercises in *Glamour*
without constantly referring back to the instructions or
photos. I had tried to get a tape measure around certain body
parts to track my progress, but it was too hard to accomplish
without help. *Glamour* recommended adding thirty minutes
of cardio to the routine "for even faster results," so in addition to walking on weekends with Jeanne, I had invited Jane,
one of my coworkers, to walk with me twice a week during
lunch. When I swung by her office to pick her up that first
day, I handed her a tape measure.

"Can you help get this around my bicep?" I asked.

"What bicep?" she answered without skipping a beat.

We bundled up and headed through Georgetown, following the same towpath that Jeanne and I took on weekends.
Our conversation, though, was markedly different.

"I'm going to miss all of your crazy stories," sighed Jane.

She began listing all the whackos I had dated, starting with the guy who once entertained me for an entire evening in his apartment wearing a ratty old wig and false teeth. "Does Karl do anything funny?" she asked hopefully.

"Not really," I said, feeling like I had let her down. "Well, the other night," I began hopefully. "I heard a lot of banging around in the kitchen and I thought, *Oh, good, Karl is cooking.* But when I walked in the room, he was hopped up on the sink, straddling the faucet, bolting our dish rack down to the windowsill in an effort to save counter space."

"I guess that's funny," Jane said, clearly crestfallen.

She didn't congratulate me on my engagement to a solid guy or admit that she was relieved that she wouldn't be hearing any more stories about clearly imbalanced gentlemen, and I wondered why certain people who claimed to like me could be so endlessly, subtly cruel. And now that I thought about it, Jane still insisted on calling me Zymie, the nickname she had derived from my former married name, even though she was repeatedly reminded that I no longer went by it, and hadn't since I was actually married.

Which led me to an equally concerning fact: my checks, driver's license, and email address all identified me by my former name. I hadn't changed it legally, though, which suggested that I secretly knew I wouldn't be staying married long enough to obtain a new social security card. Still, it had been more than three years since my divorce—what was taking me so long to perform what was clearly administrative busywork?

Sitting in Dr. Oskar's waiting room, I thought about why I hadn't gotten around to altering my name. Was it just laziness, the same type of immobility that had led me to avoid all strenuous forms of exercise? Or was removing my old name from official documents tantamount to erasing part of my identity? It was like denying a significant part of my past. However sad and traumatic, a small part of me would be going away for good.

While I sat pondering my name, I was also easily able to eavesdrop on The Loud Talker, whose appointment was still in session and who usually sounded like he was confessing all his inner turmoil through a megaphone.

"So I said to her, 'Boy, you have a beautiful body and I'd like to have some of it'"—he yelled, sounding super irritated. "And she looked at me with hatred and said, 'Fuck you, you know I don't fit into any of my jeans.' And when I asked her if it explained the pile of jeans I had just found in the Dumpster, she yelled at me and said my therapy wasn't working. So that's when I called her a bitch because, I gotta say, I think this stuff is working."

"This is all good," said Dr. Oskar more quietly. "But I think you need to try and direct your impulses."

"All right," agreed The Loud Talker.

It was so hard not to applaud when he walked through the waiting room and out the door. I really did admire his passion and vocal range.

"Let me see your finger," ordered Dr. Oskar when he came to fetch me. I offered my hand like a Southern belle.

"I'm not going to say I told you." He winked at the sight

of the ring. "But I told you." Leading me into his office, he mock-whispered, "Don't tell anyone about my special engagement predictions. I don't want to go into the wedding business."

After I gave him the blow-by-blow of Karl's proposal, I shared my name-change theory with Dr. Oskar.

"Well, yah, I think you have had enough people screwing with your identity," he mused. "Maybe now that you know who you are, you will have to take care of a little business."

When I agreed, Dr. Oskar asked what else I was doing to prepare for married life.

"This month, I'm working on getting the perfect body."

"Why?" he gasped, clutching his chest.

"Because I want to look hot in my wedding dress."

"You don't have to do anything," he argued. "You will look beautiful because you will be standing next to the person you love."

I wanted to make a joke about Karl loving wattles, but I just agreed with him. There was no use debating someone so intent on celebrating.

After two weeks of *Glamour*'s Pilates workout, I was impatient to see harder results. The circumference of my upper arm, waist, and thighs hadn't decreased by even a fraction of a millimeter. I needed more of a challenge. I could hardly believe it, but I was ready to pump up the jam.

Before I could switch into high gear, I had to make sure I wouldn't die in the process. I have never been a heavy smoker, but since dating Karl, who was at least a welter-weight, I had often gone cigarette for cigarette with him, especially on the weekends when we were really letting ourselves go. I was worried that any new and unusual activity would cause my lungs to collapse and my heart to beat straight out of my chest.

Conveniently, on the backside of the *Glamour* exercise article was one about quitting. "How I Quit Smoking" featured four inspirational stories about shaking the cancer stick. While one quit cold turkey, one underwent hypnosis, and one just stopped hanging out with her pack-a-day posse, I instantly recognized myself in Lucinda Rosenfeld, a writer who worked with a pack of Dunhills on her desk. I had just read an article about Joan Didion, who still smoked, though only five cigarettes a day and only at her typewriter. The attachment to cigarettes, admitted Rosenfeld (and I think Didion might concede), "felt almost romantic." She continued, "We were in it together, Tobacco Man and I."

After a health scare (the left side of her body went numb for a few days), Rosenfeld got herself down to one or two smokes a day. Today, Rosenfeld, who confessed she "never got over her love affair with cigarettes," smokes one Dunhill a month, usually around her period.

Not only did I need to reduce my smoking for health reasons, next month Karl and I would be boarding a sixteen-hour, smoke-free flight to Hong Kong to celebrate his grandmother's eightieth birthday. If I could cut down on my smoking now, it would help me get through a long flight without eating my hand in a fit of nicotine withdrawal.

While I was at my doctor's office getting him to write me a prescription for everything under the sun in preparation for my trip (sleeping pills to help pass the time in coach, and Cipro, prednisone, and Tylenol with Codeine for any run-ins with Asian parasites), I asked my doctor, who looked exactly like Dr. Hibbert from *The Simpsons*, if he could check out my lungs.

"I want to know if I'll heave one up," I explained.

After listening through his stethoscope, he gave me a tube and told me to blow as hard as I could.

"Keep blowing," he instructed. "Like you're Dizzy Gillespie." When my eyeballs felt like they were going to fire from their chambers he said, "Okay, now you can stop."

I was sure I had failed miserably and all the jotting he was doing on my chart was for my emergency open-heart surgery. "Your cardiopulmonary exam was completely normal," he said. "Now go run a marathon." Even though I had already downsized to Didion's daily intake, I was still more iron lung than Iron Man. Fortunately, he checked my chart again. "Actually, you better not," he countered. "You have bad knees."

Once I had been green-lighted, I wanted to find something more demanding than the rigors offered by an exercise ball and a couple of three-pound weights, the favored gewgaws in both of *Self*'s fitness articles, "Abs, Defined" and "Look Sexy, Coming and Going." I flipped through *Elle*, a magazine that rarely, if ever, offered step-by-step service pieces with models demonstrating leg kicks. Instead, writers were commissioned to guinea-pig exorbitantly priced weight-loss spas or designer boot camps and write about their experiences in feature-length articles. This month, Maggie Bullock had a piece in the magazine entitled, "It Took Seven Weeks, Five Days, and Two Hours to Lose 14 Pounds of Fat and Gain a New Addiction to Fitness." Bullock didn't accomplish all of this alone, she explained. "The stylish, two-year-old establishment [at which I already make an occasional appearance] is introducing the Life Program: an eight- to ten-week body blast that includes six no-nonsense hours of personal training and five days of meal delivery a week. Would [I] like to be the inaugural member?"

Bullock declined to reveal the cost of her Life Program, but she did reveal the price of a comparable body makeover at another posh Manhattan gym: $12,225.

Bullock's express route to fitness followed a predictable trajectory. First, she whined and resisted. "As it happens, working out every day isn't extreme," she wrote. "It's insane." Then she had her breakthrough. "Santos hands me two 12-pound weights [I started at 8] for my chest presses, and for once I don't sputter any expletives." And finally, Bullock attained her just rewards. "By week four, the worrisome bulge that once crept over the top of every low-rise waistband is gone."

I don't know why it hadn't occurred to me before now—but I could put myself through the same paces as Bullock. And I wouldn't need twelve thousand dollars to do it, because I had something even more valuable in my back pocket: my friend Danny, a personal trainer who owed me a favor for writing all the copy on his business's website, free of charge.

I would have used Danny sooner if he hadn't fallen off the wagon. And by wagon, I mean freebasing cocaine and waving around a loaded Glock. Danny, a Dubliner, was once the drug lord of D.C., supplying all kinds of illegal substances to a network of middlemen throughout the United States. He was busted in what he described as the biggest sting of all time and spent a few years in federal prison.

But Danny had since cleaned up his act. He often quoted from a book written by a monk who prescribed washing dishes as the correct pathway to God. Even better, he now taught early-morning boot camp to the well-heeled thunder thighs of Washington.

When I showed him Bullock's article, Danny crumpled it up in a ball. "This is shit," he said, kicking it across the room with the toe of his Timberland boot. Lucky if he clears five feet on a good day, Danny looks like a cross between an Irish street fighter and a koala bear. Studying me very seriously, he said, "I can help you with this." So I agreed to meet him the next day, in the gymnasium of a defunct Catholic school where he held his boot camp.

His gym smelled exactly like my worst nightmares from fourth grade: sweaty rubber balls, squeaky floor varnish, and the body odor of a million bullies gone by. But the space was remarkably clean and morbidly quiet. No grunting he-men. No flirting around the free weights. No pulsating music. And, thankfully, not one mirror.

"I don't want you to mistake my gym for a good time"

was Danny's way of saying hello. He was wearing a navy hoodie and a knit cap pulled low over his forehead. He looked like he hadn't shaved in a week.

Since it was my first day, Danny promised to go easy on me, just wanting to test my flexibility with a few squat thrusts and pushups. He correctly sensed that I have spent the majority of my life lifting nothing heavier than the remote control. Danny gave me a couple of what looked like duckpin bowling balls and asked me to hold them while lunging across the gym floor. After about four giant steps in, I felt like a tiger was ripping flesh from my thighs.

"Drop your jaw and breathe," barked Danny. "Louder," he commanded, "I want to hear you breathing from across the street."

Next, he gave me seven-pound dumbbells (even though *Self* always suggested three pounds) and told me to raise them over my head, keeping my elbows close to my ears. After three reps, my arms started to shake wildly. "Oh, you can do one more." And I did, because Danny was yelling this order at me. I also got yelled at for moving my head to shake a strand of hair from my eye, for putting a weight down to wipe my slick palms, for not lifting slowly enough, for lifting too slowly, and for wandering off between sets to get a drink of water from the ancient porcelain fountain. After forty minutes, I was released from my torture. As I hobbled out, Danny waved after me. "Next time, we'll start the real workout."

When I woke up the next day, the only thing that didn't

hurt was my hair. My inner thighs were so sore, it felt like the first time I had sex. Putting on underwear became another method of exercise.

"I don't know about this, Danny," I said when I called him an hour before our scheduled second workout. "I was hoping you wouldn't go so hard on me."

"Just get your lazy ass over here," he said, hanging up before I could weasel out.

I got the full workout: three exercises for my legs, and God help me, four for my chicken-bone arms. To get the cardiovascular benefit, I hustled from exercise to exercise, jumping between shoulder presses, bicep curls, and some horrible form of abuse for my triceps. This quickness eventually made me feel light-headed, so I soon resorted to the Ol' Shoe Tie, a stalling device that allowed me to catch my breath for a few seconds. This also gave me the opportunity to watch a young woman wrestle with the never-ending lunges across the gym's expanse. After she made it halfway across the floor she started yelling, "I ain't doin' any more." Her trainer, a soft-spoken man named Dennis, kept a silent vigil at her side. She continued lunging.

After a few more sessions with Danny, I began to notice some muscles I never knew I had before. When Danny pinched the back of my arm with his fat calipers, he remarked, somewhat shocked, "Either this thing is broken or you're a quarter inch less flabby."

I had also gotten pretty good at some of the more complex moves—the standing squat, for example. (I had a habit of sticking my butt out like one of Jay-Z's backup dancers, according to Danny.) More importantly, I was finally earning a bit of praise from Danny. "You got it . . . that's right," he said encouragingly as I swung a ten-pound medicine ball up and over my head. I felt myself grin through my sweat like an idiot. At least my constant need for male approval had finally resulted in a healthy byproduct.

"This just goes to prove the thesis of your experiment!" cried my friend EB, who was calling to congratulate me on my engagement. Since the first month of my project, he had been flagrantly hoping, despite my fears that third-wave feminists like Katie Roiphe would be placing a bounty on my head, that all good women's magazines led to proposals.

"Do you know what this means?!" he practically hollered into the receiver. "Now you can subscribe to all the bridal magazines!"

"Why would I want to do that?" It was a disgusting suggestion. I had read a bunch before my first wedding and thought they were a joke, full of advertisements for hideous dresses on the scale of parade floats and exhaustive checklists for what do to each month leading up to the big day.

"So you can create the perfect guest list, register for the gifts of your dreams, and all the other stupid stuff brides have to do."

I was resistant to adding bridal magazines to my mix. They represented mistakes and long-held resentment, carryovers from my first walk down the aisle. Especially *Martha Stewart Weddings*, the field's queen bee. My mother, who would never deign to read any of her *Martha Stewart Living* magazines ("Who has time to paint the insides of flowerpots?" she once demanded to know), became a proselyte as soon as she picked up her first *Weddings*. When I expressed a wish for daisy centerpieces, my mother spat, "Martha thinks daisies are weeds."

Besides, I doubted Martha would have had anything constructive to say about once sleeping with your officiant. Karl and I had asked Zelly to marry us, since we both saw him as the conduit that had brought us together. But what Karl didn't know was that the New Year's morning I had woken up with my black eye, I had also woken up next to Zelly. Like most of the stunts I pulled back then, this was a trick I would have preferred not to turn. But luckily, our one-time-only romp, the product of way too much wine and easy familiarity, had suffered none of the awful hangover. We were able to resume our friendship as if nothing had happened. Which was easy, since I barely remembered anything at all.

After I hung up with EB, I emailed Zelly. "Not to diminish what happened between us, but I think it wouldn't be such a bad thing if Karl went to his deathbed never knowing about our little fling."

A little while later, I received his response: "I was thinking the exact same thing," he wrote. "My lips are sealed."

▪

Whether I was looking for justification to keep my dirty little secret from Karl or just desensitized by it (as long as I was keeping Bruno underground, why not add Zelly to the bomb shelter?), my reasoning was bolstered by an article in next month's issue of *Glamour*. I was skipping ahead in my reading to February, in preparation for my trip to Hong Kong. I would be away for two weeks, and I thought I'd better get a head start so I wouldn't have to pack an additional twenty pounds of magazines in my luggage. Since I would be spending a week with Karl's mother (Karl and I were using the second week to travel alone to Vietnam), I was hunting around for articles that would help me deal with my future mother-in-law, who, let's just say, was best manageable in small doses. The thought of seven solid days together already had me feeling exhausted. And in search of clever methods to deal with her, I came across a sanctioned way to deceive Karl.

In Marjorie Ingall's "10 Things Every Relationship Needs to Survive," keeping secrets came in at number 10. "Every relationship needs a little mystery and a few boundaries," Ingall wrote. "That's why you should be allowed your stash of old love letters (from someone else), a sundae when he thinks you're on a diet, a fantasy life with your UPS delivery man." And a sexual past that should remain in the past, I added. Maggie, one of Ingall's interview subjects, agreed. "[My husband] has no idea I've slept with half of my male friends. He doesn't need to." "Total honesty," concluded Maggie, "is bull."

I remembered when I was much younger, I asked my mother her trick for keeping my father happy. Without even thinking, she said, "There's no rule that says you have to tell your husband everything."

Not that I enjoyed taking advice from my mother, but

again, like the article in *Glamour*, I was looking for a way around the truth.

"Cathy, I couldn't disagree with you more," said Jeanne, when, during our last walk before my Hong Kong trip, I confessed my secret about Zelly and my plan to keep it one.

"But it was no big deal," I tried rationalizing. "It meant nothing, and it only happened once."

"It meant nothing," she said slowly, "to *you*."

For the first time in a long time, I barely took notice of the cardinals flitting from tree to tree, the sight of deer tracks pressed into the mud, and the smell of wet earth as we passed by an inlet of pooled water. All I heard, even as we walked on in silence, was the angry refrain of Jeanne's epic warning. "A marriage that begins with a lie is a lie."

If this month was truly about fitness, I also needed to exercise Karl's right to the truth. I had no choice but to tell him.

"Take him for a walk," advised Jeanne when, upon returning from our own walk, I phoned her with doubts about confessing. "If you tell Karl at home, and he happens to be looking at a lamp when he hears the truth, then that lamp will forever be associated with that bad news. You don't want that kind of energy in your apartment."

Ironically, I decided to take Karl for a walk to buy new lamps for our bedroom nightstands. I had planned to come clean on the way home from the store, right as we passed by the Embassy of India. Across from the embassy was a small bench placed in front of a statue of Gandhi throwing handfuls of flowers. In my perfect universe, having the flora-flinging Gandhi as Karl's focal point would somehow bring him peace when he heard the news about his fiancée schtupping one of his best friends.

"I have something I have to tell you." I sounded disembodied and foreign.

"Uh-oh," Karl said, squaring his shoulders. "Is it bad?"

"It's not good."

"Just tell me."

So I did. "It was wrong of me not to tell you sooner," I said when it was all over.

"Why didn't you just come clean?" he asked, sounding confused. Not angry. Just hurt. "How can Zelly marry us now? It's weird. Don't you think it's weird?"

And this is what I can't tell him—even after telling him so much. It's not weird.

We walked in silence, which was worse than suffering through his rage. But Jeanne had reminded me that I couldn't control Karl's reaction, or the stony aftermath.

The quiet followed us home. Up until that point, the mood in our apartment had always been one of happiness and consideration. We sat down on the couch, and for a long while, I watched the dust particles hit the midafternoon sun. I watched my cat flick his tail around and wink at me. I watched Karl's chest steadily rising and falling.

"Is there anything else you want to tell me?" he finally asked. "Anyone else I don't know about?"

I had remained fairly stoic while telling Karl about Zelly, but when I realized I was just about to admit to Bruno, I hung my head in defeat, a change in gravity that caused a cascade of lumpy tears to explode onto my jeans.

"Who?" was all he said.

"I'm sorry."

"Who?" he said louder and with more panic, like I was about to explain how I got on an airplane, flew to Georgia, tracked down his father, introduced myself, and then fucked his brains out.

"Bruno."

"Bruno?" he repeated in disbelief. "Your idiot coworker?"

I was crying with relish by now. "Believe me, I'm not proud of it."

"How *could* you?" Karl may have been slow to boil, but he was at a full roll now. At least he had temporarily forgotten about Zelly.

"That's a good question," I said, still too ashamed to lift my head and look Karl in the eye. "I'm still trying to figure out the answer."

We sat quietly for a while, but it was a different kind of quiet. I no longer had control, since my control was in the telling. So in one sense, I felt calm, because my part was over. But in another sense, in what I imagined was the more Catholic definition of confession, I had no idea what kind of Hail Marys were in store for me.

I was about to meet my maker, and as a result, I was hyperaware of my time on the chopping block. The way the sun highlighted the mummified bees in the window screen; the cracking sound of Jason, our upstairs neighbor, dropping the toilet seat down after peeing; Karl's electrified foot bouncing up and down and up and down—these things were all etching their unique stamps into my memory.

Karl sighed. Most men, I realized, wouldn't have responded like this. Most men, men like Bruno, would have stormed out, phoned their gang of miscreants, and gone out carousing on the town in a passive-aggressive fit of whiskey and whores.

"What are you thinking?" he asked gently.

"Nothing," I told him.

That I hope you don't love me any less.

"What are you thinking?" he asked again.

"Nothing," I said again. "Really."

That I hope this won't change anything.

Desperate to explain how things could have gone so wrong, I showed him the article from *Glamour* and pointed to the section on secrets.

"These magazines are ruining my life," he huffed. "And it's all Oprah's fault."

"But this came from *Glamour.*"

"Well, screw her anyway. She's evil."

"I'm the evil one," I countered, tossing the magazine on the ground.

Walking into the kitchen to start dinner, he stopped and looked over his shoulder. "What month is cooking month?" he asked.

"Soon," I promised. "Soon."

Western Style

I was in the peculiar position of mistrusting the counsel I was receiving from magazines while still desperately seeking it. In a way, I was developing the same relationship with them as I had with my mother. Something was hurting, and I needed help making it stop. And just because my mother often failed with her cheery guidance (for example, whenever I sobbed to her after a routine dumping, she always said the same thing: "Just put your lipstick on, someone else is right around the corner") didn't mean I packed up my tears and went elsewhere. I was learning it wasn't about rejecting the advice I was getting—from the magazines, from my mother, from friends, from Dr. Oskar—it was about developing a better filter through which to funnel it.

Even when that advice included my own. As our trip to Hong Kong approached, I began to worry. A lot. Mostly about how I'd get along—with Karl's mother, his doting sister, and his Cantonese-speaking relatives. Not to mention an entire city of tiny people. Whose words were symbols. Who ate things with tentacles. I was afraid I'd be hospitalized within the first day. I got myself so worked up that one morning, a week before our departure, I awoke convinced that I needed a root canal and made an emergency appointment with my dentist who took one look in my mouth and asked if I was clenching my jaw for any particular reason.

So with our departure date less than a week away, I again turned to the comforts of the glossy page for help managing my teeth-grinding stress. And that's when I ran smack into my own article. About six months prior, I had proposed a story to *Self*'s Happiness editor (conveniently, the most cheerful woman on the planet) about the unique ways some women employed to help them unwind. "I find it very calming to unknot my tangled necklaces," I wrote in my pitch letter. "Nothing beats the feeling of freeing my Elsa Peretti bean from my Me&Ro lotus." She agreed and assigned me a piece we jointly titled "Offbeat Ways to Unwind." Besides my technique, I interviewed my friend Marty, who destressed by removing stains from her clothing, and a woman who replastered her entire dining room during one particularly taxing episode in her life.

Now, seeing the resulting story and accompanying byline, I wondered if anyone was ruining their lives by trying out some of my proffered advice. What if women all over the country were shaking their angry fists in my direction when wall plastering failed to soothe them?

Who was I to intrude on someone else's life with my fancy opinions? What did I know? Reading my own words in a magazine had left me feeling like a bit of a fake. It would only take so long before everyone found out and I was exposed as an impostor. It was like that scene from the movie *Happiness* in which Lara Flynn Boyle, playing a poet, has a meltdown while trying to work out a few stanzas. Throwing herself on her bed, she screams, "I'm no good! I'm no good! I am nothing! Nothing! Zero!"

This is exactly what it feels like to be a writer sometimes. And ultimately, this was what had me so stressed out about my trip. I was an interloper—in Karl's family, here and abroad. In order to survive Hong Kong, I needed to figure out how to fit in when I always felt so out of place.

If I was worried about where I stood, Karl's mother was equally unsure of her own footing. Lately, Joy was having some major boundary issues. (Or, more precisely, I was having issues with her not having any.) My parents were the boundary setters in my family—often reminding my brother and me that we were guests in their home and had to abide by their rules (which included no flushing the toilet once my father was asleep). So I wasn't accustomed to seeing a parent who was so boundaryless.

With Joy, I had the double whammy of trying to coexist with a mother who was both Jewish (she had converted when she married Karl's father) and Chinese. In case you're not familiar with this cultural combination, this is like walking around with an octopus Krazy Glued around your throat for the rest of your life. Ever since her number-one son had gotten engaged, Joy had displayed the type of abandonment issues normally associated with family dogs who get left on the side of the road. And, in a way, she had. After less than a year of marriage, her first husband was killed in a car accident. Her second husband, Karl's father, left before Karl's bar mitzvah (leaving Karl in the awkward position of literally becoming a man at thirteen), and her mother had died when Joy was barely out of diapers. Her father, who was now also deceased, had quickly remarried the family servant, to great scandal, and it was her stepmother's birthday we were attending in Hong Kong.

Life had let Joy down profoundly. Is it any wonder she expected the same betrayal from her son, who left her for another woman? From her daughter, who left her for another home, moving across the country to attend graduate school? Joy perceived any proof of her children's individuation as disloyalty.

Even her own name had betrayed her.

I couldn't help but think of Joy when I read Dani Shapiro's essay in *Real Simple*. Looking for any articles having to do with tricky family relationships, I had latched onto Shapiro's "Mommie Dearest?" In it, Shapiro wrote of her own mother's troubles in accepting her new husband. "When my mother met my future husband, I think she sensed, with the instincts of an animal in danger, that she was being threatened." But when her mother met Shapiro's in-laws, Shapiro continued, "the full force of her primal rage truly began to assert itself."

Her mother was so endangered by these outsiders that

Shapiro began to hide the frequent trips she made to her in-laws from her mother. "She hated it when we went up there, and made me pay for it weeks afterward. 'But you never bother to visit me,' she'd complain."

Joy was misbehaving in similar ways. For one, she was willfully ignoring our "no calls after 10:00 PM" policy, phoning us at exactly 10:02, night after night. When Karl calmly reminded her to please phone before bedtime, she said things like, "I could be dead on the side of the road and you wouldn't care." Then, she'd give us the silent treatment and refuse to answer her cell or respond to emails for days on end—further guaranteeing that no one would be able to find out if she was indeed dead on the side of the road.

On top of all that, there was also some indication that Joy would be an unreliable travel companion. We had all recently driven to Flushing, Queens, to attend the wedding reception of one of Joy's nephews. After picking us up at our apartment (more than two hours late) and personally helping me lay out my black cocktail dress across the backseat of the car, Joy waited until we were two hours outside of D.C., at a Burger King along I-95, before announcing, "It's bad luck to wear black to a wedding." When I burst into tears, crying something nonsensical about Round Eye Lady bringing death and destruction to the happy couple, Joy offered to loan me the extra pantsuit she had packed. "But I'm twice your size," I sobbed. Joy spent the rest of the car ride trying to determine, in rapid Cantonese yelled at full volume into her cell phone, if I would curse the family by showing up in my black frock. "Okay," she announced at one point, "Ronnie says you

can wear it." Then, her phone would ring again and she'd deliver the opposite news. "Now Stella says you can't."

By the time we hit the reception, I was a mess. Until I
saw that most of the men were wearing black tuxedos and
almost all of the women were in some form of black gown.
In the end, after I kidded her for making me a wreck for no
reason, Joy admitted that she herself was afraid of insulting
the bride's grandmother, an honored elder, by saying the
wrong thing or bowing the wrong way. Joy was merely projecting her own anxieties on me.

I knew what to expect from Joy on U.S. soil, but I was
worried that as soon as we landed in Hong Kong, a place of
sorrow and loss to which she hadn't returned in thirty years,
she would go a little Joy Nut Club. I didn't need *Real Simple*
to tell me that traveling to Hong Kong on another airline, on
another day, and staying in another hotel were all smart tac-
tical moves (and all heartily approved by Karl).

But even though I was sharp enough to get to Hong Kong
by myself, I still needed to figure out what to do once I got
there. In the same way I turned to the magazines to help me
navigate rough waters, I would need Joy to guide me through
an unfamiliar landscape—introducing me to her family, pro-
tecting me from foods that would end my life, and ultimately, teaching me how to gain her acceptance.

But before I could pull off any of that, I needed Joy to
clarify the Chinese color code when it came to birthday
party attire, which were functions, I was guessing, with

rules that were the polar opposites of those in Chinese weddings.

"Okay," I said when I finally reached Joy at the hospital where she worked (to further her theme of loss, Joy was a hospice nurse). "Let me in on your crazy Chinese rules. I don't want a repeat of Flushing."

"Just don't wear black," she said. "Or white. White is what you wear to a funeral. And nothing with black or white in the pattern."

Considering this was the color scheme of my entire closet, I was a walking Grim Reaper.

"Anything else?" I asked.

"Don't put anything in your hair that's pink."

"What could I possibly put in my hair that's pink?" It wasn't like I was prone to wearing the kind of floral hair wreaths usually seen at Renaissance festivals.

"And no white ribbons in your barrettes," she continued, speaking to me like I was dressing for my first communion.

"What about red?"

"That's a lucky color," she granted. "But maybe not on you."

"Hey!" I said in a tone of mock insult. "What's that supposed to mean?"

"It means navy might be better."

Unfortunately, the big look this month was death. *Elle* was pushing the Goth look hard, with page after page of white silk dresses with Edward Gorey–esque bats flying across the bodices and skull and crossbones done in Swarovski crystals emblazoned across the backs of jackets. A poet's blouse by Libertine displayed a silk-screened medallion of a nineteenth-century image of Abraham Lincoln (how punk!) across the front.

More unfortunate, red was the other big trend. "Red picks up where black left off," wrote *Marie Claire*. A collage of models dressed for *Sweeney Todd*'s house of ill repute paraded around the page: "Paired with black accessories, red takes on a slightly Asian influence." Apparently the fashion editors weren't aware of black's mournful impact. Finally, I found a dress in *Allure* that met my requirements: a navy print jersey-blend wrap dress by BCBG Max Azria. Not only was it appropriate in color, the wrinkle-free material would transcend even the lamest packing. (I hadn't yet come across an article on proper folding methods.)

I headed out for the BCBG store in Georgetown and, as I was now accustomed to doing, brought along the photo from the magazine.

"Well, hello there," said a fast-approaching young woman in a shiny violet blouse. "My name is Robin."

"I have a challenge for you, Robin," I said, handing her the picture of the wrap dress.

"Oh, jeez." Robin shook her head sadly. "I don't know this dress."

"Do you know another dress?" I asked. "One that's not black or white?"

"Oh, jeez," she said again, surveying the racks. "That's a tough one."

She led me to a dress that was yellow and strapless, with a faux diamond brooch pinned below the potential wearer's cleavage.

"Robin," I said, leaning in, "I realize I forgot to mention

that I'll be wearing this dress at a birthday party. In Hong Kong. For the eighty-year-old grandmother of my fiancé. Who's Chinese. Surrounded by a lot of Chinese people who don't know me."

"So, like, this dress is a bit too much?"

"If I don't want this family thinking I have a lounge act in Vegas, it is."

Eventually we found a rayon-blend wrap dress in a pointillist pattern of blues, pinks, and greens. That night I showed it to Karl, who was standing in front of the huge suitcase we were sharing, absentmindedly tossing in Gold Toe socks.

"Do you think this will be okay?" I asked, holding it up to myself like I was dressing a paper doll.

Karl studied me like a set of directions. "I don't know about this green," he said, grabbing a section with the highest concentration of that color. "Did you talk to my mother?"

"She didn't say anything about green being bad," I replied, realizing I had been clenching my teeth through Karl's appraisal.

"Then you should be fine," he said, taking the dress from me and folding it neatly into the suitcase.

Just to be safe, I packed an article I had torn from *Marie Claire* that featured Lara Flynn Boyle in her infamous pink tutu. The story was called "How to Survive a Mortifying Moment."

I woke up our first morning in Hong Kong crying.

"It's just the jet lag," Karl explained, spooning me closer.

Despite the Ambien, I hadn't slept on the plane, mostly

because a man across the aisle spent the entire flight buzzing the flight attendant and loudly complaining. Karl understood just enough Cantonese to translate. "He wants to know when we're going to eat again." Maybe there was some truth about eating Chinese food and then being hungry again twenty minutes later.

But I also knew that I woke up crying for a reason less directly causal to sleep deprivation. Later that evening, our little cocoon would be split wide open by the arrival of Karl's family—and Joy was already upset with us because we weren't going to be at the airport, which was at least an hour's taxi ride away, to receive them.

"Why don't you take a shower?" suggested Karl. "You'll feel a lot better."

As soon as I looked in the bathroom mirror, I had another reason to be upset. There was a pimple the size and color of a pencil eraser alive and well on the center of my left cheek. As holdover advice from my July camping trip, I had only packed cosmetics and toiletries in miniature form—and benzoyl peroxide was not among my petite arsenal. I doubted that any of the stores in Causeway Bay would have even one of the items suggested in *Jane*'s "Having a Bad Face Day?" And if they did, what would the exchange rate be on Fresh's Umbrian Clay Face?

Our first order of business was finding some miracle-performing pimple medicine. I was under the impression that there would be Chinese herbalists on every corner for just that purpose.

"Even if there were"—Karl laughed as we walked along a

street that looked eerily similar to Midtown Broadway—"I wouldn't know how to ask for it."

We passed by a store called Fancl that had huge photos of clear-complexioned Asian women in the window. Inside, the staff all wore white lab coats. Karl had already explained that other Asians did not easily accept the coupling of an Asian man and a Western woman, so I was not surprised when one of the staff approached us, nodding curtly to Karl and looking me up and down like I was oozing pus. Which, actually, I might have been. I pointed to my volcanic pimple, and she silently walked across the white tiled floors.

"Yes." She said this more as an order than as an affirmation, handing me what looked like a travel-sized tube of toothpaste. It was called Cleartune (did it play a song when you unscrewed the cap?), and I'm pretty sure it cost about seven American dollars. I would have gladly paid seven hundred if it would rid me of my pimple in time for the birthday party, which was only a few hours away.

The party was being held at a restaurant on the outskirts of Causeway Bay. The plan was to meet there at seven-thirty. We knew this because when we returned to our hotel after a bit more shopping, there were seven messages from Joy. Each one stressed, with mounting intensity, the importance of being on time.

Of course, Karl and I were the first to arrive. The party was on the second floor of a Trumped-out restaurant, all glass and chrome and pink marble. When we entered the banquet room, there was a group of six playing mah-jongg at a corner table. A small television set beamed down on them from the ceiling. The few in the room who weren't clicking tiles around were gazing intently up at what appeared to be a soap opera. I noted that mostly everyone was dressed in a shade of burgundy and congratulated myself for my own attire. I didn't think I'd need my navy cardigan, which I had brought just in case the green in my dress raised eyebrows.

"Hello," Karl said to a plump woman with her arm around a smaller, older woman wearing owl-like glasses.

The woman with the owl glasses approached Karl and handed him a small red envelope, the size that usually contains spare buttons. He took it and bowed slightly.

Then the woman did the same thing to me. I took the envelope and nodded my head forward. "Thank you," I said instinctively.

"Thank you," she repeated.

Karl and I took a few steps back. I wasn't sure what to make of my envelope.

"Why did we get envelopes?" I asked, palming mine.

"It's called *lai see*," he whispered, looking around the room. "There's usually a few dollars inside. All the unmarried kids get them for good luck."

"You mean I'm going to make money off this trip?" I joked. Karl was perspiring and swallowing a lot, clearly nervous. "Who was the lady who gave us the *lai see*?"

"My Pau Pau."

"THAT was your grandmother?" I said, shocked. "Why

didn't you hug and kiss her? How long has it been since you last saw her?"

My grandmother had been dead for five years, and I would have given anything to hold her soft hand again.

Karl didn't answer; he just continued to dart his eyes around. Eventually, a waiter came by with a tray of drinks. Karl grabbed something that looked like a Manhattan and took a long pull.

Finally, an hour later, Joy, Karl's sister Val, and her boyfriend Jeff walked through the door. They were accompanied by a chicly dressed woman in four-inch heels and dramatic eye makeup. I knew immediately it was Auntie Gay, Joy's older sister who lived in Australia. She was flanked by her two children, Ashlin and James, who were both at least six feet tall and gorgeous. Like Joy, Gay had married a Westerner, and her children had the same exotically unclassifiable ethnicity as Karl and Val.

"Congratulations," said Ashlin in a sexy low Australian accent. She was the first to approach and hugged me warmly. "It's so lovely to meet you. May I see your ring?"

Now that I was engaged to Karl, I had given Joy new status in her family. From what I understood, in the archaic titling of Chinese family members, being a mother was one thing, but being a mother-in-law was one thing better. As I showed Ashlin my ring, I realized that even though I was the cause of Joy's promotion, Joy had never asked to see my hand.

"So this is Cathy," said Auntie Gay, looking me up and down and handing me a red envelope. I had a glass of wine in one hand and took the envelope with the other.

Auntie Gay looked at me like I had just peeled a scab off of her hand and popped it into my mouth. I immediately felt like apologizing for my pimple. "Next time," she cautioned, "be sure to take the *lai see* with both hands."

I recalled **Truth Number 3** from *Marie Claire*'s "How to Survive a Mortifying Moment." For the third of her four listed truths, Celeste Perron wrote, "Often, you cringe inside because you think that you can read people's minds and that they're completely horrified by what you've done." But in actuality, she proposed, the embarrassment is only one still in the movie of your life. "Remember that people use thousands of different bits of information to form an opinion of you," Perron consoled. I hoped Auntie Gay wasn't viewing me as *The Towering Inferno*.

After she turned to greet arriving guests, Joy sidled up to me. "So now you've met my sister," she said out of the corner of her mouth. "Was I lying?" Joy had already prepared me for Gay's bluntness, sourpuss countenance, and smug sense of authority. With her exaggerated height and expertly made-up face, Auntie Gay actually reminded me of my mother. She was a known quantity to me, but for Joy I could see having her sister just a few feet away, after being separated by multiple oceans, was triggering some old rivalries.

I watched Joy follow after Auntie Gay. They stood on either side of their stepmother, a hand on each of her shoulders. When one would bend down to speak to her, the other would bend down to listen in. The effect was similar to the movement of an oompah band.

Val held out her hand for me to hold. We stood there for a bit surveying the crowd. Seven years younger than Karl, she was born to parents on the verge of divorce. As a result, she and Karl had a bond that, forged under an unhappy roof, was beyond close. They were each other's protectors and confidants, and at times Karl straddled the line between brother and father. If I was the other woman in Joy's life, Val—smart, beautiful, and funny—was the other woman in mine.

"You're doing great," she said. "If you want to really impress them, say 'Mmngong' the next time someone gives you *lai see*." (At least, that's what it sounded like she was saying.)

We sat down at a huge wagon wheel of a table filled with cousins, one of whom had gone to college in Canada. When I shook his hand, I noticed his eyes were cobalt blue.

"Muh gong," said Val's boyfriend Jeff when another plate of shrimp appeared before him. I was extremely worried about what I'd be able to eat, but after tray after tray of lobster, prawns, and crispy fish arrived at our table, I wasn't sure I'd actually get a chance to eat.

"I'll go talk to my mother," said Karl, getting up and moving across the room to where Joy sat at a table next to Pau Pau. I watched him point to me and gesture wildly. Auntie Gay, who had been working the room like a don, noticed the commotion and got involved, brushing away Joy's waving hand, flagging down a waiter herself, and gesturing over to me.

Joy accompanied Karl back to our table. "I'm sorry,

Cathy," she said. "Gay was in charge of the menu. I told her to make sure there was some chicken for you. But as usual, she never listens to me."

"It's fine," I said, touching her forearm and giving it a little squeeze. "You've got enough to worry about tonight."

"You can say that again." She sighed and looked over at her sister, who was sitting next to their mother looking rather pleased with herself. She gave Joy the "come here" signal.

"Her Majesty calls," she said, adopting a British accent.

Eventually, a plate of salted chicken appeared.

"That's the house specialty," said Karl's blue-eyed cousin.

By then everyone at our table had finished eating and began to focus on the dinner theater of Cathy's Spectacular Chopstick Revue. I had never learned how to correctly feed myself with chopsticks, whether due to my being left-handed in a right-handed world or just having extremely poor fine motor control. But there were no forks in sight, and I was hungry.

"Do you want help?" whispered Karl.

"Like this," offered Val, resting one stick against the fleshy part of her hand and holding the other like a pencil.

I clamped onto a glistening piece of thigh and attempted to one-two-three it into my mouth. I only could raise the chicken a few inches off the plate before it would slip from my grasp and fall back onto the plate. The more I tried to capture the chicken, the more it slid away from my grasp. It was like some bad Tom and Jerry cartoon.

I remembered **Truth Number 2** from the mortification

article. "People tend to feel vicarious embarrassment on your behalf when you make a public error." I looked at my dining companions, who were regarding me as if I were a baby giraffe trying to take her first wobbly steps.

"It's okay," said Karl's blue-eyed cousin. "I'm still trying to get the hang of them."

"Is he wearing contacts?" I asked Karl when we stepped outside for a cigarette. (Up until now, I had been below Didion's five-a-day quotient, but this trip had reinvigorated my habit.)

"Somewhere back in the family," explained Karl, "there was a little hanky-panky going on with the British colonists."

Between the grandfather marrying his former housemaid and a history of mixing it up with their British overlords, Karl's family had their own lineage of embarrassment to reconcile. After my recent display of chopstick ineptitude, I realized that mortification was relative.

By the time Joy and Gay brought out the birthday cake, each carrying one end of the serving tray with Gay a little out in the lead, I had relaxed into the evening. The blue-eyed cousin's girlfriend, thrilled to practice her English, was even more thrilled to show me the Chloé knockoff bag she had just bought.

"You must go to Kowloon," she enthused. "This is where every designer is under the sun."

I watched Karl and his Pau Pau. With Joy around—as translator and familiar buffer—he had also relaxed into the evening. He posed his grandmother next to the cake and she smiled and he took her picture. Occasionally, he waved over to me like he was on a merry-go-round.

Jeff and I watched the action from our table, poking around at some almond cookies and lost in our own thoughts. Despite mishandling both the *lai see* and the chopsticks, and mangling the pronunciation of *m'gong* every time I wanted to thank someone, I wasn't doing too badly. And when Jeff leaned over and remarked, "Have you ever seen so many Chinese people in one place?" I realized that he was way worse off than me.

Staying at another hotel spared Karl and me from the mismanagement of each day's itinerary. By the time Auntie Gay, Joy, and their respective broods had gotten their acts together, Karl and I were long gone, either on a ferry to Lantau Island to see a Buddha the size of a skyscraper, on a tram up to the sadly overcommercialized Peak, or wandering into the fog of temple incense.

"I didn't come all this way to sit around the hotel all day waiting for someone to make a decision," I had told Karl.

Gay and Joy's complete lack of planning worked to our advantage. Instead of accommodating the circus of six other people, I was thankful to be exploring the city with just Karl.

Other than the birthday party, there were two other mandated obligations: visiting the 101-year-old uncle, and paying our graveside respects to Joy's mother. Rather than dreading these pilgrimages, I was looking forward to them.

While other tourists were buying fake Prada on Nathan Lane, I'd be getting a glimpse at real life—and death—in Hong Kong.

To get to where the 101-year-old uncle lived, Karl and I had to take a wide assortment of trains, switching at underground stations that looked like gigantic morgues. The plan was to rendezvous at the other end and caravan in taxis to the uncle's house, which was in a gated community about an hour outside Hong Kong. Karl and I arrived a bit early and wandered around a nearby shopping mall. The Chinese New Year was in full swing, and in recognition of the year of the dog, there were hyperbolic white puppies everywhere we turned.

At this point in the trip, everyone had bought fancy new cell phones from the countless electronics stores that lined Causeway Bay. Before long, my phone, which was engraved with gold lotus blossoms, started ringing something out of a Suzie Wong movie.

"Is this Cathy?" Auntie Gay asked in her clipped, high-society accent. "We are here and can't find you."

The next forty minutes was like a Shakespearean comedy. Karl and I would go to meet Gay and her kids at the ice cream stand only to find that she had wandered off to meet Joy, Val, and Jeff in front of the phone booths. So Karl would call his mother and attempt to get her to stay put at the phone booths, only to discover that she had wandered back to the ice cream stand to look for Gay.

Eventually, everyone got it together and we all piled into a van. "What did you do today?" I asked James.

"Well, after we missed the ferry a few times, we finally made it to see the Big Buddha," he said, rolling his eyes at his mother. Despite his dig, it was obvious that both he and his sister were dutiful children and didn't have a choice in how they spent their time in Hong Kong. And unlike Karl and Val, they spoke perfect Cantonese.

"We're going to Macau tomorrow," I bragged. Karl and I had purchased our tickets that morning, after first phoning Joy to make sure it wouldn't conflict with visiting the cemetery. I was really excited about spending another whole day alone with Karl.

"What about having lunch with the eighty-nine-year-old aunt?" gasped Gay.

"What lunch?" said Karl.

"I told you," said Joy. "You have four things to do in Hong Kong: the birthday, the uncle, the cemetery, and lunch with the eighty-nine-year-old aunt."

"You never said anything about lunch with the aunt," countered Karl. "We asked you yesterday if we could go to Macau, and you never said anything about lunch. It's too late now, we already have our tickets."

Gay let out a snippy "ahem" and looked at her sister.

"Jeff and I had planned to go shopping," added Val. They were leaving the next day and, after spending a week across the hotel hall from Joy, I was guessing, wanted to have some time alone.

Joy was being shown up by her sister and her two obedient children. I imagined for her a lifetime of falling short of her haughty sister, of getting lost in her tall shadow, of always feeling second best. As I focused my anxieties on fitting in with a new family, I realized that Joy was probably experiencing the same feelings of alienation in her old one.

Still, I knew there was going to be hell to pay later for missing out on lunch with the aged aunt. Joy was used to running the show back home. But at the moment, I was more concerned with trying to figure out whose slippers I was about to put on. When our cab dropped us off at the 101-year-old uncle's home, I watched everyone remove their shoes at the door and select from a pile of terry-cloth flip-flops. "Is this for religious purposes?" I asked Karl. "Or to keep his carpet clean?"

"I have no idea."

The uncle was arranged on a couch next to a faux marble reproduction of *The Birth of Venus.* He looked right out of central casting, with snowy white hair and round glasses. After the kids lined up to receive his *lai see* (with both hands out, *m'gong*), Peggy, another aunt, took him by the elbow and escorted us all outside to see his swimming pool, which was a symbol of vast wealth.

"He is especially proud of his orchids," said Auntie Peggy, leading us to a sunny spot in the yard.

While we were all admiring the garden, Peggy's cell phone rang to the tune of the "Mexican Hat Dance."

"Ah yah," she answered.

There was something about hearing that music so far away from home and so completely out of context that cracked me up. I let out a stream of cackles before Karl could get close enough to clamp his hand over my mouth. Round Eye strikes again. **Truth Number 1** said, "Apologizing profusely, covering your face, or otherwise overreacting will only make people superaware of your flub when they might have barely noticed it otherwise." To save face, I needed to make a quick and casual apology.

"That was a surprising ring tone," I said breezily. As the article also suggested, I fought the urge to hang my head and let my chest cave in, a submissive stance. Instead, I pretended to be newly fascinated by a kumquat tree.

"How beautiful!" I exclaimed, and smiled at the 101-year-old uncle, who beamed and waved at me.

After we said our good-byes, Auntie Peggy took the whole lot of us out to a fancy dinner in Kowloon. The restaurant was on top of a large shopping mall, and we followed Peggy on her shortcut through the children's department of a Sears-like store. Whether Karl was annoyed with me for my cell phone outburst or just tiring of focusing a lot of his attention on me (was I eating enough, did I feel okay, was I tired, etc., etc.), he began to walk extra close to his sister, pointing to things we were passing in the store, laughing and whispering and putting her in a headlock. He continued his behavior once we sat down at the table, turning his back on me entirely and putting his head together with hers as they giggled mysteriously. For the first time since we had arrived in Hong Kong, I truly felt excluded. And jealous as hell.

After dinner, Peggy urged Karl and me to take a walk out onto the restaurant's terrace, where we could see the lights of the city in panoramic glory.

There was a "blow his mind tip" in *Cosmo*'s Love and Lust column about using a sexy vacation moment for future beddings, minus the airfare. With the warm breeze off the bay and neon lighting up the sky like fireworks, this scenario would have been a good candidate. If only I hadn't turned all Freudian analyst and said, "Sometimes you and Val behave more like lovers."

To his credit, Karl did not blow a gasket. When I told him that it hurt my feelings when he turned his back to me at the restaurant or when he behaved as if he and Val were the sole members in a secret club, he said, "I will apologize for making you feel left out because that was never my intention, but"—he continued looking at me right in the eye—"I will not apologize for my relationship with my sister."

That night, I had a dream that I caught Karl and Val in bed together. Her back was to me and she was topless, with a sheet draped across her hips. She was up on one elbow, blocking Karl from my view, but I knew it was him lying next to her because it was his laughter that caused me to open the door to our bedroom.

I tried to channel my inner Dr. Oskar. "This dream is not about sex," I heard him say. "This is about Karl's intimacy with his sister." Witnessing this closeness at dinner, quite literally catching them in the act, sparked some pretty painful memories in me. Ones of loss, of rejection, and of always sensing that I was different, an outsider, a sensitive mystery even to members of my own family.

Macau was a true respite. We spent the day visiting temples, taking photos of each other in front of every stone dragon on the island, and wandering a maze of crooked streets bursting with pink and green buildings, reminders of the island's Portuguese past. The day was a do-over of the previous evening. But even though Karl had forgiven me for my bout of insecurity ("My sister?!" he kept asking, baffled by the limitlessness of my imagination), his mother was still stewing about our decision to go to Macau instead of accompanying her to lunch with the eighty-nine-year-old aunt.

Karl and I got the cold shoulder from Joy on the subway to the cemetery. After rooting around in her purse for some imagined necessity, she finally addressed Karl. "Gay wants to know how I could look at myself in the mirror and be okay with having such disrespectful children."

Karl chose to ignore this comment. We were in a no-win situation. I knew this Macau trip was our watershed moment and would soon be brought up again and again as evidence for Karl's failure to be the devoted son. I wished I could slip her the essay from O magazine by Joyce Carol Oates. In "Love, Loss, and Transformation," Oates wrote movingly about the vulnerable side of love. "The deepest wounds in my emotional life," began Oates, "have come as a consequence of the loss of people I've loved." But, she continued, it was what you did with that loss that mattered. "I have been deeply impressed by the reinventions of personality and destiny among individuals whom I've known for years as they entered middle age," Oates confessed. "Most, but not all, are women whose children are grown and have moved away." Their empty nests, however, gave way, wrote Oates, "to the abiding values of friendship: love for friends and relatives."

As we meandered through the cemetery, I wondered if Joy would ever rediscover those same values and see others as potential enhancements to her life, rather than as proven lessons in failure.

"Do you know where your mother is?" asked Karl. The cemetery looked more like a concrete amphitheater whose seats were filled by gravestones most of which displayed laminated black-and-white photos of the deceased in younger days. The effect was a bit like standing in a giant high school gymnasium before the big game.

"I think she's over here," said Joy, climbing up another level. "Yes, she's right here."

I was startled to see that the photo on the tombstone looked so much like the woman standing next to me. The smile, the tilt of the head, the graceful neck. "She was so beautiful," I told Joy.

"Okay," said Joy. "Let me do my thing."

Karl and I watched as Joy bowed deeply in front of her mother, again and again. Then she stood and looked at the photo of her mother. I had been aware of so many of Joy's losses, but here I was actually seeing it. Karl saw it, too, and joined his mother, bowing in the same way, the same number of times. Then he put his hands on her shoulders, nodded, and drew her into a long embrace.

I did not join them, not because I thought that I wasn't

wanted, but because I knew I didn't belong. There was nothing wrong with finally knowing my place.

As we left the grounds, Joy looked back over her shoulder. "Would you believe that I haven't been able to cry for sixty years?" She dabbed her eyes for a moment and looked as if she might even blow her nose. "What do you think took me so long?"

■

Karl sat next to his mother on the subway back to Hong Kong, occasionally sliding his arm around her and patting her on the shoulder. When we passed by the stop for Kowloon, Joy looked across the aisle at me and said, "This is the wedding dress district."

I had been toying with the idea of wearing a traditional cheongsam, thinking that would be a nice nod to Karl's culture. But I still hadn't ruled out the idea of Badgley Mischka couture either.

"Do you plan on wearing white?" Joy asked.

"What are you inferring?" I smiled, thinking she was taking a dig at my misspent virginity. But then I realized that to her, white was the color of death.

I, however, happened to disagree. To me, white, if I choose to wear it, was the color of just that—my choice. Ultimately, the course of my life wasn't about taking cues from external sources like magazines or mothers. I had to learn how to listen to my own internal authority (a gut that had ironically been shaped by those very external sources).

My mother had commandeered my first wedding. I wasn't about to hand over my second. If my month began with a quest to define my boundaries, here was a good one to erect.

"When I decide on my dress," I said as we whizzed by the stop for Kowloon, "you'll be the first to know."

Recipe for Success

i walked into this month already knowing the challenge. Back in January, as penance for keeping a few choice secrets from Karl, I had promised him that March would be tagged for cooking. This was a good undertaking for many reasons, the least of which was to bone up on my woefully underdeveloped culinary skills. After one week in Hong Kong and another in Hanoi, Karl and I were scraping the bottom of the discretionary funds barrel. We simply couldn't afford to piss our money away on imported beer and Dave's Famous Chicken Sandwich, the meal of choice at the local restaurant that, at just a block away from our apartment, had un-fortunately (the true meaning of the word) become an extension of our own living room.

Furthermore, we had a wedding to finance. Now that we were back from Hong Kong, the excitement of being engaged had transmuted into a rocket-fueled urge to pick a date (I was aiming for September) and secure a venue. And unless we wanted to host our family and friends at McDonald's (our Happy Meals could contain personalized Beanie Babies as favors!), we needed to start stashing away some cash. My parents had already forked over a fat check, but since they had paid for my first wedding, I wasn't expecting them to cover the full cost of my second. ("If you screw up again," read the letter accompanying the check, "you're on your own for number three.")

While combing the magazines for recipes (the more "Cooking for Dummies," the better), I also was on the lookout for any budgeting and saving advice. Particularly, how to fund the J. Mendel dress I had seen on Natasha Richardson in *InStyle*. The color and nacre of a pearl, with the glamour and bias cut of a 1940s screen siren, it was perfect for a walk down the aisle—it was also easily ten thousand dollars. Maybe the pale gray Dior gown that Kate Beckinsale was wearing a few pages earlier was more affordable?

With the dress as the just deserts for all this impending cooking, I found an article in *Real Simple* called "Fix Your Money Leaks," which examined twenty-two minor expenditures that added up to big-dollar drains. For instance, in utilizing online bill payment, I could save over seventy dollars a year in postage alone.

I showed the article to Karl, who had taken over paying our bills practically in tandem with his proposal.

"I already do that," he said, barely taking his eyes off the television to skim the page.

"What about this one?" I asked, directing his attention to a leak authors Owen Thomas and Amy Kover called "Subscribing for cable TV, Internet access, and phone service from three different providers."

"We could save up to twenty dollars a month by switching to a package deal."

"Where have *you* been?" he said, blinking. "The first thing I did after moving in was to bundle our services."

He took the article out of my hands and worked his brow as he read. "This," he said, pointing to a leak involving cell phone plans that charged for unused minutes. "And this," he went on, tapping his finger next to one that warned about the hidden costs of paying only the minimum on credit cards, "I already know about all of this stuff."

And when I was first married, so did I. Back then, I was the one responsible for paying all our bills, which included handfuls of parking tickets (all my ex's), a whopping student loan (ditto), and a matriculation fee that would continue to visit us every month until my ex got off his ass, broke through his wall of pain, and finally finished his thesis—which was at the time seven years in the making.

So when Karl quietly and capably assumed the job of CFO in our two-person company, I was happy to hand over the reins and stick a pair of blinders over my eyes. After meeting one of my college boyfriends, my father had pulled me aside and said, "Cathy, I know, but I don't want to know." When it came to our fiscal affairs, that was my exact attitude.

This lack of interest extended to my desire to learn how to cook. I really didn't see the point of it—there had been vast improvements in the field of frozen food—and I wasn't so sure this was an area that I wanted to improve upon in the first place, especially because Karl seemed fairly happy stir-frying for us four nights a week. I had never cooked for my first husband and had always fought against the antiquated idea of domesticity, which to me represented a life of egg timers and beige food.

But if Karl was going to handle our bread, I could at least learn how to bake it. I was about to enter a marriage, after all, and maybe I should aspire to do it better this time around, to sign on for the whole deal. This was what good wives were supposed to do, right?

My horoscope confirmed my decision. "Your experiments in the kitchen will turn out delicious," read *Glamour*'s prediction for Capricorn, "so share them with a worthy guy!"

That I had no natural instincts toward baking was my mother's fault. When asked to submit a recipe to the PTA cookbook, she sent me to first grade with instructions for making a Fluffernutter sandwich. "If God had wanted me to cook," she once proclaimed, opening a twelve-piece meal from the Colonel, "I would have been born with Teflon hands." I had my own koan, stemming from an early kitchen experience at a friend's house. In fifth grade, my best friend Gail had suggested baking chocolate cookies and proceeded to gather the raw ingredients—the eggs, butter, and flour—on the counter.

Baffled by what I was seeing, I famously remarked, "Where's the mix?"

For me *joy of cooking* remained an oxymoron. While legions of women touted a twenty-two-year-old recipe from *Glamour* dubbed Engagement Chicken for its amazing properties to inspire proposals from the boyfriends who ate it, I was fixing a dish I eventually called Break-Up Chicken. I had gotten the supposedly no-fail recipe—which involved dipping chicken breasts in Seven Seas Viva Italian Salad Dressing and then rolling them in cornflake crumbs—from my cookie-making friend Gail. Without fail, whenever I prepared this meal for a new beau, instead of proposing within the month (the magical time frame of Engagement Chicken), he usually dumped me within the week.

Karl, naturally, wanted to break the curse. "We're already engaged," he reasoned. "What could happen?"

"I don't want to find out," I told him.

Back in December, I had practically severed my thumb while trying to slice a bagel. When I refused to get stitches, Karl bandaged me so zealously, I looked like I was wearing one of those giant cartoon hitchhiker thumbs.

That said, my first order of business was to find recipes that didn't require a lot of ingredients, dexterity, or prior experience. For this, I was counting on *Real Simple* to see me through, mostly because it was the only magazine to which I subscribed that offered any sort of meal preparation help. Well, I shouldn't say *only*—Oprah also came up with her own concoctions, but this month her focus was on New Orleans, reflected in an instant-death menu of crab po'boys, seafood gumbo, and grilled redfish. Besides, *Real Simple* used words like *easy* and *quick fix* in reference to their menu options. Coming from a magazine with a name like *Real Simple*, this wasn't an earth-shattering insight, but for someone who feared having more than one pot going at a time, the promise of these words held great comfort.

I tore out recipes for, among others, Mexican Chicken Soup, Pesto Pasta with Green Beans and Potatoes, and Winter Lentil Soup. But while I was at it, why not look for other kinds of "recipes," ones that held more interest for me? *Real Simple* also had all the right ingredients for "how to make the most of your time under the tap." In addition to listing shampoos that addressed various hair maladies (I made a note to run out and buy Dove Advanced Care Therapy Shampoo for my highlight-dry hair), the feature also provided a pictorial titled "Wash This Way," with step-by-step directions for lathering up and rinsing out. Most important, the article espoused the benefits of shampooing every other day, "to allow natural scalp oils to coat the hair shafts and boost shine." Maybe this would be the magic formula for transforming my hair from drab to fab (these magazine headlines were really getting to me). I decided to commit to this on-again, off-again schedule, hoping that scalp oil didn't actually have a discernibly bad odor.

After a week of hemming and hawing over menu selections, I was ready to get cooking. Not shopping, however. Whether a carryover from the days when I was married to a man who gained one hundred pounds or whether it had to do with watching my father weigh every single cantaloupe in the bin and then spend ten agonizing minutes deciding between coffee or pecan ice cream, the grocery store inspired major heart palpitations in me. I handed my list from *Real Simple* to Karl with items like "4 carrots," "1 16-ounce package of brown lentils," and "2 whole chickens" checked off. While I was drinking wine with my writers' group and workshopping a short story about a man in love with his cat, he pushed a cart up and down the aisles of our local supermarket. I arrived home just after 10:00 PM to find Karl out cold on the couch with about thirty plastic shopping bags spread all over the floor in front of him.

"Is any of this melting?" I asked.

"You think this is a lot," he said, motioning to the bags, "You should see what I put away."

Karl held high esteem for the circular coupon, especially the two-for-one variety. "Look at how much I saved," he bragged and showed me a receipt for just over $250. "See right here," he said, directing my attention to the receipt's bottom line. "It says I saved sixty dollars." Then he pumped his fist in the air a few times and congratulated himself with a drawn-out "Yessss!"

I went to bed and dreamed about making a soup out of hair and sweet potatoes. The following morning was my first off-shampoo day, so I put my hair under an old hotel shower cap (after first gathering the front section into a spiral cobra shape and securing it just above my eyebrows). I had the door to the bathroom closed, but Karl barged in to grab some cologne and caught me just before I made a clean getaway behind the shower curtain.

The look on his face said it all. "What in the world is that?" he gaped, cautiously poking at my see-through cap. I also was sporting a heavy green face mask. All I needed were cucumbers over my eyes and I'd look right out of an old *I Love Lucy* episode.

"I'm trying not to wash my hair every day," I explained, trying to get out of his sight as quickly as possible. It was bad enough I was naked—but in a shower cap with green gunk on my face? Was any woman really *that* secure?

"Oh, dirty hair. Is that what Oprah is up to this month?" He pulled open the shower curtain and pretended to look inside. "Hello, Oprah? Is the water too hot for you?"

Karl was in West Virginia. He had left the night before, riding his motorcycle just so he could get up at the crack of dawn and ride it around some more, at a speedway in the middle of nowhere with around thirty other testosterone-driven males. It was my first time sleeping alone in the bed since Karl had moved in. I was a big baby during the whole goodbye, crying and clutching at him like he was going off to war. I had read that Paul and Linda McCartney never spent one night apart during the course of their entire marriage. I loved that thought, that the former Beatle, the "cute one," the one chased and clawed at by hordes of groupies, still slept next to his beloved wife every night, presumably, until she died.

Maybe that's why Sir Paul remarried so quickly. He couldn't stand the coldness of the other side of the bed.

I decided that I would cook my first big challenge meal that evening, as a welcome-home present.

The first thing I learned about making Mexican Chicken Soup was that you need a very big pot. After digging around under the sink, the best I could come up with was a five-quarts.

I immediately phoned Jeanne in a panic. She and her husband Paul had lived in Rome for twelve years and had every kind of pasta pot known to man.

"Do you happen to have a twelve-quart pot?" I asked, like I requested large cooking items like this all the time. "I'm making soup."

"Who is this and what have you done with my friend Cathy?" she teased.

When I walked around the corner to her house, Jeanne greeted me at the door with a pot that was big enough to bathe a baby.

"Whatever you do," she cautioned, handing over the pot, "you need to boil the water and ingredients *before* adding the chicken."

"But the recipe says to put the chicken in the pot and then bring to a boil."

"Where did you get this recipe?" Her tone was one of personal insult.

"*Real Simple.*"

"*Real Simple*," she huffed. "More like *Real Crock*."

"I'm going to follow their instructions," I said, easing out of the door.

"No, Cathy, believe me," she pleaded. "I've been doing this for years. If you do that, the chicken will get all tough and dried out. I can't believe this magazine is telling you to put the chicken in first." Jeanne began to pace in her small entryway. "And after you make the stock," she continued, "you should cool it with the chicken still in it overnight in the refrigerator."

I told her that the recipe said to take the chicken out of the pot and shred it onto a plate. "The hands-on time is only twenty-five minutes," I explained. "It doesn't say to do something overnight."

"Well"—she sighed—"I'm here if you have a cooking 911."

I walked home carrying Jeanne's pot, and curious bystanders looked at me like they were expecting me to stop and serve them a free meal. "Sorry," I told one man I recognized from the building next to mine, "there's nothing under the lid."

When I got home, I discovered that the pot was too big for the kitchen counter, so I had to set it down on the living room floor. My cat Raymond traipsed over and sniffed it. The phone began to ring, and when I walked into the room to get it, I noticed he was sitting on top of it, licking one of his front paws.

"There's been an accident," came Karl's crackled voice at the other end.

I immediately had an image of him in traction, laid up in

some rinky-dink hospital in West Virginia with tubes coming out of his chest and both legs rigged up by pulleys. His roommate Bobby John, who had blown off four toes while loading his rifle, was calming himself by reciting a rosary of NASCAR drivers.

"What?" It was the first thing I could think of to say. "Oh shit," was the second.

"Not me," he said quickly, knowing that my mind immediately jumps to the worst possible outcome in the book. "I'm okay."

"Who, then?"

"Larry."

Ever since his birthday party, Karl had spared me from being around Crazy Larry. They continued to ride together occasionally on weekends when the weather was too good not to suffer his company, but he rarely mentioned his name anymore.

"Is he dead?" I immediately felt guilty for all the bad thoughts I had ever thrown his way.

"No." Karl sighed. "But his bike is."

It turned out that Crazy Larry, in an effort to impress Karl on the track, had tried to pass him on a particularly tight corner and dropped his bike. Both rider and motorcycle went sliding side by side into a wall made out of hay.

"It kind of took the fun out of things." He half-laughed. I could tell he was shaken. Seeing another rider, a friend on top of it, skidding across a graveled track with nothing but his leather pants and shiny helmet to save him from a collision, was like having it happen to yourself. "I don't feel right going back out there," he admitted. "I'm ready to call it a day."

My relief that he was unhurt and coming home gave way to a new brand of panic. He was coming home. I wasn't nearly ready to start dinner. My fantasy was that Karl, dirty and homesick, would walk through the door, and I'd have the candles lit, his slippers in hand, and food on the table. Now I'd be lucky to have twelve quarts of water boiling in time for his arrival.

I hung up the phone and began a calming mantra of *shitfuck shitfuck shitfuck.* Fortunately, the water only took about thirty minutes to boil. Once it did, I decided to follow Jeanne's instructions and let it boil for fifteen minutes before adding the chicken. (She made a very good case, that Jeanne. And I guessed if I screwed anything up, I could count on her sympathy. "I'm sorry I steered you wrong," she might say.)

While the water boiled, I needed to wash the chickens and pat them dry with paper towels. Up to this point, most of the chicken I had handled had been boneless breasts. Staring at these two whole chickens, I couldn't figure out how to remove their plastic wrap. There was no "open here" arrow or Ziploc seal. I picked up my first victim, took a knife, and cut a hole where I guessed the head once was. Once I got both chickens unwrapped, it was time to wash them off. They each weighed about three pounds, and when I held the first one under the sink, I instantly felt like I was holding a head like some shampoo girl at a salon. The way its pimply skin fell around the bones had such a human quality. Maybe this was what it felt like to prepare a body for burial.

Once I slid the clean chickens into the pot, I looked at the water, expecting the boil to continue. I consulted the recipe, looked back at the stove, looked back at the recipe, and stood there deciding what to do. The water remained flatlined. What if it never boiled again?

Karl returned home, dirty and a bit homesick. He was in the next room, laughing. Having lived on his own since he was sixteen, he was as relaxed in the kitchen as he was on his bike taking turns at 90 mph.

"You look perplexed. Can I help you?" he asked, wandering into the kitchen. He studied the quiet sea of chicken and told me to be patient. "That's what happens when you boil a lot of water," he said, as if he were explaining how air blown into a balloon causes it to inflate.

"It smells good," he added before going back to the couch to watch a movie.

After an hour, Karl reached into the pot with two wooden spatulas and transferred the chickens onto the plate I was shakily holding. They looked slimy and raw. "Are they done?" I asked him. He cut into one and declared it perfect.

I burned the tips of my thumbs and index fingers while trying to yank the yellowed and puckered skin off each chicken. I continued to burn them while pulling the tender meat off the bones and shredding it onto a plate. I refused to use any meat that was irregular in texture—no funny veins or dark spots, nothing that looked fatty. My mother always

made turkey soup after Thanksgiving and wasn't as discrimi-
nating. If you didn't chew with caution, you were likely to
bite into gristle and small bones.

Next, I added the rice to the broth and threw the chicken
back in. Since I had removed the carrots and onions, Mexican soup wasn't really more than just stock, rice, and a load
of chicken. It looked nothing like the picture in *Real Simple*.
But miraculously, it tasted delicious. The chicken was so
moist it was practically liquefying. And the broth, infused
with lime, was light and slightly tangy. It was so good, I
wanted to jump in the pot and soak in it.

"I love when you cook for me," said Karl. "For us," he corrected himself. "I love when you cook for us."

We left the soup simmering, and after a short while, the
rice had turned into a thick paste. But Karl still served himself
a second bowl, and even with this new consistency, it wasn't
half bad. We also had enough leftovers to feed a family of nine.
And the only damage that resulted, other than a few blistered
fingers, was a large, jagged line trailing across the countertop,
caused by dragging Jeanne's pot from the stove to the sink. No
amount of scrubbing or Clorox would remove it. It was my
only battle scar in the line of cooking duty.

I couldn't believe it. Whenever I ordered chicken at a restaurant, my parents' favorite joke was for one of them to
lean over and ask me, "Do you need me to cut that for you?"
They had long held the belief that I was ungraceful and un-
coordinated, and I had been dissuaded from trying out for
cheerleading, taking up percussion, and doing anything in
the kitchen that required a hot oven.

But the funny thing was, after believing myself to be all thumbs, clunky, and without rhythm, I was realizing that that might not have been an accurate picture of who I really was, even though it certainly helped shape who I had become. But by proving myself in the kitchen, maybe I would begin to create a new, more flattering photo album for myself.

Even though I was experiencing my share of gastronomical victories (the ensuing nights featured impressive entrees such as Pasta Pesto with Green Beans and Potatoes, Winter Lentil Soup, and Chicken Riesling), I was having a hard time not washing my hair every day. I began to dread the mornings when I had to don the shower cap. I found myself making social plans only on my clean hair days, when I scrubbed my head with even more alacrity than the *Real Simple* article condoned. However, most of my bad hair days were of my own doing. For years, I've had an anxious habit of grabbing strands of my hair, guiding the bundles up to my eyes, and examining everything at close range for split ends. (Come to think of it, this exercise, while being bad for my hair, probably isn't very good for my vision, either.) When I once visited a friend in Los Angeles, we drove by the Paramount lot and she told me that she once saw Jennifer Aniston, pulled over in her car by the gate, cell phone in one hand and a clump of hair in the other, checking for split ends. And more recently, I was absentmindedly checking the status of my ends in the backseat of a car and one of Karl's friends turned around and said, "I know what you're doing. My sister does the same thing." I wondered if we girls were all gorillas; if his sister and Jennifer Aniston and I would one day all sit around grooming one another.

The act of guiding the strands over and over between my thumb and index finger also spread around a lot of oil. A long time ago, before I picked up this habit, my mother told me that when she was a girl, she had a duckling that she petted so fervently, it died. All her stroking had spread around the oil that naturally lived in the feathers, essentially clogging all the duck's pores and suffocating it in its own feathers.

I studied my reflection in the bathroom mirror, visualizing myself as a giant duck, gasping for air, dying by my own nervous hand. On the counter in front of me was Oprah's seven-minute-eyelift article, her recipe this month for looking "instantly livelier and more awake." I was planning on going under the knife, or tweezer, in an effort to "offset droopy lids and make the eyes appear wider." As I administered the first pluck to the arch, just above the outer rim of the iris, the phone rang.

"Hi, pet."

It was Richard, the better half of the fabulously gay duo. He had been complaining of stomach pain, which we had both chalked up to his days as a heavy drinker. Even though he had been sober for months, I had still seen him double over more than once, usually after eating just a birdlike portion of his meal.

"What did the doctor say?" I asked, absentmindedly working the tweezers in the air.

"It's not good," he whispered.

"Tell me."

"I have pancreatic cancer."

I swallowed hard and tried to squelch back the wail that was rising out of my belly. "Oh, my sweet."

Although I considered him one of my closest friends, Richard was very guarded about his life away from our social one. A traditional Southern gentleman, he stood whenever a lady entered the room, treated me to all our fancy nights out, and phoned me whenever he was en route anywhere—from the grocery store to the Gap—to ask if he could pick up anything for me, like I was an infirm grandmother. Like someone from my parents' generation, which he was not, Richard would have never wanted to burden me with anything as troubling as his personal tragedy. And other than telling me he had cancer, he offered very little further detail.

I scanned my brain for anything I knew about cancer. In the past, I had interviewed a slew of breast cancer survivors for a series of articles that appeared on Lifetime Television's website. Years later, I still emailed many of my favorite women; their unfailingly upbeat responses—and just the fact that they were still alive to email back—provided me with a bit of hope. The one characteristic these survivors all shared was a healthy sense of humor.

"At least you don't have to worry about your hair falling out," I said. Richard was already completely bald.

"You know what they say," he said, perking up although I could tell he was weeping. "The sense of humor is the last thing to go."

I got off the phone and had a good, hard cry. Then, I called my father. Even though he was technically an optometrist, I still continued to run to him with all of my medical questions. He had met Richard during my parents' last visit to D.C., when Richard sprang for an expensive Sunday brunch. My father fell instantly in love—with his generosity and with the sweet way in which Richard looked after me.

"Richard has pancreatic cancer," I told him.

There was a long silence at the other end, like maybe my call had been dropped. As I was about to repeat myself, I heard my father exhale a deep breath. "Oh, Jesus," he said in an oddly measured tone. "That's a death sentence."

"What do you mean?" All this time, I had been under the grossly naive impression that the doctors would just remove the offending organ and Richard would get better.

"Cathy," my father said seriously. "You need to prepare yourself."

"What do you mean?" I could feel myself unraveling. My hands started shaking, and my face felt red and hot.

"This is a fast-moving cancer," he said gently. "He probably has about three months left."

Up until that point, I had thought my magazines had the power to prepare me for anything. But not this. I may have known how to throw a party or handle a difficult coworker— even poach a chicken—but I had no idea how to handle the pain of losing someone right in front of my eyes. I felt stupid and humiliated for being so self-absorbed in my own unwashed hair and sitcom experiences in the kitchen.

What made it worse, if that was possible, was that this

month, *Jane* had an article about a woman who died from cervical cancer, written by her best friend and titled "I Hate Tumors" (winning the award for title in the poorest taste). The first photo showed the friends in better days, almost identical, with long sun-bleached hair and perfect complexions. The subsequent photos were a timeline of her slow decline. The last image, of the author cradling her gaunt and gasping friend in her hospital bed, was so awful, I had to stop reading the article and turn the page—which revealed the last photo of the story, a sweetly reposed woman in an open casket.

When I was younger, if I ever saw a disturbing photo or drawing in one of my books, I'd ask my parents to throw the book away. They had to destroy the evidence because to my highly imaginative mind, just knowing that photo (usually of a ghost or monster) was still somewhere in the house meant it could still crawl out of the bookcase, pop out from the top of the stairs, seep into my dreams, and haunt me.

That night, long after Karl had fallen asleep, the image of me holding an emaciated Richard like the *Pietà* continued to play across my closed eyes. Planning tomorrow night's menu was the last thing I wanted to think about.

The slick pages of my magazines had left me bereft, and I sought solace from Dr. Oskar.

I told him about Richard's diagnosis, how life was so unfair, how Richard had spent the last year renovating his home with a fantastically expensive Aero Thermostatic shower and wouldn't be around long enough to enjoy it. "I sound like a cliché," I complained, reaching for a Kleenex.

Whenever I cried, Dr. Oskar usually joined in. After I had pulled a tissue from the box, he leaned over and took one as well. We both blew our noses and looked at each other.

"Oh, boy," he said. "This is really bad stuff."

He asked me exactly what the doctors had told Richard. "I don't know," I admitted. "He didn't tell me very much."

I did know that Richard had scheduled an appointment with a specialist at Georgetown Hospital for the following week. "I think the doctor wants him to go in and get a biopsy."

Dr. Oskar nodded, his signal for me to continue talking.

"I want to do something to make him feel better," I said, more to myself than to Dr. Oskar. "Something that will give him a bit of relief before the doctors rip him wide open."

"Yah. Wow. Okay," remarked Dr. Oskar. After he'd borne witness to my bluntness week after week, I could still manage to offend his senses. "So I think you just gave me a head job," he said, shaking his head.

"You know what I mean." I shrugged. "I want to make him feel good before things start to get bad."

"Just remember to take care of yourself," he said, finger wagging. On the scale of cancer and things that aren't cancer, it amazed me that Dr. Oskar was still concerned about my welfare. "I don't want this to eat you up."

Whether he recognized the irony or not, Dr. Oskar's bad pun gave me an idea. There was something I could do for Richard, something that I had been preparing for all month. I had cooked for Karl, at first, out of assigned obligation. But as the month went on and as the meals continued to roll out, I began to rethink my place in the kitchen. When Karl jokingly asked one night, "Did you ever think you'd be cooking a Spanish omelet for a Chew?" I had to admit to myself, *No. I never thought I would ever have that chance.* And when I admitted to my mother that, well, I actually didn't mind making dinner every so often, my mother merely pointed out the obvious. "It makes a difference," she acknowledged, "when you cook for someone you love."

Inviting someone else to the table, I would be able to offer the love and generosity that cooking had come to represent for me. This was the gift I could give to Richard. *This* was why people cooked.

I invited Richard over the night before he was to switch to a bland diet in preparation for his surgery. I was going all out with the menu and was even stepping way out of my comfort zone and making an actual appetizer—a bruschetta with smashed chickpeas, garlic, flat parsley leaves, and balsamic vinegar. It was the first time in my life I had ever peeled and chopped a clove of garlic. And for some reason of science, the parsley stung my fingers. But the mix tasted good, and before I set the bruschetta aside in the refrigerator, Karl took a picture of me posing with my creation.

My timing had improved since the beginning of the month, and there was still forty-five minutes before Richard was due to arrive to cook up *Cosmo*'s recipe for jerk chicken (complete with Scotch bonnet chili, a spice as fantastical to me as myrrh). Looking at our dining room table, which I had set with celery-green plates, crystal wineglasses, and pairs of Victorian candleholders ready to be ignited, I felt like my mother, who usually had our house decked out at least three days prior to her annual New Year's Eve party. She may have preferred to feed my father Lean Cuisines, but my mother could arrange a centerpiece like an Oscar-winning set designer.

"Oh, sweetie," Richard exclaimed when he saw the table. "You even put out real plates!" We had a joke that I was going to register my china pattern with Chinet.

"I hope you're hungry!" I sang, even though I knew he probably wasn't. There was no need to ask him how he was feeling. "I slaved all day over a hot stove for you."

"Everything smells delicious, pet," he said.

We sat down and clinked forks. "Here's to hoping this is not the last of Cathy's forays into the kitchen," toasted Karl.

I sat back and watched them take their first bite. "Mmm, mmm," they both said, delivering the verdict. Richard winked at me and patted my knee. I smiled at him and took my own taste of the jerk chicken. It didn't take long before my mouth was on fire. I turned to Karl and saw that sweat was dripping down his face. I turned back to Richard and saw that he had since drained his glass of ginger ale.

"Oh shit," I said. "It's too spicy."

Tears were now streaming out of Karl's eyes, but he kept on eating, mopping his face with one hand and feeding himself with the other.

I didn't know what else to do, so I just started laughing.

"Should we call out for pizza?" Karl said, and began to cough. "Fuck!" he coughed. "I think I'm burping up flames."

Richard, who was now laughing so hard he was hiccupping, held my hand under the table. "I'm sorry," I said. "This was probably the worst thing I could have made for you."

"Pet," he said, heroically picking up his fork, "everything is perfect."

At that moment, I truly saw the value in learning how to cook, no matter how disastrous the results. It was the reason we were all sitting here together, laughing and holding hands. I was amazed that such a small gesture could provide me, at least for this one brief moment, with so much fullness.

APRIL

Booty Calls

Karl was definitely pro–cooking month. He informed me that I was less neurotic when I used the magazines for productive endeavors—to him, "anything that doesn't have to do with feeding into women's insecurities about how all men are evil cheaters." If Karl was satisfied with my new skills in the kitchen, I was about to deliver a one-two punch and knock his socks off as I took my act into the bedroom.

Which begged the question: with sex-on-the-brain magazines like *Cosmo* flashing me in the face month after month, why was I continuing to demurely sidestep the elephant in the boudoir?

Bad knees, I supposed. They were what kept me from any activity that required bending, squatting, or lunging. My knees were also the reason I avoided most of the positions depicted in *Cosmo*, especially the ones with "Cowgirl" in the title.

But ultimately, I think I spent the prior months attending to other business before, ahem, getting down to business because, contrary to what a hankering for cubicle sex suggested, I was actually shy. Past relationships, the good ones, all shared one curious paradox: the more I trusted and loved someone, the more repressed I got. Let me explain. I think I'd make a great one-night stand. I'd go as crazy as I wanted—wax dripping, spanking, role playing—because I'd never have to see that person again. In a way, Bruno was just a string of one-night stands, a disastrous basis for a love affair. I did things with him that I had never done with anyone else (sex in the hallway of my apartment building comes to mind) and will never do again. Our relationship, which was based on recklessness instead of being grounded in normal activities like laundry and actual conversation, was completely unsustainable.

But with someone who really mattered, a man whom I imagined was in for the long haul, a man like Karl, I was going to have to hold conversations as mundane as our monthly budget in between all of the dirty talk. This was a hard concept to wrap my mind around. As of yet, I hadn't figured out a way to successfully marry my virgin/whore routine. And I thought Karl deserved to have a dirty slut in his bed every once in a while.

Just the other night, Karl had asked me, postcoital, if I still enjoyed sex.

"Is there something I'm doing to suggest that I don't?" I

questioned, even though I had just spent most of our love-making focused on what I was going to wear to work the next day.

"No." He sighed. "You just seem tired, that's all."

He was right, of course. Early on in our relationship, I took pleasure counting the frequency of how often we had sex—we averaged around four times a night. Which had rendered me a different kind of tired. Lately, I was the kind of tired that presented itself as lazy.

It was time to spice things up. But truth was, I was extremely uncomfortable with the idea of receiving my carnal education from a magazine like *Marie Claire*, whose survey this month revealed that nearly half of their readers (45 percent) would rather have sex with their favorite celebrity than win a Nobel Prize. (What about sex with Linus Pauling?) The thought of relying on *Cosmo* was even more distressing. I had already made the mistake of appropriating one of their moves way back when I was desperate to make Glen, the cowhide guy from next door, fall in love with me.

I believe the article was called "Find His Seven Secret Pleasure Triggers." According to *Cosmo*, the region just above the bow of his lips was a hotbed of pleasure. Ditto the pathway along his jawline, the outer area of his nipple, and the inside of his thigh. But with Glen, my particular area of concern was the region just north of his package.

Glen had always been a bit of a Pesci, a term my friends and I reserved for guys who, à la Joe Pesci in *Casino*, man-handled a woman's head down to their crotch as a helpful hint. But I remembered thinking, as I peeled off Glen's microfiber boxer-briefs (the only kind he wore), *tonight*, Cosmo *Cathy is in charge.*

I also remembered thinking that I had to act quickly. I was afraid Glen would come to his senses and wonder what I was doing poking around on his belly trying to locate, through a haze of bourbon, the "feel-good minefield," which *Cosmo* described as a narrow strip of skin between his hip crease and just above his pubic hair.

"Make like a cat," I recalled, spreading my palm over the center of Glen's groin, just between his hipbones. I imagined Raymond, my adoring cat, kneading his favorite blanket. I wasn't really sure whether to pull my fingers in a horizontal or vertical motion. So I tried it both ways. As I was concentrating on my inner kitty, I felt one of Glen's hands brush against my, uh, paw. I took it as a sign of encouragement. Until he did it again. But I was undeterred. This was one of *Cosmo*'s 101 best sex moves of all time, after all. So I continued doing my pawing and even added in a bit of the Pesci. It was the equivalent of simultaneously patting my head and rubbing my stomach. After a few minutes, Glen reached down, picked up my hand, and placed it on the bed next to his thigh. When I wrongly assumed that he, in awe of my catlike prowess, just wanted to hold the hand of a sex goddess, I just switched to my other hand and resumed pawing.

"Can you not do that?" Glen called down from the headboard. "It's really irritating."

Remembering the sting of Glen's critique made me hesitant to pick up the same playbook that had once steered me so off course. I wasn't so game on being a cat or a cowgirl—

but I wasn't so sure I was happy just rooting for myself either. I was just getting to know myself outside of the bedroom. Who I was between the sheets was even more of a mystery to me.

■

It's been clearly established that my mother contributed both positively and usually negatively to my physical and emotional sense of self. But I cannot blame her for doing any damage to my sexual identity. As far back as I can remember, she was a lusty role model. She once told me that when she was a little girl, she overheard her parents, my heavenly grandparents, having sex. Instead of being as repulsed as I was by the mental image, she admitted that she couldn't wait to start having sex for herself because it sounded like so much fun. (In turn, when my five-year-old brother asked what making love felt like, she calmly replied, "It feels like having your back scratched," a sensation he could easily understand. "That's what I thought," he said, shrugging.)

In seventh grade, when I was struggling with a home-ec sewing project, I asked her if she knew how to tie a French knot. "No," she candidly replied, "but I know how to French kiss."

In ninth grade she encouraged me, already close to six feet tall, to dress in tight jeans and to go braless. When we went shopping for my prom dress, she asked the saleswoman at Lord & Taylor if she had "anything sexy for my daughter."

Regardless of her own sexual enlightenment, I remained quaintly in the dark. For a long time, I thought kissing *was* sex. And when a boy in my advanced placement English class posited that I was frigid, I had to ask my mother the definition of the word. (I'm pretty sure my classmate didn't know what it meant either.) My mother was horrified that someone would call me that and assured me I wasn't—a kindness for which I have never thanked her. And when I told her, on the eve of leaving for freshman year at college, that my friends and I had made a pact to remain virgins until our wedding nights, she laughed her head off and said, "I give it one semester." (It actually took three.)

My mother's openness and somewhat relaxed ideas about my virginity did nothing to unlock my legs. Her words were of little solace compared to what the boys were saying about me. And it was their cruel and incisive language that I appropriated as my own. In elementary school, I overheard some older boys talking about me. "She has a nice body," said the ringleader, a popular boy with dark hair and a puka bead necklace, "but her face is nothing much." The other boys all nodded in agreement. "Yeah," they said. "Nice body but ugly face." (At summer camp the following year, another boy would sign my autograph book with, "You have one of the most interesting faces I've ever seen.")

The poor reviews continued to roll in. In college, a year after my mother predicted, I lost my virginity to a guy on my hall, an eerily quiet coke fiend named Phil whose nightly head-butting parties left him with a swollen forehead and a pair of black eyes. A week after my deflowering, I was sitting at his desk doing homework when I noticed a note Phil had scribbled down on the corner of his desk mat. It read, "Just

one month at college and all I have to show for it is a painful blow job and a bony fuck." It would take me another year to screw up the courage for oral sex, so I knew who I was in Phil's dry assessment.

There was the guy who told me I kissed like a fish, the boyfriend who told me I had no ass, another who told me I had interesting breasts (again, that horrible word!), and another, a Brit, who, every time I initiated sex, called me a "horny little bitch." Delivered in his clipped tone, this was not a compliment.

The labels stuck. Like the layers of wallpaper found in old homes, if I managed to peel one off, another era of tender pain was just underneath.

Normally, historical dismantling would have been the perfect project for Dr. Oskar. He and I could have gotten there with our scrapers and gone to town stripping away the man-made perceptions that had colored and influenced my own hang-ups. But ever since I ruined his halibut lunch by telling him about my ex-husband's midnight snack boogers, I had viewed Dr. Oskar as a bit of a shrinking violet. Maybe it was unfair of me to think that Dr. Oskar could handle a little sex talk without blushing himself on fire, but for the life of me, I just couldn't imagine sitting down on the couch, staring him in the eyes, and announcing, "It's time I fucked my fiancé like a porn star. If only I wasn't so scared."

Or maybe I was the one who couldn't handle the embarrassment. Dr. Oskar probably had way more perverse patients than me. The loud talker with the time slot ahead of me clearly LOVED FUCKING, since that was usually

he was yelling about when I arrived for my sessions. And once I heard a woman with clear transference issues adopt a flirtatious widdle-girl voice. "Oh, wrats," she said before exiting his office, "is it time to go alweddy?" Perhaps at this point in his career, Dr. Oskar had heard it all and found even the most extreme fetish to be pretty run-of-the-mill stuff.

Luckily, magazines made easy confessors. This month in O, Martha Beck, creator of the Index of Dread and my patron saint of camping, was back with another saving grace. In "Here's Looking at You, Kid!" Beck offered a much-needed course in self-appreciation. When we derive our sense of self-worth from someone else, ("turning it over to some longed-for or long-suffering lover," wrote Beck) eventually that person—whether a friend, a parent, or a partner—will disappoint us. "Realizing that we've surrendered our self-esteem to others and choosing to be accountable for our own self-worth would mean absorbing the terrifying fact that we're always vulnerable to pain and loss." But good looks, according to Beck, were not lodged in physical appearance. Rather, "it's the mind that mixes up beauty and acceptability, that misperceives the cause of emotional pain, and sends us down the class IV rapids of self-loathing."

I wasn't the only one going to bed with Karl. My interesting boobs, bony body, and fish lips were also tangled up in the sheets. "If you've ever let yourself feel lovable and lovely, only to be deeply hurt, you may see accepting your body as a setup for severe emotional wounding," explained Beck. "After all, you let down your guard before and look what happened! You'll never go *there* again."

But of course, I had to go there again. And again and again, if Karl had anything to say about it. The first step, wrote Beck, was trusting that I was lovable. "I'm not asking you to do it all the time, or even in large doses," Beck assured. "I'd just like you to experiment with a new mind-set, a few minutes at a time."

Getting it into my head involved taking out a sheet of paper, providing written examples of six of her listed scenarios, and pushing my mind to "attack its own protective strategy of self-denigration." Beck suggested this would take approximately ten minutes. But after spending nearly half an hour racking my brain and trying to come up with examples of **occasions when someone loved or praised you, even though you didn't look perfect,** I was convinced my regression would take a lot longer.

Slowly, though, after I had closed my eyes for a while and envisioned myself time-traveling through life's high points, I remembered one time last month, when I was on my off-day for shampooing, when a coworker saw me in the bathroom and remarked, "Your hair looks so pretty today." When she complimented me, I immediately zoomed back in time to when my grandfather was alive. Whenever he'd see me, he too, would admire my hair. "Did you wash it?" he'd always ask. When I was in seventh grade, I went through a brief period when I protested all forms of soap and water, and I think my grandfather was relieved to see evidence that I was actually bathing.

Obviously, people through time must have told me I looked nice even when I was feeling fat or had a huge zit on my chin, and I was sure Karl had told me he loved me on days when I was curled in the fetal position with period cramps, but I couldn't come up with any more concrete examples. "If you're deeply mired in self-loathing," wrote Beck, "it might take you a while to come up with examples for a given topic." But I didn't think poor self-esteem had anything to do with my failure to come up with more anecdotal evidence. It had more to do with why Madonna refused to read any of her own press. She was afraid that she'd only remember the negative reviews.

For her next question, Beck wanted me to come up with examples of **people you've loved even though they didn't look perfect.**

I thought about my ex-husband and his hundred-pound weight gain. Did I stop loving him because he had gotten fat? No, I didn't think so, although I still asked myself whether his bloated appearance wasn't a contributing factor to our demise. It had created a barrier, after all. But there were other walls, invisible ones that were more imposing and unforgiving. And when Karl, who knew of the weight gain, asked if I'd kick him to the curb if he ever got fat, I didn't think twice before insisting, "No, of course not." Come to think of it, I had seen Karl looking pretty grisly, hair matted down after being in his helmet or sitting on our couch in a stained wife beater, contentedly clipping away at his toenails. "I love you," I had told him when he pushed his pile of discarded nails into my open palm for disposal.

The next one was easy: **stunning people who act so awful.** I wrote "Bruno" down before I even finished reading

they begin to appear ugly. I remembered his first day at work, when he shook my hand and I swooned. Or the early stages of our sexcapades, when I looked at him and announced (so stupidly), "You have forever ruined my attraction to any other man." In the last months, though, I had begun to appraise him as coolly as a livestock buyer. "His eyes bug out," I noted, "and his chin recedes like a failed aristocracy."

I began to have fun with this exercise and came up with **famous people who are dazzling despite physical imperfection.** Anjelica Huston popped into my head. So did, inexplicably, Stephen Hawking.

By the time I was done with the last one—**women who are so perfectly at ease with themselves that they set a new cultural standard of goddessness** (hmmm, I wonder what Beck's subliminal message was here, considering she writes for Oprah)—I was ready to drop some emotional shields. Going through Beck's exercise didn't help me create a new self-concept; her questions just made me realize that I had been already building, over the past year, a pretty decent place for myself. Maybe the construction would never be completely finished, there was always work to do, but what I had to offer, inside and out, was solid enough.

Karl was in for a treat. The final step in Beck's exercise was to take my new and improved self out for a test drive. "Go out in public and pretend for, say, half an hour that you're lovely enough to be loved," Beck suggested. "No, go to a coffee shop and have a tasty beverage."

Instead, I opened up my Kama Sutra Bedside Box and pulled out an array of edible treats. A few months previously, while I was working on a story for *Self* about the advanced measures a woman might employ to get herself in the mood for love, a PR person had mailed me a small wooden box whose outside had been faux-finished to resemble a Victorian jewelry chest with chubby-kneed cherubs and purple garlands decorating every available surface. Inside, however, was a whole other story. There were trial-size tubes of Love Liquid, a pot of Vanilla Crème Massage Cream, edible Honey Dust with its own feather applicator (a white plume that looked like the one that was used to sign the Declaration of Independence), and something called Oriental Oil of Love, which according to the label promised to be spicy and tingly. It was a sample case that a traveling salesman might bring to a floozy convention.

"If you've done your homework," promised Beck, "you'll find something miraculous beginning, like the first tiny green crocus shoots emerging from the snowy earth."

Well, something would definitely be shooting up.

"What's all this?" said Karl, walking into the bedroom and finding me camped out on the bed, reading the box's product brochure and running the feather up and down my leg. "Just lie down and enjoy the show," I smiled, sweeping the feather across his side of the bed.

I squirted a big gob of Love Liquid into my palm and got to work. I straddled his waist and rubbed my hands together to warm up the gel. One of *Cosmo*'s "Sex Goddess Secrets" was, "They engage in liquid lust." According to these deified sources, "adding store-bought moisture can boost the sensation, no mater how turned on you are."

"Yuck," said Karl as I rubbed his stomach. "This stuff stinks." I had forgotten he was picky about smells. I couldn't try any new perfume without first getting his olfactory approval. I distracted him by putting my finger in his mouth and giving him a look like the lead model in the sex goddess article. "Forget about how it smells," I commanded. "Do you like how this tastes?" I whisper-asked, waiting a beat before adding, "Karl."

This was the number-one tip from *Cosmo*'s second sex feature this month, "7 Ways to Make Him Ache for You," which was aimed at rekindling the fires of the early stages of romance. "As lovey-dovey as pet names make him feel, they still don't compare to the electrifying rush your man gets when his name crosses your lips," wrote Colleen Rush.

Karl already knew this tip. He often whispered my name in my ear as he pressed himself closer and tighter. Even though I loved hearing his soft voice filling my head, I had never been much of a talker during sex. I once slept with a guy I had known in college. He had been a minor celebrity on campus for having a recurring role on *The Young and the Restless*. We reconnected in New York City a few years after graduation, and went out on a couple of dates. When we finally slept together, he narrated his entire performance, Harry Caray–style: "Now I'm putting it in, now I'm taking it out, now I'm putting it back in, and now I'm coming."

Still, I wanted to say something. I considered sex talk part of the desensitization. "Karl," I began again, lightly drawing my lubed finger along his lower lip. "Is it good?"

"Oh my god," he said turning his head, "it tastes like Goo Gone."

By now, I felt as if a piercing knife was going through my knees. I rolled off him and reached for the spicy oriental love oil. "You should like this," I said, pointing to the word *oriental* and giving him a wink. "Karl."

"What are you planning on doing with that?" He looked concerned.

"Whatever you want, Karl."

When I unscrewed the cap, the overwhelming smell of Big Red chewing gum burst forth, causing my eyes to water.

"Holy crap," said Karl, sitting up, "that's lethal."

"Don't you want to know how it tastes?" I knew I was curious.

"What, are you trying to torture me or something?" I hadn't told Karl about sex month. I figured he'd be pleasantly surprised when I pulled out the kind of tricks I was actually trying to demonstrate at the present moment.

"I wasn't planning on it," I said, "But I could, if that's what you're into."

This comment caused us both to crack up. "And what the fuck is this for?" Karl asked, picking up the plume.

"Tickle your ass with a feather?"

"What?"

"I said, 'Particularly nasty weather.'" This was my father's favorite joke.

We lay naked on the bed, laughing and sniffing all the Karma Sutra's foul odors. Why didn't any of my magazines suggest some hearty guffawing as an aphrodisiac? What about a tip for playing the sexy fool? It was what made my stupendous failure with edible massage cream so much more palatable. Even if I couldn't wrap my ankles around my ears, I was still flexible enough to realize that getting over past rejections was just another step toward conquering an aftermath of displaced fears.

"Just so you know," said Karl, aiming the feather under my nose, "I'm a simple guy with simple tastes."

"And what simple thing would you like to do now?"

"Take a shower and wash this shit off of me."

Predictably, no one wanted to hear about sex month. When I was concentrating on other months, I was information central for my girlfriends. One night, I had dinner with two sisters from Chicago who spent the entire meal pummeling me with questions about hair products, eye makeup and, of course, men.

"How do I get Andy to listen to me when I talk?" asked Moira, who had just passed the D.C. bar. "I feel like he's always tuning me out."

"What about a guy who says he's ready for a relationship, and then just falls off the face of the earth?" added Moira's sister Cassie, a stage actress who had recently broken up with a guy who was more in love with his BlackBerry.

My male friends, on the other hand, were completely baffled. One afternoon I visited Glen at his design studio, a second-floor walk-up that displayed his leather goods (or his "lifestyles," as he referred to them, with a straight face). Glen had conveniently forgotten that we had ever seen each other naked, and I had since acquired a fiancé, which had made the idea of a friendship at least a little possible. Glen was in the middle of trying to sell a hide rug to our friend Jim, a gregarious financial adviser who was moving to London. I entertained them with a synopsis of *Cosmo*'s Sex Hall of Fame story, explaining the mechanics of moves like the Sit 'n' Spin and the Lusty Lotus.

"Did you do everything all at once?" wondered Jim. When I informed him that I had only performed a few, one at a time, he interrupted me.

"That's cheating," he complained. "You have to do all of them at the same time. Otherwise you're not really following the article correctly."

I wondered if Glen recognized his own bust in the Hall of Fame—if, at any point in my raunchy narration, he remembered the night he was being pawed and kneaded, courtesy of the very magazine whose tips I was now using on Karl.

I read something in *Self* that had a surprising impact on me. In an article about body confidence called "Feel 100% Sexy," Natasha, a self-proclaimed "big girl," revealed that "not everyone is going to think I'm sexy, but there's going to be someone. And I only need to date one really great guy, not a thousand."

Natasha's wisdom made me weep. Maybe it was because I was reading her words right before shopping for my wedding dress, and I was feeling blessed to have found my one really great guy. Or maybe it was because I was going shopping with Richard, whose pancreatic cancer had been downgraded, after a series of biopsies and specialists, to pancreatitis, which meant he was going to live (on a diet of bland food that certainly wouldn't involve my jerk chicken), and I was feeling incredibly thankful and overjoyed in general.

As I got into Richard's humongous Ford Expedition, I considered what Natasha might find sexy about herself. I imagined her with long, pre-Raphaelite hair, chesty, with an admirable five-inch cleavage. And I thought about my own physical virtues, especially now that I was going to dress them up for my wedding day, which was now nailed down for the end of September. In their Love and Lust column this month, *Cosmo*'s "Blow-His-Mind Tip" was to "Play Up Your Hottest Asset." I once asked Karl if he was a leg man, since I thought that compared to the remaining choices, ass and tits, my legs were higher ranking. "I like it all," he said diplomatically. "But you do have the sexiest back of all time."

This had been a surprise. Since I never really spent much time looking at myself from that angle (except to check for panty lines), I hadn't considered the erogenous possibilities back there. I knew I had one dark freckle, like a beauty mark in the middle (pointed out to me not by a lover, but by a dermatologist). And I could feel the way Karl dragged his fingers again and again down my spine, or rested his hand on the small of my back as we walked down the aisles of the grocery store. Still, ever since he had pointed out his predilection, I had made extra efforts to expose as much of my nape, shoulder blades, and the V-shaped slope downward— as weather permitted anyway.

"What are we in the market for, pet?" asked Richard while I buckled my seat belt.

"Something that looks just as good coming as going." He had lost a lot of weight; he looked so fragile sitting behind the wheel, like a kid who's allowed to sit in the driver's seat while Daddy pumps the gas. I leaned over and gave him a kiss on his cheek. He smelled like cocoa butter.

Richard and I hit all the fancy stores in Chevy Chase. I wasn't interested in looking like a bride with a poofy white dress and layers of tulle. I heard my mother's voice as we stepped into Christian Dior. "I'm getting married," I told the saleswoman. "What do you have that's sexy?"

I brought into the fitting room a floor-length pale gray silk charmeuse gown that had so many covered buttons down the left side, I asked Richard to join me. Other than a zillion small buttons, there was no other ornamentation. A modified cowl rested just off my shoulders, and the back draped suggestively low. It was cut on the bias and molded to my body; I was happy I had started exercise month in January.

"Oooh," said Richard as he secured the last button and took a step back to survey me. "Very Rita Hayworth."

The dress did have that old Hollywood glamour look and the color was a definite bonus. I knew Joy would appreciate it if my dress weren't the color of death. And I thought my own mother, who had agreed to help me pay for the dress, would applaud my sophisticated retro taste. She had always imagined me getting married in a vintage white suit and dramatically brimmed hat, which she thought was, for some reason, very Italian.

"Get real," was what she said when I told her about the $2,600 price tag. I had put the Dior dress on hold while Richard and I hit another store, a small decades-old boutique owned by a real dame named Harriet Kassman. By the end of our day, I had narrowed the competition down to the Dior and another dress, a Bob Mackie–influenced va-va-voom number with a back that dipped all the way to the crack in my ass. "Very red carpet," proclaimed Richard. It was a pale green floral print, and the bottom was slit all around, like a plastic-flapped curtain at a carwash.

"Come down out of the clouds," my mother had continued as I tried to argue my case. I didn't even tell her that the red-carpet dress was $2,950.

"Aren't any of these places having a sale?" she wondered. I could hear my dad in the background repeating the price of the Dior over and over like a nut in a mental institution.

I told her about another dress I had seen at Kassman's store, by the same French designer (whom I had never heard of), with the same stunningly low back. This dress was bolder in color, with fuchsia and pink flowers cascading down the front and silver embroidery at the waist.

"How much?" my mother asked, sounding like she was bartering in the Cairo bazaar.

"I think it was around five hundred." In revealing the sale price, I knew I had lost the retail battle.

"Could you learn to love the five-hundred-dollar dress?" She sounded like the Godfather. "Could you get behind this dress?"

It did have a nice behind, after all. Karl would enjoy the view—and appreciate my not blowing our honeymoon fund. "I guess so," I agreed.

"Then hang up with me," she instructed as forcefully as one of my magazines, "call the store, and charge it."

It took me a few days to get excited about my wedding dress. Not because I hadn't learned to love it, as my mother had hoped, but because I realized why I was so hesitant to buy it in the first place. My first wedding dress, a traditional ivory lace, had been on sale. I guess I didn't want this wedding to be discounted as well. To me, the dress represented how much my marriage to Karl was worth to me. I just didn't want to feel cheated out of what I finally, *FINALLY* thought I deserved.

I didn't want to get my wedding dress off the sale rack because I wanted to do everything differently this time. And that's why this dress was so tied to sex. Married sex. The only kind I had grown to despise. So much so that I had eventually refused it, slamming my legs shut and making up every excuse in the book until my ex eventually just stopped asking. The thought of sex had sickened me, since by that point in my marriage I was more mother than unfettered wife, and it would have been grossly oedipal. Eventually, I accepted the fact that I had no libido whatsoever, that if I ever wanted children, I'd have to lie back and think of England.

But then, Bruno changed all that. And perhaps that was what made me more grateful to him than I should have been.

And so what would married sex be like with Karl? Would I be casting the die with this marked-down wedding dress, or breaking the mold with the help of *Cosmo*? In the coming weeks, I tried most of the sex goddess secrets, the biggest hits being:

PUSH THE PEAK

At the moment of climax, incorporate a small but powerful move to heighten the experience. Squeeze his thighs with your hands when you're on top, kiss him hard, or arch your back so that your breasts thrust up against him in missionary position.

DOUBLE THE PLEASURE

If he's on top, tug his hair with one hand while kneading his butt with the other.

I actually combined the two and did the thigh grabbing with one hand and the hair pulling with the other. Karl likes to cut his hair close to the head, so it was a little like tugging at sisal carpet, but he seemed to enjoy the two-handed play.

"That was new," he told me one night, after I "squeezed from within."

Even though I was proud of myself for taking a few mattress risks, I couldn't help but think that great sex was about totally letting go. I didn't want to think about it, plan my attack, or memorize step-by-step instructions like I was preparing for a test in auto shop.

Looking for a different kind of connection, I decided to give Karl the questionnaire found in *Glamour*'s "The Bedroom Diaries," where three couples wrote down answers, reprinted in their own handwriting, to a list of inquiries ranging from the frequency of their sex to foreplay techniques and favorite sex accessories.

In a sort of He Said/She Said duel, Jason thinks their sex usually lasts twenty minutes. Karen, using blue felt pen, writes over his answer, "No! It's longer."

Pea thinks that she and Monté have sex four times a day. In red pen, Monté writes, "I wish!" and replaces Pea's 4 with the number 2 and changes *day* to *week*.

I was curious to see where Karl's and my answers overlapped, where they diverged, and where they suggested we didn't know each other at all.

"I just emailed you some questions," I told Karl.

He noticed the issue of *Glamour* on my lap and rolled his eyes. "Oh, no."

"Come on." I laughed. All along, Karl had been such a good sport. "I'm going to answer the same questions and then we can compare."

This seemed to pique his interest. "What are the questions about?"

"Sex."

"Oh, boy," he said, heading off to his computer, which was in our bedroom. "I'm going to nail this one."

I heard his desk chair slide back and the creak of him sitting down. Then, after a few minutes, the rapid clicking of keys.

I sat down at my computer and started typing the way I often journaled—free-form, no self-editing, just a loose, stream-of-conscious mind purge. I'd estimate it took me ten minutes to complete twenty questions.

"Are you almost done?" I called in to Karl.

"No," he called back.

"What question are you on?"

"Number two."

He was taking this pretty seriously. I reviewed my own answers to see if I could elaborate on any.

"Now are you almost done?" I had already watched one episode of *The Real World: Key West* marathon and was about ten minutes into another. "Now what question are you on?"

"Number eight."

I wondered if I was the guy in the relationship. While Karl was quietly composing sonnets to me in the bedroom, I had barreled through the questions as quickly as possible, with, I was afraid I'd soon learn, even less sentimentality.

Finally, Karl came out of the bedroom and wiped his brow in a display of fine exertion.

"Okay," he said. "I just emailed you back with my answers."

As I sat down to read his answers, I was startled by how similar they were to mine. We had even used the same phrases in some instances. Responding to **We usually go to bed wearing . . . ,** we had both written BIRTHDAY SUITS. We agreed on the frequency of sex (seven times a week), the duration of sex (one hour), our favorite sex accessories (our tongues), and, eerily, our favorite thing to do after sex—SNUGGLE TOGETHER, wrote Karl, UNTIL CATHY GETS UP TO PEE. We had also both had identical answers to **You'd never know it by looking at us, but . . . .** Wrote Karl, WE SOMETIMES ACT LIKE STUPID KIDS. Wrote I, WE BEHAVE LIKE A COUPLE OF 9-YEAR-OLDS WHEN NO ONE ELSE IS AROUND.

What struck me even more, though, was seeing myself laid out so exquisitely on the page. Karl followed **I love her: . . .** with EVERYTHING. REALLY. I WANT TO EAT MY GIRL UP ALL OVER. I LOVE HER BRAIN, TOO. As far as the sexiest thing I did? GOOD-NESS KNOWS, he wrote, I GET EXCITED JUST LOOKING AT HER EYES PEEKING OUT OF A MOTORCYCLE HELMET!

Every one of his answers was a little love story. THE RELA-TIONSHIP HAS TAUGHT ME WHAT HOME IS, began one answer. I SPEND MOST OF MY TIME IN BOXER SHORTS AND BLACK SOCKS [Mmmm. Sexy!]. I'M A CLOSET COUPON CLIPPER AND CATHY LIKES TO WATCH *THE REAL WORLD*.

His answers conveyed a brilliantly simple sense of satisfaction. Our foreplay was VERY DELICIOUS. And he recalled that **The first time we had sex, we . . .** THOROUGHLY ENJOYED OURSELVES and that **The last time we had sex, we . . .** THOR-OUGHLY ENJOYED OURSELVES.

In the end, Karl's answers functioned as my report card. I didn't need to master the Celestial Cowgirl or spank my man with a spatula. I was already a sex goddess.

"How did we do on the test?" asked Karl, who had moved behind me and was reading over my shoulder.

"We could totally clean up on *The Newlywed Game.*"

"By the way," he said, winking and wandering off into the kitchen, "when is sex month?"

MAY

Living It Up!

*J*ane was the first to tell me it was over. Then, *Marie Claire* announced the news; then *Lucky*. They informed me that my year with them had come to an end, and they all were wondering the same thing: did I want to stay in the relationship?

My answer was no. Partly because the thrill was gone. What had once been a guilty pleasure, taken at nail and hair salons, had since become a full-time job. I was not only reading fourteen magazines a month, I was actively participating in their content, checking in with faceless writers and editors at all times, and constantly analyzing the results. It was an exhausting way to live out a life, however successful the end result.

More so, as my year progressed, I felt further away from the material. In the beginning, I had stood in front of that wall of magazines like a disciple. And I had heard the call. But now, I just didn't feel as connected to these magazines anymore. And looking back over the past twelve months, I hadn't even relied on many of them for help. Reading *Jane*, for example, usually made me feel like I was standing in the corner, watching all the other girls dance and flirt with boys. This wasn't surprising. *Jane*'s target audience, according to their mission statement (which I had looked up on the Condé Nast website as a way to understand my alienation), was a twenty-something woman "who is the ultimate front-row influencer." I was more comfortable taking a position along the sidelines, observing life from a distance. Which explained why, in my freelance writing, I preferred to comment on the action rather than take part in it, like Alice Roosevelt Longworth, who famously jibed, "If you haven't got anything nice to say about anybody, come sit next to me."

Lucky's raison d'être, according to their mission statement, was "100% shopping and nothing else." I'm sure for some of the magazine's million subscribers that was the only mission. But for me, the more I read, the more choices in handbags (to clutch or to tote?), the more ways to wear the new cropped jacket, the more I started to yearn to wear a uniform. I had the same feelings of overstimulation with *In-Style*, plus my fascination with Jennifer Aniston's preferred brand of jeans felt like a guilty pleasure with none of the pleasure.

Even the magazines I had most relied upon, *Cosmopolitan*, for one, had worn out their welcome. In fact, *Cosmo* should consider offering three-month subscriptions, which was the loop their content seemed to take. How many ways could the editors repackage and sell the same sex tips? I remember my friend Dave telling me that before he moved to D.C. to work at our company, he had a brief stint at Hearst, in the research department. Part of his job was comparing buzzwords on covers of competing magazines. "I was just trying to find new ways to say the same things," he told me. "It was ridiculous. I used to come up with my own cover lines—'50 Ways to Decorate Your Uterine Walls,' 'How to Squeeze His Balls Until You Get What You Want.'"

That was the problem for me. As an aspirant magazine, *Cosmo* was pretty schizophrenic, mashing together two competing ideals—feminism and femininity. Both rationales were empowering in a sort of "use your stiletto heels to confound and crush men—and then steal their corner office" way. But the end result for the reader, or for me, at least, was confusing. To be seen as a woman, went their message, was to be seen as desirable. But for me, being a woman also meant rejecting the trappings—the lacily attired 34Cs, the thoughtfully painted lips—that pegged me as one. These were seriously competing worlds and I was tired of trying to hold them all, let alone reconcile them.

With its gentle tone and inviting layouts, *Real Simple* was a bit too mild-mannered to hang out with a potty mouth like me. It was the kind of reading material I'd be happy to see on my hotel nightstand or find abandoned in the seat pocket on an airplane. Occasionally, there was an excellent personal essay, the kind I wished I'd written, full of insight and forgiveness. But ultimately, the magazine was too nice for me, like the friend who is incapable of gossip and has never gotten shit-faced or enjoyed a brief whiff of schadenfreude.

And I loved Oprah, I really did, but frankly, I was just tired of seeing her face month after month.

And so I decided not to renew *any* of my subscriptions, except for *Self,* for which I continued to freelance. Maybe with some distance, I'd learn to read them for enjoyment again. Maybe with some perspective, I'd be able to distinguish their collective work on me and, more significantly, take credit for the work I'd done on myself. As June issues started to straggle in, I put them all facedown in the corner and breathed a sigh of relief. I did not have to read another magazine for as long as I lived.

However, before I could begin my monthly detox, I had to get through May. I considered rewarding myself with a free-for-all buffet of shoes and eye cream. But after spending a few days tearing out photos of Jimmy Choos and two-hundred-dollar wrinkle erasers, these outward pursuits seemed pretty trivial in comparison to the strides I had made that were more personal and less showy. Since I had worked so hard to create a better place for myself internally, I wanted my outside world to appear just as put together.

"Karl," I said one night. "Let's paint the living room."

Our apartment had no color scheme—unless wood counted as a color. Compared to Jeanne's brownstone, a Middle Eastern bazaar of amethyst, oxblood, and burnt ocher, or Richard's bungalow, which was like stepping into a Noël Coward play, Karl and I lived in the land of the bland. After a lifetime of antiquing, I had some great pieces—a French deco coffee table, a mid-century modern teak credenza, and a hard-won collection of English art pottery—but it all disappeared against the backdrop of apartment rental beige.

Real Simple chastised another couple, Patti and Todd Bender, for allowing a boring color scheme to rule the roost. "White walls do nothing to define or enliven a room," wrote Sara Bliss, perfectly named for an article on domestic harmony. In an article called "One Room, One Weekend, One Easy Makeover," Bliss documented how the couple turned their lackluster space "from blah to beautiful" with a few coats of paint.

The Benders' used Benjamin Moore's China Blue, which was about three shades paler than a Tiffany box. This same blue hue was touted in the decorating sections of multiple magazines this month. *InStyle* used it on the walls of "The Nester," and *Glamour*'s "How to do Anything Better Guide" featured Benjamin Moore's Icy Blue 2057-70 as an example of how to "bring a little nature home." Even Oprah, in her "Here we go!" letter from the editor, posed against a sky-blue backdrop.

In every layout, this eggshell blue was teamed with chocolate brown. *Glamour* thought the pairing looked sophisticated, yet rustic. And *InStyle* explained that a "limited color palette works best in a room you spend lots of time in."

They don't call it a living room for nothing. I looked around ours and noticed that sitting on our brown couch were two silk pillows in blue and brown stripes. And above the couch hung a Danish silkscreen of a bejeweled woman reclining on a curlicued chaise. *Vanitas*, the title of the picture, was printed in, I was sure, a Benjamin Moore shade of blue. Without even realizing it, I was already riding the blue/brown trend. I was reasonable enough to know that I'd never have Scarlett Johansson's lips or Jessica Alba's ass. But looking at the Benders' living room, I thought, for the first time ever, that I could actually make my physical reality match what I saw in a magazine.

In the past, I had flipped right past all the home improvement articles in magazines, finding the idea of painting or rearranging furniture too overwhelming and costly. Back then, I would rather have spent the extra cash on myself, especially after my divorce, when I was buying diamond huggies and eight hundred dollar custom-made cowboy boots. But nesting, really nesting, was bringing out my Suzy Homemaker side. It was the difference between pleasure seeking and deep and true gratification.

On the brink of marriage, I was finally ready to fully embrace the trimmings that went along with domestic life. And once again, the magazines were reminding me what that life looked like—at least on the outside. It was up to me to create a real home, the kind of safe haven that I knew, from last month's sex survey, was truly where Karl's heart resided. And that's why blue, like calm water, was the perfect color.

I had never seen the inside of a Home Depot. It's exactly the kind of place I hate, in the same circle of hell as bulk club warehouses and computer stores. Wandering the cement floors, listening to a surreal mix of the Pretenders and 50 Cent (music that was occasionally interrupted with breaking news like, "Shoppers, if you come up front to the registers, we're offering a four-piece patio set with two lounge chairs for eighty-nine dollars."), I was convinced that Home Depot was really a controlled study, and that the people in the orange aprons were all socioanthropologists or some form of research assistants. On this particular Saturday afternoon, everyone here fell into a category—**the Know-It-Alls,** who stood scrutinizing hundreds of jewel-colored electrical wires like they were appraising diamonds; **the Time-Killers,** who maybe had come in for a circuit breaker but wound up spending an hour fantasizing in the outdoor grill aisle; **the Wanderers,** who either didn't have anything in mind to buy, or did and just refused to ask for help (these were the same people who wouldn't pull in to a gas station to ask for directions); **the Masochists,** who had a child or other family members along just to spread the torture to greater numbers.

Karl, one of the Know-It-Alls, loved this place. Before we had even set foot in the paint aisle, he had gotten caught up in a Sophie's Choice between 4 mm or 3.98 mm bolts.

A Time-Killer stood next to him, looking at acorn screws like he was deciding what Godiva chocolate to eat. "If I knew what I was doing"—he chuckled to himself—"I'd be dangerous."

I had brought along my articles and insisted on buying a three-inch Performance Select brush.

"But this one is cheaper," noticed Karl, pointing to a Home Depot brand.

"I want the brush *InStyle* says to get." This was the first time I had put Karl, instead of some silver-panted salesperson, through the magazine rigmarole. Like those who came before him, Karl accepted the rules.

"Okay." He shrugged. "We can get the *InStyle* paintbrush."

As per *Real Simple*'s checklist, we also picked up a can of latex primer, four rolls of blue painter's tape, a drop cloth, two paint rollers, and a paint tray for each of us. Then we had a brief negotiation over paint color. Karl liked Benjamin Moore's Jamestown Blue, a "deep, dirty turquoise" from *InStyle*, but I preferred Moore's Icy Blue from *Glamour*'s "How to Do Anything Better Guide." "I want to bring a little nature home," I told Karl, pointing to the article.

"Fine," he said, grabbing the Icy Blue. "*Glamour* wins."

◼

"Isn't it exciting to do home stuff?" Karl remarked, organizing our purchases in order of use.

Real Simple had provided a weekend timeline, breaking the living room renovation into bulleted three-hour tasks: tape, prime, paint, and, at 3:30 PM on Sunday, "Kick up your heels. Then put up your feet and enjoy."

But as soon as we returned from Home Depot, at 7:30 PM, Karl wanted to get right to work.

Being stucco, the walls in our apartment look like the ropy veins of a hundred old hands. Karl made the executive decision to paint the smoother surfaces of the window moldings and the trim around the doors. "Accent walls," he chirped, stealing a phrase from *Real Simple*.

Even though he agreed to act as my assistant, as soon as we began to work, Karl immediately took charge, first showing me how to scrape off the flaking paint along the windowsill, then patiently teaching me how to place the blue tape along the aluminum window frame, and then, when I got more tape stuck on my arm than on the window, impatiently finishing the job himself.

Jeanne phoned to confirm our Sunday-morning walk, and in the five minutes I took to talk to her (joking that I was planning on painting the blades of the ceiling fan a nice pinstripe), Karl had hung a plastic sheet like a stage curtain. Half the room was under wraps; the curtain extended around the window, over the couch, and covered the credenza, the television, and the stereo.

"Hey," I said after I hung up with Jeanne. "You have to let me do something, or else it won't count."

"It's time," Karl said, "to prime."

This was like invisible painting, a smooth base that would soon be covered up. But Karl still watched me paint my section like a hawk.

"Not too thick," he said. "Like this," he said, walking over to his side and demonstrating his even strokes.

I had helped to paint a few apartments in my day, all belonging to former boyfriends who had all given me the sort of insignificant painting, a touch-up or an outlet, that I couldn't possibly screw up.

"I know what I'm doing," I insisted, a well-timed blob of primer dripping on my shoe.

While the primer dried, we took a break and watched the season finale of *Little People Big World*, a reality television show about a family where the mother, father, and one of their three children were dwarves. Karl and I idolized the father, Matt Roloff, and loved to discuss how Matt always managed to get everyone around him to carry out his big plans—from building a pumpkin-tossing trebuchet to pulling up a thousand square feet of old carpet—while he sat back and supervised. Watching Mr. Roloff in action also allowed Karl to dwell upon one of his favorite fantasies—of being a little person himself. "Can all this," he said, pointing to his own brain, "actually be shrunk down to a smaller size?"

About halfway into the show (and halfway into the drying time) Karl got antsy and decided to put on the first coat of paint. I didn't make a move to help (the Roloff twins were going to their first prom!), and before long, I had a glass of wine and a bowl of tortilla chips in front of me.

Karl regarded me from above, as he stood balanced on the radiator and painted the top of the window frame. A swipe of blue, like war paint, lay across the bridge of his nose. I ate a chip and put my feet up on the coffee table in an exaggerated display of repose.

"Typical," he said, shaking his head.

When he finished with the window, we hung another plastic tarp in front of the window, draping it carefully around the sides. The effect was that of a fallen sail, tipping into an invisible swell.

"That wasn't so bad," said Karl upon reflection, when we went outside to breathe some fresh air. It was a little past midnight. Considering he had done most of the work, it really wasn't so bad. "Tomorrow," he said, pointing his finger at me, "you're painting all the door trim. Alone."

While Karl spent the day tooling around Northern Virginia with his gang of gentlemen riders (designer leathers and Italian bikes), I threw on an old T-shirt and a pair of Karl's frayed chinos, and using *Real Simple*'s timeline as my guide, began my artistic endeavor.

- Cover door frames and trim with painter's tape; put down drop cloths (90 minutes)

I was having a hard time taping off my territory. The bumpy stucco wall caused the blue tape to warp and pucker. I predicted great calamity later, when after painting, I peeled off the tape, only to find that the blue paint had migrated underneath it. I imagined having company over for dinner and, looking up and seeing wavy blue lines everywhere, one of our friends asking us why we had hired a painter with Parkinson's disease.

But after nearly two hours of botched taping, I was determined to continue. Not for my benefit, however. I had just spent a whole year impressing myself with my grit and determination to see things through: I had ensured that Bruno would be my last jerk, worked hard to understand and redefine the relationship with my mother, ventured out into the wilds of a Porta-John and into the uncharted territory of my kitchen. I had hurdled over so many personal obstacles; I wasn't about to let Karl come home and find me crying and heaped on a plastic drop cloth.

- Paint trim with a brush (45 minutes)

Paint was flying everywhere; even though I had put drop cloths down, the paint merely used the drop cloth as its launching pad, bouncing off the plastic and turning our hardwood floor into a Jackson Pollack. Karl phoned in the middle of all this, and when I crossed the room to pick up his call, I made even more of a mess by stepping in a puddle of primer and tracking my ghost prints all over the living room as I paced around. "Everything looks great," I assured him.

But once I got all the paint up and the tape off, I wasn't so sure about the eggshell blue. It was sort of a wimpy putt-putt steam color. I recalled the day my brother painted the bathroom of his East Village studio entirely in metallic silver, like what the restrooms must have looked like in Andy Warhol's factory.

"Maybe we should have gone more peacock," I told Karl. I was standing in the center of the living room surveying my work when he arrived home, dirty with miles of open road plastered to his neck.

"I disagree," he said, setting his helmet down and joining me. He used his hands like a conductor, pointing out how the room seemed more tied together, how the eye danced from blue pillow to blue door to blue vase.

"If *Real Simple* doesn't put us on their cover next month," he said, moving over to the window for another vantage point, "fuck them."

I sat down for lunch with Lynn, one of my favorite editors in D.C., and showed off the callus I got from painting along the rough stucco walls of our apartment. It reminded me of the small tough patches I used to get on the fingertips of my left hand from playing my guitar nonstop all through junior high.

"My latest round of self-improvement," I bragged.

Sharp-eyed and endlessly curious, Lynn had a mop of blond curls that shook when she laughed, which was often. I had followed her rising star all over town, first writing for her when she was a features editor at a now-defunct D.C. magazine, and continuing to rise up the food chain with her as she landed a job at the *Washington Post*. When I started my magazine experiment, I had begged off assignments from her, but we still met for lunch, where I'd update her on my year of magical tinkering over salad and iced tea.

"So," she said slyly, "what's the most important thing you've learned?"

"That if you're ever in a pinch, you can use a crumpled-up piece of aluminum foil as a scouring pad." I delivered this with a straight face, and I could tell Lynn was debating whether I was serious or not.

"That's your big take-away?" She sounded a little amused and a little disgusted by my answer. "Give me another lesson."

"That I'll never find an eye cream that makes me look ten years younger."

This truth caught her by surprise. She leaned back in the booth and laughed like I had just delivered the funniest punch line of all time.

"Let me tell you," she said, still laughing, "I've got a few years on you, and you don't really start to look old until you get to be fifty. And there's nothing you can do about it." She took a quick bite of salad and continued, "I'm sure if I were to see you at fifty, I'd probably look at you and say, 'Wow, you look old.'"

Being this matter-of-fact served Lynn well as an editor. It occurred to me that these magazines had often functioned, for better or worse, as a really frank friend.

"Don't you think," she asked, pushing deeper, "that these magazines are designed so that women feel bad about themselves? Like they'll never have the right skirt, the perfect lipstick, or the chicest haircut?"

I squinted at her and grinned. "Have you been talking to Karl or something?"

Of course I knew that Lynn was looking for the big picture, the deeper meaning of my year-long investment. But didn't every woman know, whether in a private moment of self-doubt or in a public viewing of her carefully made-up face, that these magazines' whole livelihood was based on inadequacy? Wasn't that the first thing you learned in Feminism 101? Even Oprah, who focused on honing inner beauty, still had articles about taking ten years off your face by plucking your eyebrows.

The fact of the matter was, I did need to be better. And that's why I had found these magazines so surprisingly liberating.

"I realize that you can't solve life's mysteries with the right pair of shoes or the perfect shade of lipstick," I acknowledged. "But at least I tried."

"What do you mean?" Lynn took a bite of salad and motioned with her fork for me to continue.

"I mean that a year ago, I truly hated my life—my poor taste in men, unhealthy diet, whacked-out priorities," I explained, ticking off my past regrets on my fingers. "But all of my miseries were self-inflicted. That was my choice. I knew that if I wanted to fix my life, to change the equation, I had to start somewhere."

A wall of women's magazines was as good a place as any.

Lynn took a sip of her iced tea and leaned back in the booth. "So," she wondered. "Are you perfect now?"

Was I? I didn't know the answer. But maybe that was the point.

"I'm a work in progress," I told her.

"Maybe you're an example of progress," she said, editing me.

On the walk home from lunch, I thought about all the other questions hurled at me over the year. "Are women's magazines a necessary evil?" "Do you hate them?" "Are you a better person for reading *Cosmo*?"

I always responded with the same answer, "Yes. And no."

Because while it wasn't exactly true to say women's magazines changed my life, it wasn't exactly false, either. The truth was I opened myself up for change when I opened up my first magazine. The truth was, I believed magazines would help me get a better life. The truth was, my optimism was justified. But the other truth was, these women's magazines were just the vehicles (ambulances during some months) I took on the road to self-discovery. I was the one who was willing to put on the miles.

Renewal

I began my walk down the stairs. As my silver sandals alighted upon each step, I was able to read lines from Homer's *Odyssey*, a single line of which appeared on each tread of the staircase in gilded lettering.

> *But come now, stay with me,*
> *eager though you are*
> *for your journey*

My parents were waiting for me at the bottom, watching my descent and smiling like potheads. I saw my mother, who had dressed up her standard black Armani suit with three strands of opera-length pearls, and thought how relieved she must have felt to be standing in such a beautiful, air-conditioned space, thankful that she wouldn't have to apologize to her

friends in attendance for her daughter's typically kooky ideas
(like a Fat Elvis wedding in Vegas). I watched my father do a
last-minute check on his suit, the first suit he'd bought since
my brother's wedding, which was seven years ago. Just a few
moments earlier, we had been forced to station people on
each floor of the inn to wrangle my father, who had been
giving tours of the place, back downstairs and into position.

I sandwiched myself in between them. "Ready to go?" I
asked, linking their arms with mine.

"I love you, kid," said my father.

"You look gorgeous," said my mother.

The Beatles' "Because" floated high above the room as we
crossed the portal. I could hear everyone's feet shift as we, a
Moses in collective, parted the standing-room-only crowd
into a neat aisle.

"Slow down," I whispered to my mother, who was strain-
ing to the finish line. I wanted to take my time, to take inventory, to see as many loving faces as I could as I ended one
journey and began another. The first person I spotted was
Dave, who was hard to miss since he was waving me down
like he had saved a seat for me at the movies. I hadn't seen
him since the beginning of July, when I had slid my letter of
resignation under my manager's door and never looked
back.

It was a move prompted not by any magazine article but
out of an "emergency" meeting where my boss's boss demanded to know why I "refused to work with Bruno," and informed me that if we couldn't get along, I'd be put on
probation. "Believe me," he warned, "you do not want to find

yourself back in this office." He was absolutely right. I quit the following day, leaving the contents of my cubicle in a time-capsule limbo, like I had gone off to college. Eventually, my manager was the one who packed up ten boxes of my crap and arranged for their delivery, a fitting fuck-you for his wimpy behavior and silent defense of my nemesis.

As I continued down the aisle, I spotted Dr. Oskar, his white-blond hair standing out in the sea of Asians who surrounded him. He was elbow-to-elbow with Karl's Auntie Gay, and I remembered something I had told him the week before. "This will be like the last two years of therapy come to life," I had only half joked. "Too bad I can't make everyone wear name tags." I noticed Dr. Oskar paying close attention to my mother and hoped he wouldn't try and analyze her at the reception.

Jeanne and Richard were right up in front. Without ever having met, they had miraculously chosen to stand together, my two most dear and beloved friends. I paused for just a moment in front of them. "Can you believe it?" I said, feeling like I was just about to burst into song. Jeanne had already started to cry. She used an antique linen hankie to dab her eyes. Richard, who had served as my de facto wedding planner and had accompanied me to the nail salon every Friday for two months until I found the perfect shade of nude for my fingernails, put his hand on Jeanne's shoulder and patted it gently. "Don't get me started," he told her, which caused everyone around them to laugh.

All weddings, I suppose, are a trip down memory lane. But this one felt even more trippy, like some sort of *Cathy*

Alter, This Is Your Life television show. If I had just walked down Odysseus's staircase, I was now frolicking among my Greek chorus, who had been with me throughout my journey, remarking on my progress, encouraging me onward, and now banding together to sing my praises.

Before I could kiss her, my mother was off to join my brother David, his wife Abby, and their two little girls, Sophie and Josie, who were running around the chuppah, tossing a flurry of silk rose petals. Joy and Val, both dressed in red, stood across from my family, smiling as Sophie tentatively approached them and dropped a few petals next to their feet. Joy bent down and put her hand on Sophie's blond head and gently steered her back over to my family.

My father and I watched Sophie drop a few more petals before he turned to take his place next to my mother. "Not so fast," I told my father, kissing him on both cheeks like I was suddenly in Europe.

Karl stood in front of me, leaning on a cane, his left leg completely obscured by a hip-to-ankle brace that was Velcroed over the leg of his Paul Smith suit. In August, he had crashed his motorcycle when his front tire hit a patch of sand in the road. He sailed over the handlebars, his knee smashing into the metal pole of a bus stop, the surgery to follow . . . all of my magazine knowledge had come rushing back at me. For the past month, I had been a nurse, maid, short-order cook, and even a sex therapist. When we were sitting in the emergency room the night of the accident, I had overheard a woman who was holding up her bandaged index finger in an "I'm number one!" pose turn to her husband

and say, "I'm barely holding on by a thread." I had repeated that sentiment more than once in the weeks after the accident. But making sacrifices, being a caregiver and being open to receiving care, was a big part of what got me to this place, under the chuppah, next to Karl.

"Family and friends," began Zelly, reading from his green leather journal. "We are gathered here today to witness and celebrate the joining of Cathy and Karl in marriage."

Make no mistake. I did not set out with the intention of turning my life over to magazines in order to nab a man (although that part was certainly nice). When I thought about the past year, it really wasn't about this moment, this wedding. It was about everything that had allowed for this moment. If I had learned anything over the year, it was that the only constant thing in life is change. To truly grow is to suffer these transitions—getting out of a damaging relationship or a rotten job, enduring the illness of a loved one, etc. Because without knowing pain and vulnerability, how do we express gratitude and appreciation? Looking back, I realized that I subscribed to these magazines because I was also subscribing to change.

I hovered over the room like an angel in a Chagall painting and saw that I was about to set off on another adventure, an obvious wedding-day truth that was echoed much better and more profoundly in the Walt Whitman poem I had asked Zelly to read. "Will you give me yourself? Will you come travel with me? Shall we stick by each other as long as we live?" Zelly's voice cracked as he slowly delivered those last lines, which caused waterworks all around. Even Karl choked up.

"Cathy and Karl," said Zelly, refocusing our happy tears. "Please face each other and take each other's hands."

As Karl recited his vows, he gave my hands a few tight squeezes. "I do," he said, his face arranged in pure schmaltz. I thought about what was next for me. The stuff all brides think of—a starter house, our first family Thanksgiving, the sweet delight of a baby.

Then, it was my turn.

ACKNOWLEDGMENTS

I am grateful most of all to Bonita Brindley, who began this book, and to Karl, who provided the spectacularly happy ending.

I am forever indebted to Billy Fox, who contemplated women's magazines way more seriously than any man ever should. Billy is a supremely talented writer and composer, and if he's not already famous by the time this book goes to press, he ought to be. Please look him up and hire him to do anything his heart desires.

Many thanks and the naming of any first borns shall go to Dan Mandel and Greer Hendricks, who believed I could do it long before I did and who always treated me to fancy meals.

Equal thanks goes to my writing compadres, who provided endless amounts of support, inspiration, and willingness to read whatever was put in front of them: Dana Scarton, Melissa Vanefsky, Maria Streshinsky, Sarah Schmelling, Denise Kersten Wills, Sean O'Neill, Matt Summers, Karl Adams, Josh Levine, Gail Lisa Sullivan, Cari Ugent, Tony Schwartz, Page Evans, and Carrington Tarr.

Speaking of writing, I'd like to thank my aunt, Hava Dunn, for encouraging me to write from a very young age and my cousin Stephanie Dunn for continuing to egg me on.

I am endlessly grateful to Stefan Lund and Christopher Lively for seeing me through tough times, and to Terry Gerace for supplying the glorious finish line.

Lastly and always, to my parents, Susan and Elliott, my brother, David, his wife, Abby, and their disgustingly beautiful daughters, Sophie and Josie, all for showing me what a happy life really looks like.